FRRLS -
31022007.
J 921 MCCARTHY
$22.00
Giblin, James
The rise and fall of
Senator Joe McCarthy

W9-CDI-237

5-10

GEORGIA LAW REQUIRES LIBRARY
MATERIALS TO BE RETURNED OR
REPLACEMENT COSTS PAID.
(O.C.G.A. 20-5-53)

1190L

PEACHTREE CITY LIBRARY
201 Willowbend Road
Peachtree City, GA 30269-1623
Phone: 770-631-2520
Fax: 770-631-2522

THE RISE AND FALL OF

Senator Joe McCarthy

THE RISE AND FALL OF

Senator Joe McCarthy

JAMES CROSS GIBLIN

Clarion Books

HOUGHTON MIFFLIN HARCOURT

BOSTON   NEW YORK   2009

ACKNOWLEDGMENTS

Thanks to the following institutions that provided illustrations and information for this book: AP/WIDE WORLD PHOTOS, New York; The Library of Congress, Washington, D.C.; Department of Special Collections and University Archives, Raynor Memorial Library, Marquette University, Milwaukee, Wisc.; The National Archives, Washington, D.C.; Outagamie County Historical Society and Museum, Appleton, Wisc.; and the Wisconsin Historical Society, Madison, Wisc.

Special thanks to Michael Cooper, who researched the photographs and cartoons from the Library of Congress and the National Archives, and to my assistant, Mordechai Czellak, who listened to me read aloud drafts of many chapters and offered helpful comments.

Clarion Books
215 Park Avenue South, New York, New York 10003
Copyright © 2009 by James Cross Giblin

The text was set in 12-point Minion Pro.
Book design by Carol Goldenberg
Map by Kayley LeFaiver

All rights reserved.
For information about permission to reproduce selections from this book, write to Permissions, Houghton Mifflin Harcourt Publishing Company, 215 Park Avenue South, New York, NY 10003.

Clarion Books is an imprint of Houghton Mifflin Harcourt Publishing Company.

www.hmhbooks.com

Printed in the United States of America.
VB   10 9 8 7 6 5 4 3 2 1

Library of Congress Cataloging-in-Publication Data
Giblin, James.
The rise and fall of Senator Joe McCarthy / by James Cross Giblin.
p. cm.
ISBN 978-0-618-61058-7
1. McCarthy, Joseph, 1908–1957—Juvenile literature. 2. Anti-communist movements—United States—History—Juvenile literature. 3. Legislators—United States—Biography—Juvenile literature. 4. United States. Congress. Senate—Biography—Juvenile literature. I. Title.
E748.M143G535 2009   973.921092—dc22   [B]   2009015005

FRONTISPIECE:
Joe McCarthy, at the height of his political power, leaves the Waldorf-Astoria Hotel in New York City, March 8, 1954. *The Library of Congress*

For Dinah Stevenson

Contents

Prologue: More Powerful Than the President ■ ix

1. Chickens, Groceries, and a High School Diploma ■ 1

2. Days and Nights at Marquette ■ 8

3. Joe's First Campaign ■ 14

4. Judge McCarthy ■ 20

5. "Tail Gunner Joe" ■ 29

6. One Fight Ends, Another Begins ■ 39

7. Defeating a Legend ■ 46

8. Newcomer in Washington ■ 54

9. Charges of Torture ■ 64

10. The Speech That Started It All ■ 76

11. Where's the Evidence? ■ 86

12. The Top Russian Spy ■ 96

13. War Breaks Out in Korea ■ 105

14. Revenge ■ 114

15. "We Like Ike!" ■ 126

16. The Missing Paragraph ▪ 137

17. "I Can Investigate Anybody" ▪ 146

18. Cohn and Schine Go to Europe ▪ 158

19. McCarthy Gets Married ▪ 169

20. The Dangerous Dentist ▪ 177

21. Grilling General Zwicker ▪ 187

22. Exposed on Television ▪ 197

23. A Devastating Report ▪ 208

24. McCarthy on the Receiving End ▪ 220

25. "Have You No Sense of Decency, Sir?" ▪ 232

26. Censured ▪ 241

27. "His Time to Die" ▪ 258

Epilogue: Another McCarthy? ▪ 266

After McCarthy's Death . . . ▪ 268

Bibliography and Source Notes ▪ 271

Index ▪ 283

An Uncomfortable Situation

—By Hungerford

Cartoon by Hungerford, published December 3, 1953. *The Library of Congress*

More Powerful Than the President

THE CARTOON TO THE LEFT, published in December 1953, bears the title "An Uncomfortable Situation"—which is certainly an understatement. It shows President Dwight D. Eisenhower sitting at his desk and confronting three folders labeled "National Issues," "Foreign Policy," and "GOP Political Plans." The initials GOP stand for Grand Old Party, a nickname for the Republican Party.

The president is startled to look up and find a determined-looking man sitting on the left arm of his chair. The man, whose last name appears on his trousers, is Senator Joseph R. McCarthy of Wisconsin. He dips a pen in ink, and his intended action is clear; he, not Eisenhower, will sign the papers awaiting the president's attention. Or perhaps he plans to hand the pen to the president, then tell him how to sign the documents, which would be just as bad.

The cartoon raises many questions. Who, exactly, was Senator Joe McCarthy? (His given names were Joseph Raymond, but he wanted everyone, strangers and friends alike, to call him Joe.) And what made him think he could dictate policy to the president of the United States?

Joe McCarthy was a complex, fascinating, and highly controversial figure who left an indelible mark on the political life of America in the late 1940s and early 1950s, and whose influence is still felt today. This book will explore the questions about him that the cartoon raises, and many others. The story does not begin in Washington, D.C., where Joe McCarthy reached his zenith, but in the tiny farm community of Grand Chute, Wisconsin, where he was born on November 15, 1908, the fifth of seven children.

The McCarthy family's farm near Grand Chute, Wisconsin, around 1908, the year of Joe McCarthy's birth. *Outagamie County Historical Society, Appleton, Wisconsin*

Chickens, Groceries, and a High School Diploma

EVEN AS A BOY, Joe McCarthy was ambitious. "Joe always wanted to do something," his younger sister Anna Mae recalled in a 1970s interview. "He never kept still. He was always exploding on something."

Joe grew up in a large Irish American family on his father's 141-acre farm. The farm had been purchased for his father, Tim, by *his* father, who had emigrated from Ireland during the deadly potato famine of the mid-1800s and homesteaded in Wisconsin in 1855. All the McCarthys—Tim, his wife Bridget, and their seven children—helped to keep the farm going. They raised corn, oats, barley, cabbage, and hay, and had several dozen cows, a coop full of chickens, and a few horses. The 1920s were a prosperous time in America, and the McCarthys did reasonably well, although they never seemed to have any extra money.

They were a close family. The boys worked with Tim in the fields and the cattle barn, while the girls helped Bridget with the household chores. Every Sunday, even in the snows of midwinter, the family drove to the nearby town of Appleton to attend mass at St. Mary's Roman Catholic Church.

When he was seven, Joe entered Underhill Elementary School, about a mile south of the McCarthy farm. It was a one-room schoolhouse in which a single teacher taught all eight grades, usually between twenty and thirty students. Joe was no scholar, but he had a quick mind and an excellent memory, and always got decent grades. He completed the seventh and eighth grades in just one year, and graduated in 1923 at the age of fourteen.

Joe was a good-looking boy whose features reflected his Irish heritage. Thick

Joe McCarthy (at right, in shadow), with his brothers William (left) and Howard (center) on the family farm.
Outagamie County Historical Society, Appleton, Wisconsin

black hair topped his broad face. He had heavy eyebrows, blue eyes, and pale skin. Although he loved a good joke and laughed a lot, his expression could change in a flash from a smile to a frown.

Joe was strong physically. His father had taught him how to box when he was twelve, and he put this skill to good use in boxing matches with neighborhood boys. In his teens, Joe also liked to wrestle with his pals at church picnics. He never seemed to run out of energy and could get by on just a few hours of sleep a night. But he was dogged by a chronic health problem. From childhood on, he suffered from frequent bouts of acute sinusitis, an infection of the sinuses. It was an affliction he was never able to conquer.

The fall after his graduation from elementary school, Joe's parents expected he would go on to high school. But at that point he wasn't interested in any further education. Ready to make his way in the world, he wanted to make some money on his own. He bought two dozen chickens with sixty-five dollars he had earned working for an uncle in his spare time, fenced the birds into a corner of his father's property, and built a shed for them.

Joe sold the chickens' eggs to stores in Appleton and with the profits bought more chicks. Soon he was making enough money to buy a beat-up used truck.

Making deliveries to stores in an even wider area, he increased his sales. By the time he was seventeen, in 1925, Joe owned two thousand egg-laying hens and ten thousand broilers for eating, and was driving as far as Chicago to market his eggs and poultry. The future looked bright indeed for Joe McCarthy, chicken farmer.

Disaster struck in the spring of 1928. On one Chicago trip, Joe's truck overturned. He was unhurt, but many of his chickens were killed, which was a major setback to his business. That was just the beginning. The following winter was unusually cold, and Joe came down with a bad case of the flu after making midnight trips to the chicken house to check that the birds weren't freezing. The flu, complicated by his recurring sinusitis, kept Joe in bed for more than two weeks. He hired some local boys to look after his chickens, but they neglected their duties, and a fatal poultry disease, coccidiosis, infected the birds. In a short time, thousands of Joe's chickens lay dead and he himself was broke.

When he recovered fully from the flu, Joe tried to rebuild the flock, but his heart wasn't in it. He had been a success as a chicken farmer, but he didn't want

Joe McCarthy (third row, fourth from right) at the one-room Underhill Elementary School, less than a mile from his home, around 1918.
Outagamie County Historical Society, Appleton, Wisconsin

to spend the rest of his life on a farm. After handing over the surviving chickens to his father, he found a job as a clerk at a Cash-Way grocery store. He performed so well that the higher-ups soon promoted him to manager, then assigned him to open a new Cash-Way store in the small town of Manawa, thirty miles from Appleton.

Joe plunged enthusiastically into his duties and tried some unusual tactics to draw attention to the store. He drove along country roads near Manawa, knocked on farmhouse doors, introduced himself to the farmers and their families, and invited them to stop by the new Cash-Way. Later, he would put this tactic of meet, greet, and make the sale to good use in his political campaigns.

At the store, he shelved the merchandise along aisles instead of putting it behind counters, and urged customers to wait on themselves. This practice—standard in supermarkets today—was novel in the late 1920s, when most products were kept behind the counter and a clerk picked them out for each customer. Joe also bought merchandise in large quantities, thus getting it at better prices, and kept the store open late on Saturday evenings to increase business. Before long, the new store was operating at a profit, and in a few months it led the twenty-four-store Cash-Way chain in sales.

Joe wasn't satisfied with his success as a storekeeper. Again, he wanted something more—something that would take him beyond the small Wisconsin towns where he had lived and worked thus far. He had no idea what that something might be, but he knew he would need more than an eighth-grade education to achieve it. His expanded life would require at least a high school diploma, and probably a college degree. But how could he go back to high school now? He was twenty years old, and he had heard that the Little Wolf High School in Manawa did not admit anyone over the age of nineteen.

He mentioned the problem to his rooming house landlady, and she suggested he talk it over with the high school principal, Leo D. Hershberger. The principal was impressed by Joe's earnestness and agreed to admit him as a freshman in the fall. He went on to tell Joe about a new, experimental program the school was introducing. It would permit students to advance at their own pace, depending on how hard they were willing to work.

Joe leaped at the idea and signed up for it as soon as he entered Little Wolf High School that September. He was nervous all the same. Years later, he confided to an interviewer, "The day I first walked into that classroom, and sat down with those thirteen and fourteen-year-old kids, I would have sold out for two cents on the dollar. But they all knew me pretty well [from the Cash-Way store, which had become a young people's hangout], so I got along all right."

Joe requested the hardest assignments and took on a heavy load of homework. After closing the store in the evening, he studied in his room until the early hours of the morning, snatched a couple of hours of sleep, and then downed a quick cup of coffee before opening the store at eight A.M. This demanding schedule began to tell on him, and it wasn't long before a Cash-Way official informed him he would have to choose between running the store and going to school. Without hesitation, Joe chose school.

Fortunately, he had saved enough money from his job to pay his basic expenses in Manawa. He also picked up a little extra cash by coaching the high school boxing team. But he felt a need to speed up his studies and started working at his books on weekends as well as weekdays. By Thanksgiving, he had passed his freshman tests and begun classes on the sophomore level. Early in the new year, he progressed to the junior level, and by Easter he was working on senior class assignments.

A page from McCarthy's Little Wolf High School record. *Marquette University Archives*

LITTLE WOLF HIGH SCHOOL RECORD

STUDENT McCarthy, Joseph R. ADDRESS Manawa, Wisconsi

AGE AT ENTRANCE 20 YEAR ENTERED H. S. 1929 DATE ENTERED HERE Sept.

ENTERED FROM Underhill School CREDENTIALS Dipl

✳ *mw. correspond.*

Studies	Wks.	Rec.	Final	Studies	Wks.	Rec.	Final	Studies	Wks.	Rec.	Final	Studie
glish 1	36	5	90	Economics 4				Dom. Sc. 1				Bookkeeping 2
glish 2 ✳	36	5	87	Soc. Probs. 4				Dom. Sc. 2				Shorthand 3
glish 3	36	5	86	German 1				Dom. Sc. 3				Shorthand 4
glish 4				German 2				Dom. Sc. 4				Typing 3 (½)
tin 1	36	5	84	Algebra 1	36	5	92	Agriculture 1				Typing 4 (½)
tin 2	36	5	80	Bus. Arith. 1	18	5	92	Agriculture 2				Com. Geog. 1	18	5	91
tin 3				Pl. Geom. 3	36	5	95	Agriculture 3				Commer. Law
tin 4				Solid Geom. 4				Agriculture 4				Bus. Practice 4
S. History 4	36	5	92	Ad. Algebra 4 ✳			93	Man. Train. 1				Orchestra (¼)
c. History 2	36	5	93	Biology 2	36	5	91	Man. Train. 2				Music (¼)
& M. Hist. 3	36	5	93	Science 1	36	5	92	Man. Train. 3				Penmanship
izenship 2	36	5	91	Physics 4	36	5	91	Man. Train. 4				Spelling
								Soc. Prob.	18	5		

Joe McCarthy's high school graduation photograph. *Wisconsin Historical Society, Madison, Wisconsin*

The faculty backed Joe strongly as he sped ahead. Later he recalled, "The teachers were swell, and gave me special instruction after school, and at noon, and even at night." All this hard work paid off, and twenty-one-year-old Joseph Raymond McCarthy graduated from Little Wolf High School in June 1930. Joe was by far the oldest of the thirty-nine seniors who received their diplomas at the graduation ceremony. He was also the school's only student to complete four years of high school in nine months.

Principal Hershberger waited until the end of the proceedings to present Joe with his diploma. As Joe's mother and father, his brothers and sisters, looked on with pride, the principal said of Joe, "We never graduated a student more capable of graduating." He went on to describe Joe as "the irresistible force who overcame the immovable object."

By the summer of 1930, the effects of the stock market crash on Wall Street the previous October were felt in rural Wisconsin. The prices farmers got for their milk, wheat, and corn were heading down, like everything else in the economy, while jobs were harder and harder to find. It was anything but an encouraging prospect for a recent high school graduate.

Joe tried not to let the prevailing mood get to him. Because of his record with Cash-Way, he was able to obtain a job for the summer at a store in the town of Shiocton, twenty miles from Manawa. He already knew what he'd be doing in the fall. Despite the hard times, he'd applied for admission to Marquette University in Milwaukee and, with the help of a strong recommendation from Principal Hershberger, had been accepted. How would he pay for a college education? Joe had no doubt he would find a way.

Days and Nights at Marquette

JOE'S HIGH ENERGY LEVEL and ability to get along on a minimum of sleep came in handy at Marquette. He moved into a boarding house where eighteen other young men lived, and he took part-time jobs to pay the eight-dollar-a-week charge for his room and meals. On top of that, he had to cover his tuition and other university expenses.

He couldn't afford to be choosy about the jobs he took. At various times, he worked as janitor for a somewhat shady tavernkeeper known as Dirty Helen; he washed dishes and was a short-order cook in a diner; he sold flypaper door to door; and when things got really tight, he sold pints of his blood to city hospitals. By the end of his second year at Marquette, he had worked out a deal that provided him with a steadier income. He managed two gas stations, working ten to twelve hours a day for thirty-five cents an hour, plus tips.

Along with the jobs, Joe somehow managed to carry a full load of classwork. He started at Marquette as an engineering major, taking courses in science, mathematics, English, economics, and public speaking. In a class called Debate and Argumentation, he was so nervous at first that he could barely speak in front of his fellow students. He shifted his feet uneasily from side to side and extended his arms for no apparent reason. But with encouragement from the teacher, he learned to stand still, move his arms only when he wanted to make a point, and speak clearly and with expression. His only failing was the flat, nasal quality of his voice, a result of his chronic sinusitis.

McCarthy (center) leaning on the shoulders of two Marquette University classmates, October 1931. *Marquette University Archives*

Joe's success at public speaking was one of the reasons he changed direction in his junior year at Marquette and decided to study law instead of engineering. He was also influenced by the legal students he had met at the boarding house. Their spirited conversations about shaping the arguments for cases, and cross-examining witnesses in the courtroom, made the practice of law sound much more interesting than engineering. Marquette's law school accepted the credits Joe had amassed in his first two years at the university, and he made the transfer at the beginning of his junior year.

Classes in the law school met from eight A.M. until noon. After lunch, the students were expected to study in the library or observe proceedings at the federal courthouse downtown. Instead, Joe headed for one of the two gas stations, where he worked most nights until eleven P.M. Afterward, he often met friends at a saloon that offered a free lunch to customers all day long.

Amazingly, Joe's life at Marquette was by no means all work and no play. He went out for the boxing squad at the university. Training started in the fall and climaxed with two boxing shows in the spring. The activity counted for the gym credits Joe needed. One of his sparring partners, Charles Hanratty, recalled later that Joe was strong and fearless, more of a slugger than a boxer. He would charge his opponent with blow after blow, ignoring the need to defend himself. He won praise from a sports reporter for the *Marquette Tribune,* who wrote: "McCarthy is a husky, hard-hitting middleweight who promises an evening's work for any foe."

Soon after switching to the law school, Joe joined a law students' fraternity and moved into an old house that he and the thirty or so other members pooled funds to rent. Most of the fun at the house started around midnight. Although Prohibition was in effect, the members somehow managed to obtain beer. They cracked open bottles and rounded up players for card games.

At one of the tables, Joe learned to play poker. He wasn't a particularly good player; however, he was a daring one. He lost frequently, but when a risky move paid off, he won big. And he was generous with his winnings, often using them to buy beers for everyone in the room. These fraternity house games introduced Joe to gambling, which would become a major preoccupation in his later life—at the table, at the racetrack, and in the stock market.

When he had a winning streak at poker, Joe splurged. He became the first member of the fraternity to own a car—a convertible roadster that he got at a good price. Because of the car, Joe's friends lined up to go on double dates with him. He went out with some of the most attractive young women on campus but never seemed to become emotionally involved with any of them. Once, when he and his fraternity brothers were discussing marriage, Joe remarked that he didn't intend to get married until late in life. Marriage, he said, would bring responsibilities that could interfere with building a career.

To perfect his speaking skills, Joe joined the law school's Debating Society. Members met weekly to debate one another, and they had to be ready to argue both sides of the given topic. Joe proved to be an effective debater, but he would have been even better, the debating coach said, if he'd taken more time to prepare his arguments. Instead, he talked off the top of his head and bluffed his way through. He got away with it because of his quick-witted skill on the platform.

Joe was usually good-natured, but sometimes his mood would change abruptly. If he got into an argument over something that concerned him deeply, he could become extremely angry and lash out at his opponent with harsh and abusive language. Then, just as abruptly, he would usually drop the argument, slap his opponent on the back in a friendly fashion, and exchange a joke with him. Years later, erratic behavior like this would become a common occurrence in McCarthy's political life.

The United States was a country in turmoil during Joe's college years, the early 1930s. The worldwide economic slump known as the Great Depression was raging everywhere. Unemployment rose to more than 20 percent in the United States, and there was no unemployment insurance to help jobless workers get through the hard times. Unable to make their mortgage payments, many

Hundreds of unemployed men and women wait in line on a Times Square traffic island in New York City for a free sandwich and cup of coffee. Photo taken on February 13, 1932, during the Great Depression. *AP/WIDE WORLD PHOTOS*

families lost their homes, and hungry people lined up to get free food from soup kitchens that charities had set up throughout the country.

Faced with the harsh realities of the Depression, many college students questioned whether free-market capitalism, as practiced in the United States, was the most desirable economic philosophy. As an alternative, some looked to Russia, which had formed a Communist government following the 1917 revolution and was now the core of a group of affiliated nations known as the Soviet Union. In the 1930s, the people of the Soviet Union, under the leadership of Joseph Stalin, were "building socialism." All across the land, factories were under construction and individual farms were being combined into giant collectives, all for the good of the people, the Communists said.

Much later, observant reporters found out that slave labor built many of the factories, and large numbers of peasants resisted the collectivization of their farms. But at the time, the Soviet media presented a glowing picture of what was going on, and many foreign visitors, impressed by what their guides had shown them, wrote enthusiastic accounts of Soviet accomplishments.

On college campuses, including Marquette, many idealistic students responded to such reports by joining organizations that supported the Soviet Union, including the American Communist Party (officially, the Communist Party U.S.A.). Joe McCarthy, who wasn't particularly idealistic, did not. Like most of the Catholic Irish Americans in Wisconsin, he supported the Democratic Party and had voted for Franklin D. Roosevelt for president in 1932. At Marquette, he was too busy working and studying and partying to pay much attention to politics.

Joe graduated from law school on schedule in the spring of 1935, despite all the time he'd spent on extracurricular activities. His friends helped him prepare for the final exams by coaching him on likely questions, and his almost photographic memory for facts and figures ultimately saw him through. Joe's grades were good enough to win him his law degree, and with it membership in the Wisconsin Bar Association.

He and his friend Charles Hanratty had planned to drive together to the state capital, Madison, to be sworn in as attorneys. Joe showed up in a brand-new Ford with six new suits draped over the back seat. After he and Hanratty had finished their business in Madison, Joe suggested they drive to Waupaca, a small town near Manawa. Joe said he had heard there was need for another lawyer in Waupaca. After they got there, Joe stopped by an office building on the town's main street, and Hanratty gasped when Joe pointed to the lettering on a second-story window: JOSEPH MCCARTHY, ATTORNEY AT LAW.

Joe explained that he had made a bet with a fellow student that he would open a law office within six hours of being sworn in. To make sure he won the bet, Joe had borrowed enough money—he wouldn't say from whom—not only to rent an office in Waupaca, but also to buy the new Ford and the six new suits so that he'd look like a successful attorney before he'd even started.

Joe's First Campaign

JOE RENTED A ROOM in the house of a Waupaca dentist, bought a set of law books, and acquired scarred wooden office furniture from a secondhand shop. There wasn't enough left of the money he'd borrowed to buy anything better.

He soon discovered that, contrary to what he'd heard, Waupaca, a town of just 3,000, already had five lawyers. Competition for cases was fierce, especially in the ongoing Depression. People put off getting divorces and filing lawsuits because they didn't have the money to pay for them. Joe kept his office open late to attract business, and he joined the Lions Club and other civic organizations to make himself better known.

He often played poker, taking the game seriously and frequently winning pots of twenty dollars or more—a sizable amount at the time. His biggest wins usually came from daring bluffs.

When Joe was playing poker, he concentrated entirely on the game. One evening, a young woman drove all the way from Milwaukee to keep a date with him, but Joe got so involved in a poker game at a bar that he ignored her. Fed up with his behavior, the young woman finally left and drove back to Milwaukee, while Joe played on until four A.M. A colleague of McCarthy's told an interviewer later that he didn't think Joe was very interested in women except as attractive accessories, like his suits and his car.

Joe's poker winnings helped to pay his living expenses. Even so, when he added up his total income after nine months of practicing law in Waupaca, it came to only $771.81. That wasn't much, even by Depression standards. Consequently, he was more than open to an offer he received early in 1936 from Michael G. Eberlein, a lawyer practicing in the larger town of Shawano, forty-five miles from Waupaca.

Eberlein specialized in accident and insurance cases, which could be extremely lucrative. He maintained a large office and employed several young lawyers to assist him with the workload. One of the lawyers on his staff had left recently, and Eberlein was looking for a replacement. He had observed Joe in action at the local courthouse and was impressed by his confident, aggressive style. At their meeting, Eberlein was blunt: "Why don't you close up this dump of yours and come to work for me?" He clinched the deal when he said Joe's starting salary would be $200.00 a month.

The notion that he'd have a steady income for a change appealed to Joe. He accepted Eberlein's offer without hesitation, and a few weeks later—in mid-February 1936—he was on the road to Shawano. He rented a room in a boarding house and set out for Eberlein's office at the intersection of Main and Division streets.

The older lawyer introduced Joe to his secretary, May Voy. Joe shook her hand firmly and said: "You watch. In a few years, I'll be at the top of the heap here in Shawano."

Eberlein wasn't bothered by Joe's brashness—he could be pretty brash himself. He said: "Mrs. Voy's been here quite a few years, Joe, and I'll wager for the first six months she'll be able to teach *you* some law."

Joe didn't bring in much business at first, but he quickly became known around town. Most people liked his cheerful, outgoing manner. He'd enter a store or tavern and greet perfect strangers with handshakes, compliments, and funny stories. Others were put off by his tactics. When he played cards, he often cheated and then would laugh uproariously if he was caught. He didn't cheat for the money, he'd say; he just wanted to see how much he could get away with. Not all his fellow card players believed him.

There were few Democrats in Shawano, but Joe joined the local Young Democratic Club and before long was elected president of all the Democratic clubs in a ten-county area. He liked this first taste of the political life and decided to run for district attorney in the upcoming primary election.

At age twenty-seven, and with few qualifications for the job beyond his law degree, his confidence, and his ambition, Joe was definitely the long shot in the race. The frontrunner was the man who currently held the job, Louis Cattau. Cattau was the candidate of the popular Progressive Party, which wielded considerable power in Wisconsin in the 1930s. Next in line came the Republican candidate, Ed Aschenbrenner, who could count on the fact that there were more registered Republicans in the district than there were Democrats.

Even though he faced no Democratic challengers in the primary, Joe campaigned vigorously. He plastered his car with "Elect Joe McCarthy" signs. He greeted potential voters on the streets of Shawano and the other towns in the district with handshakes and hugs. And he addressed several Democratic rallies, employing the public speaking techniques he'd learned at Marquette.

Despite Joe's efforts, the primary election results came in as expected. Louis Cattau received the most votes, 3,014, and Ed Aschenbrenner was second with 692. Joe placed last with 577 votes. Even so, he didn't resign himself to defeat in the general election. Instead, he plunged into campaigning more aggressively than before, making speech after speech, including fourteen in a single two-day period. In his speeches, Joe belittled the Republican Party and its 1936 presidential candidate, Alf Landon, and heaped praise on President Roosevelt, who was running for a second term.

Joe also tried another, more damaging tactic. He published a pamphlet accusing District Attorney Cattau of violating a local law by continuing to practice law while at the same time serving as district attorney. This, Joe claimed, was a clear conflict of interest. Although Cattau actually spent little time on his private practice, and made almost no money from it, the charge was accurate. Cattau responded angrily to the pamphlet via a full-page newspaper ad. In it, he called Joe an "unscrupulous" politician and claimed he had "grossly misstated" the facts.

Joe's pamphlet didn't influence the outcome of the general election in a significant way. He lost again when the ballots were counted: Cattau came in first with 6,175 votes. But Joe did advance to second place with 3,422 votes, while the Republican candidate, Aschenbrenner, dropped back to last with 2,842. Joe credited his improved showing to the pamphlet, which people were still talking about after the election was over. This experience taught him an important lesson about campaigning: Voters are much more likely to remember an accusation of wrongdoing than a subsequent denial by the accused.

In 1937, Mike Eberlein made Joe a partner in the law firm. Now the sign on the office window read EBERLEIN & MCCARTHY, ATTORNEYS AT LAW. Joe beamed when he looked up at the sign, even though the promotion did not come with a raise. He was still making the same $200 a month.

At this time, the effects of the Depression in the United States were easing somewhat. President Roosevelt had been reelected by a landslide, and the mood of the country was a little more optimistic. In Europe and Asia, however, major wars were being fought. Right-wing forces in Spain, under the leadership of General Francisco Franco, had revolted against the elected republican government in 1936 and were now besieging the capital, Madrid. Nazi Germany, under Adolf Hitler, and Fascist Italy, under Benito Mussolini, supported Franco and had sent soldiers, tanks, and planes to reinforce his rebel army. The Soviet Union

Student volunteers from New York University serve on the front line with the Abraham Lincoln Brigade during the Spanish Civil War. *AP/WIDE WORLD PHOTOS*

backed the republican side and had dispatched soldiers and equipment to aid the republican troops.

England and France tried to remain neutral in the conflict, but left-wing volunteers from those countries rallied to the republican cause and traveled to Spain to join in the fight. So did volunteer groups from the United States, most of them grouping into a unit known as the Abraham Lincoln Brigade. Many of the American volunteers were idealistic young people. Some of them were among those who had earlier joined protest groups to demand that the government take stronger measures to alleviate the Great Depression in the United States.

Meanwhile, on the other side of the world, in China, another bloody struggle was in progress. Japan had seized China's northeastern province, Manchuria, in 1931. Now, in 1937, the Japanese invaded northern China proper and occupied the key cities of Tientsin and Beijing, then called Peking. The Chinese Nationalist army under President Chiang Kai-shek was no match for the superior Japanese forces.

As they retreated south, the Nationalists had to contend not only with the Japanese, but also with the growing strength of the Chinese Communists led by Mao Tse-tung (today spelled Zedong). The Communists controlled large stretches of western China. They had won over the local peasants by dealing fairly with them, unlike the Nationalist government, which was known for its corruption.

In 1936 and 1937, the American journalist Edgar Snow was one of the first westerners to visit the Chinese Communist strongholds. He sent back reports of a strong and dedicated group, prepared to fight both the invading Japanese and the unpopular Nationalists for the sake of their country's future. Snow's writings swayed many American college students. They studied Chinese history, past and present, and informed themselves about the current situation in the vast country. After graduation, some of them obtained positions as college professors; others joined the State Department, where they hoped to influence U.S. policy toward China.

Joe McCarthy probably didn't pay much attention to what was going on in faraway Spain and China. He had never been much of a reader. He read what he had to in order to pass his high school and college courses, but not much else. From his days as a chicken farmer on, he had always been on the go, racing from one class or job to the next. In time, what had happened in China and Spain in the 1930s, and the Americans who had played a part in those events, would be very much on his mind. But now, in late 1937, Joe was most concerned with his next move in Shawano. He had become a partner in Mike Eberlein's law firm, but that was old news. Joe needed a fresh challenge.

He'd enjoyed running for district attorney—maybe he could run for some other office. He noted that the 10th Circuit judge in the Shawano district, Edgar V. Werner, would be up for reelection in 1939. Judge Werner had been in the job a long time, and Joe had heard he wasn't all that efficient. Why not oppose Werner for the judgeship?

Judge McCarthy

WHEN JOE MENTIONED his plan to several other lawyers in Shawano, they thought he was crazy. Judge Werner had enjoyed a distinguished career in the law. He had served as a judge for more than twenty years, and before that had been district attorney for six years and Shawano's city attorney for another six years. How could Joe possibly compete against a man with so much experience?

"Watch me," Joe replied.

Mike Eberlein supported Joe's entry into the race. Campaigning might take time away from Joe's law office duties, but it brought welcome publicity to the firm.

The campaign began in earnest late in 1938. To help establish himself as a mature, thoughtful man, Joe gave a speech to the Shawano Junior Women's Club on the rise and fall of great civilizations, ending with a section on why America was great. Urban Van Susteren, a young lawyer in Appleton, called it an example of McCarthy's "pure Irish bullshit."

To finance his campaign, Joe borrowed money from everyone he knew—$50 here, $500 there. If he was defeated, he'd have a hard time repaying these loans, but Joe was confident he would win. He opened a small campaign office to avoid any possible conflict of interest with the Eberlein firm, hired a secretary, and bought a new Oldsmobile on credit.

Except for Appleton and a few small towns like Shawano, the 10th Judicial District was largely farm country. Joe planned to campaign throughout the district in his new car. He would introduce himself to the farmers and their families, chat with them about their concerns, and get their names and addresses so he could follow up his visits with "personal" notes composed, typed, and signed by his secretary.

What about his views on the issues? some of his friends asked. Wouldn't voters want to know about them? Not necessarily, McCarthy replied. In his opinion, voters didn't care all that much about political issues. How they voted depended more on their feelings about a candidate. A handshake, a smile, a personal note on a postcard letting them know the candidate remembered them—those were much more important.

Joe didn't rely on the personal touch alone to win the election. From his earlier campaign for district attorney, he'd learned how effective a strong attack could be. Now he thought he'd found the perfect weapon with which to confront Judge Werner. The judge was sixty-six years old and appeared to be in good physical and mental health. But he'd lied about his age in the past. When he first ran for judge back in 1916, he told voters he'd been born in 1866 instead of the actual year, 1872. Werner apparently believed people would be more likely to choose an older, and presumably wiser, man to fill the role of judge. Judge Werner had never corrected his erroneous birth date, which Joe discovered in a 1938 directory of Wisconsin attorneys.

Even though he knew the date was inaccurate, Joe decided to risk making it public. Early in 1939, he informed the press that Werner was in his seventy-third year and, if reelected, would be eighty by the time his term ended. Joe hoped that with this information in hand, voters would decide Werner was too old for the job.

The judge reacted angrily to the story when it appeared in the local newspapers. He told reporters his real age and demanded that Joe retract his statement. Joe responded cagily with a letter that implied it was Werner who wasn't telling the truth, and went on to make further use of the judge's advanced age. "Even though a sense of loyalty to the office makes him willing to sacrifice himself and his health," Joe wrote, "perhaps as a kindness to him and in fairness to the public, he should not be burdened with another six-year term."

This was Joe the poker player, gambling that voters would put more stock in his original disclosure than in the judge's rebuttal. And they did. When the election results were tallied on April 5, 1939, Joe had defeated Judge Werner, 15,160 to 11,154. A third candidate in the race trailed with 9,071 votes. The *Appleton Post-Crescent* said it was "one of the most astonishing upsets in the history of the Tenth Judicial District."

Joe, at thirty, was the youngest man ever to be elected a circuit judge in Wisconsin. When he was interviewed about his victory, he adopted a modest tone: "The campaign was a big job, but I have a bigger one ahead of me. The only thing that will overcome the handicap of my youth is unremitting hard work." He would have to repay more than $7000 he had borrowed to keep his campaign going. His annual salary as a judge was $8000, but he wouldn't start to collect it until he took office on January 1, 1940. Until then, he would have only his income as a lawyer, and he would need that to live on.

Joe didn't seem to be worried, though. Ever the optimist, he arranged to take out an additional loan to start paying off his campaign debts. Since he had no assets to guarantee the loan, he agreed to sign over his future judge's salary to the bank. It would deduct the repayments on the new loan and pass along what was left to Joe.

Meanwhile, Judge Werner, his friends, and his family found it almost impossible to accept Joe's victory. How could this young upstart, in one blow, have destroyed the reputation of a man so respected and honored in his community? Werner and his supporters demanded that the authorities investigate the campaign, and especially Joe's tactics. A lengthy inquiry followed, but in the end no reason was found to file criminal charges. Joe might have employed questionable methods, but he had done nothing illegal. During the summer of 1939, Joe stayed in Shawano and tried to bring some business into the Eberlein-McCarthy law office.

A cloud of unwelcome tension hung over much of the Western world that summer. After annexing Austria in 1937 and Czechoslovakia in 1938, Adolf Hitler's Nazi Germany now seemed poised to invade Poland. England and France had protested the German dictator's earlier aggression but had done nothing to stop him. As British Prime Minister Neville Chamberlain had stated, his country and France were pursuing a policy of compromise with Hitler, seeking "peace in our time." But Poland was different. Both England and France had promised to help defend Poland if it was attacked—and that would inevitably mean war with Germany.

If war did come, many Americans believed strongly that the United States should stay out of it: "It's a European problem; let the Europeans solve it." Joe reflected that isolationist view in a speech he gave at a Fourth of July celebration in Appleton. He deplored "the damnable flow of war propaganda" that filled the media, and feared that it would lead to "another futile slaughter" like World War I. "We would like to see all the peoples of the world enjoying the liberty and freedom that we have," Joe said. "But it is written in history that when an autocracy [like the Nazi government of Germany] is removed by powers other than the people themselves, that autocracy will be replaced by an autocracy even more vicious. Democracy has never been bestowed upon a people by an outside paternal hand."

According to newspaper accounts, the speech was well received, as Joe expected it would be. From personal contacts, he knew that a majority of his audience supported an isolationist stance. Still, the speech offers a rare glimpse into Joe's thinking on U.S. foreign policy. And by the time he was sworn in as a judge in January, the war was a frightening reality. Poland had fallen to the Nazis in September 1939, England and France had declared war on Germany, and the world waited anxiously to see what would happen next.

Other European developments troubled American leftists who, earlier in the 1930s, had endorsed the policies of the Soviet Union. In 1937 and 1938 Joseph Stalin, a deeply suspicious man, decided that some of his associates in the Communist Party were plotting against him. These so-called traitors were given hasty trials in Soviet courts and sentenced to hard labor in the icy wastes of Siberia, where thousands of them died.

Then, in the late summer of 1939, just before Germany invaded Poland, the Soviet Union signed a nonaggression pact with the Nazis by which each party agreed it would not attack the other. Stalin had a good, if cynical, reason for doing so. He feared Hitler would not be satisfied with occupying Poland and would send his armies on into the Soviet Union.

The Russian dictator's 180-degree change in policy badly shook the loyalties of his idealistic Western supporters. They had allied themselves with the Russians in the fight against the Fascists in Spain—a fight that had been lost earlier that year when the right-wing general, Franco, finally defeated his republican opponents. Now these Western leftists, including many Americans, were expected to shift gears and join the Soviet Union in shaking hands with the Nazis.

Those most committed to their belief in Communism, including leaders of the Communist Party U.S.A. and the staff of its newspaper, the *Daily Worker,* remained faithful to the party's political line. But many other American leftists couldn't bring themselves to do so. Almost overnight, they changed from fervent supporters of the Soviet Union and its policies to equally fervent enemies. Later, many of them would play major roles as witnesses in Joe McCarthy's investigations of Communist influence in high places.

In January 1940, Joe's focus was on his new duties as circuit judge. He put a down payment on a small house in Appleton and took possession of the judge's office at the courthouse. Immediately, he found himself confronted by a backlog of almost 250 cases. Judge Werner, it seemed, had worked at a slow, deliberate pace, often interrupting court proceedings to give lectures on the law to the opposing lawyers.

Joe reversed all that. To move through the backlog, he often kept his courtroom open more than twelve hours a day and sometimes worked until midnight. The rapid pace he maintained wore out his court reporter, Pat Howlett. "Joe always drove himself," Howlett said. "Sometimes I couldn't keep up." Later, Joe

McCarthy serving as a circuit court judge in 1942. *Marquette University Archives*

would boast that he had once heard and judged forty complicated cases in just forty days.

Few complained of the haste with which Judge McCarthy made his decisions. It was a welcome change after Judge Werner's long delays. Although Joe lacked a deep knowledge of the law, lawyers who tried cases in his court respected him as a judge. He displayed an ability to get quickly to the heart of a matter and a sincere concern for justice. The lawyers forgave him if he sometimes grilled witnesses harshly or held them up to ridicule. On the whole, they found him hard working and fair-minded.

Joe established an informal atmosphere in his courtroom and often injected a note of humor into the proceedings. In a traffic accident case, he once told the attorney for the plaintiff, "Every time a doctor comes in here, he tells me his patient was seriously injured and his bill was reasonable. I'm waiting for the day when a doctor comes in and says, 'No, my patient wasn't hurt so bad, and my bill was way too high.'"

Word of Joe's performance as a judge spread around the state. In a feature article, the *Milwaukee Journal* wrote: "Breaking with the 'horse-and-buggy' tradition that has tied up the calendars of most Wisconsin circuit courts, young Judge Joseph R. McCarthy of Appleton has streamlined his Tenth District . . . and has made a hit with lawyers and litigants alike."

Being a judge didn't change the way Joe went about his personal life. Unless he was trying to impress someone, he didn't pay much attention to material things. His house was sparsely furnished, and he often left his suits and other clothes scattered about his bedroom.

He had a hard time organizing his judicial papers and was always losing or forgetting something. His speeches were cobbled together at the last minute, often containing muddled passages that revealed a lack of preparation. Friends like Urban Van Susteren overlooked his faults because they appreciated Joe's good qualities: his generosity, his loyalty, his spontaneity, and his sense of humor.

Joe hadn't forgotten his family; he made frequent trips to Grand Chute to visit his parents. Nor had he abandoned his religion. He attended Sunday mass regularly, knelt for evening prayers whenever possible, and often recited the rosary while driving.

And he still loved to gamble. He particularly enjoyed the card games that started at midnight at the Appleton Elks Club. Once he kept on playing until seven-fifteen A.M., took a quick shower at home, put on a different suit, and got to the courthouse before nine.

Most of his friends thought Joe was satisfied with being a judge. Early in 1941, he surprised them all when he said he was thinking seriously of running for the U.S. Senate. His closest friends didn't reject the notion; after all, Joe had won his race for circuit judge against seemingly impossible odds. However, they did remind him of certain realities. He was known in only a relatively small area of Wisconsin; both of the incumbent senators, Robert M. La Follette, Jr., and Alexander Wiley, had good reputations; and besides, it was illegal for a sitting judge in Wisconsin to run for any other office.

Joe brushed aside their objections, saying he wasn't sure just when he would run. He already had a plan for becoming better known around the state. He would seek opportunities to exchange positions with other circuit judges, and would accept invitations to speak anywhere and everywhere in Wisconsin. And wherever he went, he would gather names of people who might be helpful when he did make a run for the U.S. Senate. In the summer and fall of 1941, McCarthy raced from one Wisconsin city and small town to another, getting his name in the newspapers and impressing potential voters with his energy, his cheerfulness, and his firm handshake.

All this groundwork came to an abrupt end on Sunday, December 7, 1941. That day everyone in the United States was stunned by the surprise Japanese air attack on the American naval base at Pearl Harbor in the Hawaiian Islands. In response, President Roosevelt declared war on Japan on December 8. Nazi Germany entered the fight on December 11 when it backed its close ally, Japan, by declaring war on the United States also. President Roosevelt and the U.S. Congress reacted in the only way they could, with a declaration of war against Germany. Within less than a week, the United States found itself involved in a war that was being fought in both Asia and Europe.

Now it no longer mattered whether you were a right-winger or a left-winger, an isolationist or an internationalist. Almost every American male of military age, except for those who opposed war because of their religious beliefs, had a single purpose in mind: to help defend his country.

As a judge, Joe was automatically deferred from military service, but he felt guilty about accepting the deferment. Besides, he sensed it would be a drawback to his future political ambitions if he stayed out of the fight. He decided to enlist in the Army, but Urban Van Susteren persuaded him to think again. Knowing

Joe's love of the limelight, Van Susteren told him that if he wanted to be a hero, he should join the Marines.

McCarthy took his friend's advice. On June 2, 1942, he applied for an officer's commission in the Marines and then arranged for a leave of absence from his duties as a judge. Later that week, he drove to Milwaukee and enlisted. In an interview, he told reporters he hoped to get into officers' training school but was enlisting without any guarantee of a commission. "At the moment," Joe said, "I'm much more interested in a gun than a commission."

One reporter misinterpreted his words and wrote that Judge McCarthy had enlisted as a buck private. Joe didn't correct the error when the story appeared in print. Instead, he told anyone who asked that he had entered the Marines as a private, and only later earned a second lieutenant's commission. In fact, he received his commission as a first lieutenant on July 29, 1942, and was sworn in at that rank on August 4.

Why would Joe promote a lie that could so easily be exposed—and eventually was, nine years later, in 1951? Probably because he thought it would enhance his image in future political campaigns: People would believe that Joe McCarthy's desire to serve his country was so great that he enlisted in the Marines as a buck private. And probably, too, because he thought he could get away with it.

After being sworn in, Joe was ordered to report to the Marine base at Quantico, Virginia, for basic training. He was thirty-three years old. Joe had no idea where he would be sent after his training was completed; the war was being waged on two fronts and was not going well on either in the summer of 1942.

Nazi Germany occupied much of western Europe, and German armies were advancing into the Soviet Union. Hitler had broken the 1939 nonaggression pact he had signed with Stalin and had invaded the Soviet Union in June 1941. Now the Soviet armies were fighting on the side of Great Britain and the United States, and even some archfoes of Communism in the U.S. were making contributions to Russian war relief.

In the Pacific, Japan had followed up its attack on Pearl Harbor by sweeping down on the Philippine Islands, and on what are now Malaysia and Indonesia. The Japanese already controlled the coastal areas of China, including the port cities of Shanghai and Canton, and still held Peking. General Chiang Kai-shek, the leader of free China, had been forced to move his capital to the inland city of Chungking.

Japan had also seized many key islands in the western Pacific, from Guam to

Wake. The United States had just begun to fight back, engaging a Japanese fleet at Midway Island and launching an invasion of the Solomon Islands. But the U.S. Navy, Air Force, and Marines faced a long, bloody struggle as they attempted to push the Japanese back across the Pacific, island by island.

This was the overall military situation that confronted First Lieutenant Joseph R. McCarthy and hundreds of other Marine recruits when they reported for duty at Quantico in early August 1942.

5

"Tail Gunner Joe"

JOE SPENT THE REST of 1942 and the first months of 1943 in training. After Quantico, he was stationed at Camp Lejeune in North Carolina and then at the Marine Corps Air Station in El Centro, California. Along the way, his rank was raised from first lieutenant to captain.

At El Centro, Joe was named the intelligence officer for a dive-bomber squadron. His duties would include briefing the forty pilots in the squadron before their flights and—on their return—debriefing them about the success they'd had in hitting their targets, the enemy resistance they'd faced, and any problems they'd encountered while airborne. Then he'd write intelligence reports for officers higher up the chain of command. His responsibilities would not involve taking part in combat missions, at least not according to the job description.

In March 1943, the squadron was sent to Pearl Harbor for two months of further training in Hawaii. In June, they embarked again, this time for the South Pacific, where U.S. Marines had recently taken Guadalcanal Island from the Japanese after months of fierce fighting.

A Marine traveling on the same ship as Joe kept a diary of the voyage, excerpts from which appeared in the *Milwaukee Journal.* "We weren't long out of Pearl," the Marine wrote, "before I decided that McCarthy was the most interesting character aboard." Joe was popular with the officers because "he had found a way around the regulation banning liquor on board. He had three trunks marked 'office supplies—squadron 235' and all those supplies were liquid."

The Marine diarist thought Joe was a terrific poker player—although a tricky

Joe interviewing Marine pilots who have just returned from air raids on Japanese installations in the Solomon Islands, 1943. *Wisconsin Historical Society*

one. "He'd sit in a game and suddenly, for no reason at all, bet $101.15 or $97.90. Not only would the bet knock other players off balance, but they'd have the problem of counting out the exact sum. Most times, they'd let him have the pot just to get on to the next hand."

When Joe's ship crossed the equator, the commander permitted the men aboard to stage an initiation ceremony. The participants wore pajamas, and those crossing for the first time were paddled, soaked with hoses, and subjected to other indignities. Joe's tormenters had tied a bucket to his right foot, then forced him to climb down a ladder. Just before he reached the bottom, his left foot caught on a rung and he fell backward to the deck, fracturing the foot. It had to be put in a cast.

A week later, when the cast was about to be removed, the medical corpsman assigned to the task mistakenly used a strong acid instead of the usual vinegar to soften the plaster first. Joe winced in pain as the acid passed quickly through the cast and burned his lower leg. The burn took several weeks to heal and left what the medical corpsman termed a "fairly large" scar.

Joe thought of a way to turn these two accidents into a political plus. He let friends back in Wisconsin know about the injuries, exaggerating their seriousness. As a result, newspapers in Appleton and Milwaukee ran stories saying Judge Joseph McCarthy, serving with the Marines in the Pacific, had suffered serious injuries to a foot and leg. That fall, his Wisconsin office issued a press release stating he had been wounded in action.

On July 3, 1943, Joe's squadron arrived in the New Hebrides island chain, and two months later, on September 1, its planes landed at Henderson Field on Guadalcanal Island. From there the squadron's pilots flew daily combat missions over islands the Japanese still held in the Solomon chain. They took out artillery sites and bombed fortifications while trying to elude antiaircraft fire from the ground and attacks by Japanese fighter pilots.

Meanwhile, back at the base, Joe carried out his assigned duties as intelligence officer. He also arranged for hard-to-get foodstuffs and beverages to be shipped to the airfield. Beer, canned turkeys, medicinal brandy, and canned grapefruit juice were just a few of the items that were flown in. Enlisted men and officers alike were delighted to get the delicacies, and didn't ask questions about how Joe had obtained them. As one grateful airman recalled, "You'd see Joe McCarthy come up with an airplane full of goodies from the rear area . . . kind of like Santa Claus coming in the Macy's parade."

Although he was thousands of miles from Wisconsin, Joe hadn't set aside his political ambitions. He told a close friend, Master Sergeant Jerome Wander, that he was planning to run for the U.S. Senate, and said that newspaper stories and photos of him in combat would help his future campaign. He persuaded Wander, the unit's chief gunner, to teach him how to shoot the two machine guns located at the back of the squadron's bombers—the tail guns. He also learned how to take high-altitude photographs of the plane's targets with a camera positioned near the guns.

After mastering the basics, Joe wangled his way onto a number of combat missions. Sitting in the tail gunner's seat, he got some good pictures of the plane's targets as it dive-bombed them. Then he turned to the guns, strafing Japanese antiaircraft positions and firing at fuel dumps, truck convoys, and bridges. "The judge loved to shoot guns," one of the pilots Joe flew with said later. "He was really eager in that rear seat." It was then that Joe acquired the nickname "Tail Gunner Joe."

As a joke, the men in the squadron awarded Joe a plaque "for destroying more coconut trees than anyone else in the South Pacific." Joe laughed at the joke along with everyone else. Meanwhile, he cajoled the squadron's photographers into taking dramatic pictures of him in his flight uniform, standing by his plane, manning his camera, and aiming his guns. He stashed the photos away for use later in his Senate campaign.

Joe McCarthy, wearing a pilot's uniform, poses in front of a military airplane, 1943. *Wisconsin Historical Society*

McCarthy with two of his soldier buddies in the South Pacific, 1943. *Marquette University Archives*

Next he embarked on a risky ploy that he must have known would have serious consequences if he was caught. In the spring of 1944, he proudly showed close friends in the squadron a citation he said he had just received. It bore the signature of Admiral Chester Nimitz, commander of the Pacific Fleet, and commended Joe for his participation as a rear gunner and aerial photographer "from September 1 to December 31, 1943." The citation read in part:

He [McCarthy] obtained excellent photographs of enemy gun positions, despite intense antiaircraft fire, thereby gaining valuable information which contributed materially to the success of subsequent strikes in the area.

Up to that point, the citation was basically correct. But then it deviated from the facts:

> Although suffering from a severe leg injury, he [McCarthy] refused to be hospitalized and continued to carry out his duties as an intelligence officer in a highly efficient manner. His courageous devotion to duty was in keeping with the highest traditions of the naval service.

A later inquiry revealed that the citation had been triggered by a letter of recommendation dated February 19, 1944, and signed by Major Glenn A. Todd, then Joe's commanding officer. However, in an interview conducted in 1977, Todd denied having written or signed such a letter. He offered a possible alternative explanation: "Intelligence officers had so little work to do, we gave them all sorts of odd jobs. One was to write citations for awards." In other words, Todd concluded that Joe himself wrote the citation, forged the major's signature, then sent the citation up through channels to Admiral Nimitz. The admiral's signature was genuine, but he signed thousands of such citations during the war and probably did not read all of them.

However it was obtained, Joe had his citation, and he wasn't shy about showing it to reporters, then and later. He also inflated the number of combat missions he had flown. His official flight log, signed by Major Todd, listed eleven missions, but in 1944 Joe claimed to have flown fourteen. Two years later, he said he had been a tail gunner on seventeen missions, and later still the number rose to thirty-two. By then, Joe was at the height of his influence and power, and no one challenged the larger figure. Instead, sympathetic Marine Corps officials used it as the basis for awarding him the Distinguished Flying Cross in 1952.

In April 1944, Joe announced that he would run for the Senate that fall. He also told reporters that he had decided to leave the Democratic Party and enter the primary election as a Republican. Joe had never been that committed a Democrat despite heading clubs in the Shawano area, and he figured he would be in a better position to challenge the incumbent, Alexander Wiley, if he ran as a Republican in largely Republican Wisconsin.

It wouldn't be easy to campaign from the South Pacific, and Joe didn't expect to wrest the nomination from the popular Wiley. He saw the primary as a chance to become better known throughout the state and build a foundation for another run for the Senate in 1946.

Two things worked in Joe's favor as he prepared for the primary. The Wisconsin state legislature had recently repealed the law that prohibited a sitting judge from seeking any other office. And Joe had made a windfall in the stock market with which to finance his campaign. Before joining the Marines, he gave $2,200 he had scraped together to a broker who said he had a tip on several slumping railroad stocks. The tip proved to be correct. Wartime shipments boosted the railroads' earnings, their stock prices jumped, and in 1943 Joe realized a $40,000 profit on his investment.

Joe opened his campaign on the island where he was stationed. Military regulations forbade servicemen from speaking on political issues while in uniform, but Joe found other ways to promote his candidacy. He put signs on military vehicles reading MCCARTHY FOR U.S. SENATE, and painted HEADQUARTERS: MCCARTHY FOR U.S. SENATOR on his tent. He tracked down enlisted men from Wisconsin, introduced himself, and asked them to vote for him on their absentee ballots.

Marine Captain McCarthy examines a piece of campaign literature for his 1944 U.S. Senate race. *Wisconsin Historical Society*

During a leave from the Marines in July 1944, McCarthy visits an office in Wisconsin, where five workers in his Senate campaign are writing and addressing "personal" postcards in his name. *Outagamie County Historical Society, Appleton, Wisconsin*

Back in Wisconsin, Joe's friends and supporters got busy with his campaign. In a few weeks, they produced 2.5 million pamphlets and fliers and mailed them to more than 80,000 families throughout the state. These publications extolled Joe's performance as a judge and a Marine captain and were filled with photos of him in uniform. One brochure summed up his qualifications this way: "He is ably qualified [to be a senator] by training and experience—much of which he obtained on the battlefields of the South Pacific."

Joe told reporters he didn't expect to get back to the United States before the August 15 primary, but he was actually making arrangements to do just that. He had served with his squadron on two combat tours, from September 15, 1943, through March 1944, and was due a leave. In early July he obtained a transfer to the Marine Air Fleet in San Diego, and there he was given a standard fifteen-day leave. He flew immediately to Wisconsin, arriving in Milwaukee on July 20.

Dressed in his captain's uniform, Joe granted numerous interviews and proudly displayed the citation he had received from Admiral Nimitz. He appeared at several rallies and gave brief talks to the Milwaukee and Appleton chapters of the League of Women Voters. He also found time to visit the room in his campaign headquarters where young women volunteers were busy writing and signing Joe's name to "personal" notes to voters, urging them to cast their ballots for him.

Four newspapers endorsed Joe, three of them in communities where he had lived and worked. The *Appleton Post-Crescent* wrote: "McCarthy, about 35 years of age, had the wholesome judgment to hang his robe as circuit judge in the closet, ignore the adequate income to which the law entitled him, and shove off with the tough young fellows in the Marines. If a combination of the McCarthy qualities cannot make a statesman, what can?"

Despite such endorsements and Joe's last-minute campaigning, Senator Wiley won renomination in the primary. But Joe was satisfied with the results. He had never expected to win, and was pleased that he had done as well as he had. He got almost 80,000 votes statewide, had come in first in the three counties within his judicial district, and had lost only narrowly in seven others. More important, he had reached beyond his base in the Appleton area and had become a known political figure throughout Wisconsin.

In August, his leave over, Joe reported to the El Centro Marine Corps Air Station in California, where he had trained, and was soon transferred to the El Toro Marine training base. He knew he would be eligible for another overseas tour of duty early in the new year and decided to try to head off the assignment. He would be up for reelection as a judge in April 1945, and he wanted to get ready for the campaign. On October 19, he applied for a four-month leave, claiming he had urgent duties to tend to at home.

The Marines turned down Joe's request but gave him the option of resigning his commission. He accepted the offer on December 11 and was home in Wisconsin by late January. When asked about his swift return, he didn't say he'd resigned. Instead, he told questioners he was on furlough until February, and then would go on inactive duty. Within a few days, and still wearing his uniform, he was once again presiding over his courtroom in Appleton.

No one opposed Joe for the judgeship, so he had to mount only a minimum campaign for reelection. As soon as the election was over, he began to make plans for his next Senate race, in 1946. This time, he would face stiff opposition in the form of the incumbent, Robert M. La Follette, Jr. And this time he was determined to win.

6

One Fight Ends, Another Begins

THE EARLY MONTHS OF 1945 were a time of great changes throughout the world. In Europe, the Soviet army had broken the back of the invading German army at Stalingrad in 1943. Now the Russians, having driven
the Germans out of the Soviet Union, were advancing swiftly through eastern
European nations and pressing into eastern Germany.

Meanwhile, the armies of the western Allies, under the leadership of General
Dwight D. Eisenhower, had landed on the beaches of northern France in June
1944. They liberated Paris from German occupation in August of that year, and
by the beginning of 1945 had fought their way into western Germany and were
about to cross the Rhine River.

In February, when Joe was on his way back to Wisconsin, the leaders of
the major Allied powers—Franklin Roosevelt, Winston Churchill, and Joseph
Stalin—met in the southern Russian resort of Yalta. There they decided on the
shape of postwar Europe. Germany and its capital city, Berlin, would both be divided, and the nations of Eastern Europe that the Russian army had occupied—
Poland, Czechoslovakia, Hungary, and the rest—would be considered a Soviet
sphere of influence. Later, Republican politicians, including Joe, would charge
that President Roosevelt had "sold out" Eastern Europe to the Russians at the
Yalta Conference.

Roosevelt and Churchill wanted Stalin to invade Manchuria and other
Japanese holdings in China in order to hasten the end of the war in the Pacific.
Stalin agreed to enter the war against Japan within three months of the end of the

war in Europe but exacted a high price for doing so: control of several Japanese-held islands, and an occupation zone in north Korea.

Almost exactly two months later, on April 12, President Roosevelt died of a cerebral hemorrhage. He was succeeded by his vice-president, Harry S. Truman. Roosevelt had been president for an unprecedented twelve years and had seen the United States through the worst of the Great Depression and most of World War II. Much of the nation was plunged into deep grief, but Joe, savoring his reelection as a circuit judge, made no public comment on Roosevelt's passing.

On April 25, the Allied and Soviet armies met at the Elbe River in eastern Germany. The remnants of the Nazi regime were surrounded on all sides. The Germans fought back fiercely, but by April 28 the Allied and Soviet armies were on the outskirts of Berlin. Adolf Hitler, realizing the war was lost, committed suicide on April 30 before the Russians could take him prisoner. Just over a week later, on May 8, 1945, Germany surrendered unconditionally to the Allies. The war in Europe, which had gone on for almost six years, was over.

Now the Allies' entire attention could be concentrated on the war in the Pacific—the war that Joe McCarthy had opted out of. In February, U.S. forces had landed on the Japanese-held island of Iwo Jima. A month later, on March 16, the main fighting on Iwo Jima ended, and a U.S. Navy military government was established on the island. The cost: 4,000 American dead and 15,000 wounded.

On April 1, a large U.S. force launched a massive invasion of Okinawa, an island even closer to Japan. The Japanese responded with a desperate kamikaze (suicide) attack on the landing ships by more than 350 planes, but the Americans pressed forward. The Japanese continued their resistance for almost three months, but finally surrendered the island on June 22. The final toll: 12,500 Americans dead, and an estimated 100,000 Japanese dead.

A month later, on July 17, the Allied leaders, Truman, Churchill, and Stalin, met for the first and only time, in Potsdam, Germany, just outside the devastated capital, Berlin. They clashed almost immediately over the postwar situation in Eastern Europe. Stalin insisted on recognition of the pro-Soviet regimes the Russians were busily installing in Poland, Czechoslovakia, and the other nations their armies had liberated from German occupation. Churchill and Truman argued that free elections should be held in those countries. Truman later called it the "bitterest debate of the conference."

The leaders were closer to agreement when it came to the ongoing war with

Japan. Stalin, keeping the promise he had made at Yalta, said his armies would invade Japanese-held Manchuria on August 8. Then President Truman revealed to Stalin a secret he had already disclosed to Churchill: The United States had developed a powerful new weapon that would bring the Japanese to their knees. He had already gotten Churchill's approval to use it; now he wanted to get Stalin's. The weapon was the atomic bomb, which had been tested successfully for the first time in the New Mexico desert on July 16. Truman had received news of the test while on his way to Potsdam.

Stalin didn't seem particularly surprised by Truman's news—he probably had learned of the bomb's existence from Soviet spies—and told the president he hoped the United States would "make good use of it." On July 26, the Allied leaders issued the Potsdam Declaration, which included an ultimatum, a demand that Japan surrender unconditionally or face "prompt and utter destruction." The ultimatum did not mention the new bomb.

The Japanese prime minister, Kantaro Suzuki, responded to the Declaration on July 28. At a press conference, he said it was no more than a rehash of earlier Allied declarations, and that the Japanese government intended to ignore it.

Now President Truman and his advisors had to make perhaps the most fateful decision of his presidency: when and where to drop the atomic bomb. On August 6, an American B-29 bomber dropped the bomb, nicknamed "Little Boy," on the port city of Hiroshima. A huge mushroom cloud rose into the sky, fires raged, and an estimated 80,000 of the city's 255,000 civilians died. In a White House press release later that day, President Truman referred to the Potsdam ultimatum that the Japanese had rejected and warned: "If they do not now accept our terms, they may expect a rain of ruin from the air the like of which has never been seen on this earth."

There was no reaction from the Japanese government to the president's new threat, but events moved swiftly in the next few days. On August 8, as scheduled, the Soviet Union declared war on Japan and Soviet troops launched an invasion of Manchuria. Then the next day, having received no response from Japan, President Truman gave the order to drop a second atomic bomb on another Japanese port city, Nagasaki. The resulting explosion had a blast yield equivalent to twenty-one kilotons of TNT. It is estimated that about 70,000 of the city's 240,000 residents were killed instantly.

The Nagasaki bombing, following so closely on the destruction of Hiroshima and the Soviet invasion, finally compelled the Japanese emperor, Hirohito, to surrender. On August 14, he recorded the announcement of his decision, which was broadcast to the Japanese people and the world the following day. Hirohito said: "Should we continue to fight, not only would it result in an ultimate collapse and obliteration of the Japanese nation, but also it could lead to the total extinction of human civilization."

Although Joe must have been aware of these crucial developments in the war, his reactions were not recorded. He spent much of the summer of 1945 indulging his longtime passion for gambling, on a grand scale. He borrowed money to invest in the stock market, used his gains to obtain additional loans, and then made more investments. The profits he derived from the stock market would help to finance his Senate campaign, which was bound to be expensive.

Joe took other steps in preparation for the election, which was more than a year away. In order to become more widely known, he resumed his prewar practice of seeking invitations to fill in for other circuit judges across the state. When he went to work in a new community, he sought out lists of local Republicans, tried to learn their nicknames, and then made phone calls asking for their support.

Joe also befriended Loyal Eddy, the energetic president of the Young Republican Federation of Wisconsin. More than 300,000 men and women from Wisconsin had served in the armed forces in World War II, and Eddy's main job was to reach out to these veterans, ages 21 to 36, and persuade them to join the Republican Party. At 37, Joe was too old to join the Young Republicans, but he saw them as potential supporters. Whenever the organization held an evening meeting near Appleton, Joe did his best to be there. He'd shake hands with those attending, introduce himself, and give a brief talk about his campaign if there was time.

Loyal Eddy welcomed Joe's visits, and afterward the two men often went to a local tavern for a drink. Eddy admired the way Joe commanded the attention of the tavern patrons. They'd flock around him, basking in his charm and good humor, and listen intently as he told stories of his wartime experiences in the South Pacific. But Eddy found himself questioning some of Joe's stories, especially the one about his severe leg wound. His friend appeared to be in excellent health, and never limped. One evening, Eddy asked jokingly if Joe had gotten the injury from a fall off a bar stool. McCarthy just laughed.

Eddy was close to Thomas E. Coleman, a wealthy bank president in Madison and a powerful figure in Wisconsin's Republican Party. The party had long been divided into two factions, the more liberal Progressives and the staunchly conservative Stalwarts. Coleman had been the leader of the Stalwarts since the late 1920s, while members of the La Follette family controlled the dominant Progressives.

The La Follettes were a true political dynasty. Robert M. La Follette, Sr., served as governor of Wisconsin from 1902 to 1906, and then as a senator in Washington from 1906 until his death in 1925. His wife, Belle Case La Follette, was a leader in the feminist movement and a fighter for the right of women to vote. Their two sons both followed in their father's political footsteps. Philip La Follette served twice as governor of Wisconsin. Robert M. La Follette, Jr., was elected in 1925 to fill his late father's vacant Senate seat, and was reelected as a Republican for a full term in 1928.

Senator Robert M. La Follette, Jr.
Wisconsin Historical Society

The La Follette brothers shook up Wisconsin politics in 1934 when they broke away from the Republican Party to form their own Progressive Party. Now Wisconsin had four active political parties: the Republican, the Democratic, the Progressive, and—by far the smallest—the Communist. For the rest of the 1930s, the Progressives dominated the Wisconsin political scene. Robert La Follette was reelected to the Senate as a Progressive in 1934 and again in 1940.

Unlike the Republicans, whose party he had left, Sen. La Follette supported President Roosevelt's New Deal domestic initiatives, such as unemployment insurance and Social Security. He differed from the president when it came to foreign policy. Faced with the looming threat of Adolf Hitler's Germany, Roosevelt believed that the United States should begin to rearm, while Sen. La Follette believed just as strongly that the nation should adopt an isolationist policy and stay out of any future European conflict.

America's forced entry into World War II ended the discussion. La Follette, along with other prominent isolationists, abandoned his previous position and joined the rest of the country in backing the fight against Japan and Germany. But the Progressive Party had been badly weakened by La Follette's changing positions. By 1946, it had virtually disappeared in many parts of Wisconsin.

The party's collapse presented a difficult choice for Sen. La Follette. He intended to run for reelection in 1946, but would he run as a Republican or a Democrat? Rumor had it that he leaned toward returning to the Republican Party—which meant that he would be Joe McCarthy's chief opponent in the Republican primary. However, La Follette faced another major hurdle: Would the Republican Party and its unofficial leader, Tom Coleman, want him back? It was well known that Coleman thoroughly disliked the senator because of his earlier rejection of the party and his support for President Roosevelt's New Deal.

Joe was well aware of the complicated political situation he'd have to navigate on the way to the Republican nomination. He also knew how important it would be for him to obtain the endorsement of Tom Coleman. But that was by no means a sure thing.

Loyal Eddy had talked up Joe to Coleman, and had arranged for the two men to meet. The meeting did not go particularly well. Joe was not the type of man Coleman was used to dealing with. Coleman was accustomed to socializing with wealthy upper-class Republicans at elegant fundraisers for the party. Joe came from a rural background, his education was limited, and his manners were somewhat uncouth. Moreover, he had been a Democrat—a serious drawback in Coleman's eyes. And he was relatively young, a disadvantage in an era when most senators were older men who had been rewarded for long years of service to their party.

Joe must have sensed how Coleman felt about him, but that didn't stop him from continuing to campaign energetically. His efforts received a major boost in March 1946, when La Follette announced officially that he would run for reelection as a Republican and at the same time managed to alienate Tom Coleman. "True, we have had no invitation from the self-appointed boss of the Wisconsin Republican Party or from the Communist Party," La Follette said sarcastically. "But Progressives would be insulted if they received engraved invitations to join up with either Colemanism or Communism."

Coleman responded in kind: "Their [the Progressives'] shift is not to the Republican Party. It is to the Republican primary. Pure expediency is the motive." In other words, Coleman was charging that La Follette had returned to the Republican Party only in order to enter and win the Republican primary and then the election.

Joe joined the discussion with a statement calculated to appeal directly to Coleman and his Republican Stalwarts:

The party history of the La Follette brothers (Robert and Phil) is one of successive and successful party destruction. Twelve years ago they temporarily wrecked the Republican Party. Then, by playing with the New Dealers in Washington, they wrecked the Democratic Party in Wisconsin. They now allow their own child—the Progressive Party—to die. And they are about to attempt their fourth wrecking job.

The fight for Wisconsin's second Senate seat was on.

7

Defeating a Legend

Even though Joe had failed to win an immediate endorsement from Tom Coleman, Loyal Eddy arranged for him to give the keynote speech at the Young Republicans' state convention in Eau Claire in April. Joe seized on the invitation as an opportunity to state his position on a number of important issues. Sounding a familiar Republican theme, he accused the Democrats in Washington of assuming "that for every problem that arises, a new bureau should be created." The many war veterans in the audience cheered when Joe said they were "being plowed under a smothering mass of red tape" when all they wanted "was the right to live under a sane, sensible form of government rather than a stifling type of bureaucracy."

Joe's manner became even more intense when he discussed foreign affairs. A month earlier, in a speech at Westminster College in Fulton, Missouri, Winston Churchill had painted a dark picture of the postwar European scene. Referring to the Soviet domination of the formerly independent nations of central and eastern Europe, Churchill said, "An iron curtain has descended across the Continent." The description "iron curtain" would be frequently used in the years that followed.

Joe picked up on Churchill's message, blaming the Soviet Union's empowerment on the weakness and indecision of two Democratic presidents, Roosevelt and Truman. "We retreated mentally and morally in Austria, in Poland, in the Baltic States, in the Balkans, in Manchuria," Joe said. It was a charge he would repeat over and over, and the Young Republicans in Eau Claire nodded in solemn agreement as he made it for the first time.

Although Joe didn't win an official endorsement from the Young Republicans, his speech was enthusiastically received. Many of those applauding would be attending the Republican Stalwarts' nominating convention in Oshkosh two weeks later. Loyal Eddy obtained their names and learned they would comprise more than 20 percent of the voting delegates. On the last day of the Young Republican gathering, Joe threw a beer party for the future delegates, and almost all of those who came said they planned to vote for him.

There was much more work to do, though, and only two weeks to do it in. As he had during his campaign for circuit judge, Joe bought a new car—perhaps for luck—and raced around the state from one political meeting to another, often driving at eighty miles an hour or more. At the same time, he somehow managed to perform all of his duties as a judge. Mike McMillin, a journalist and columnist in Madison, observed: "It is doubtful whether Wisconsin has ever seen a politician who is more ambitious politically or more untiring and unremitting in his campaigning. He never ceases to campaign. He seems to have no other interest than political power."

As the day of the convention neared, Joe paid visits to potential rivals for the nomination and persuaded all but two of them to drop out of the race. With the holdouts, he employed stronger tactics. He threatened to make a campaign issue of one contender's divorce, which was sure to damage the man's chances in largely Catholic Wisconsin. The contender soon announced he was no longer in the running.

Joe used a more indirect approach with the remaining rival. The evening before the convention, one delegate after another came up to the man in the lobby of the convention hotel and told him they planned to support him even though all the other members of their delegation were for McCarthy. After the man had heard the same story more than ten times, he withdrew his name from consideration. Only later did he learn that all of those who had approached him had lied. They were Young Republicans acting on instructions from Joe.

One more person needed to be persuaded to support Joe's candidacy: Tom Coleman. Loyal Eddy made another strong pitch to Coleman on Joe's behalf. McCarthy was young, energetic, a war veteran who'd been commended for his heroism by Admiral Nimitz himself. All of these qualities added up to a man who could run a successful primary campaign and defeat Coleman's longtime enemy, La Follette.

Coleman still wasn't convinced and told Eddy he wanted to think about it overnight. The next morning, just before the convention opened, Coleman sought the advice of a prominent Stalwart Republican donor who had had several meetings with Joe. The man told Coleman that he and a number of other important contributors were strongly behind the judge from Appleton. After hearing this, Coleman came to a reluctant decision. He told the donor he, too, would back the nomination, and the election, of Joe McCarthy.

Once Coleman's endorsement became known in the convention hall, the voting itself was little more than a formality. On the first ballot, Joe received 2,328 votes to 298 for a little-known attorney from Milwaukee whom no one took seriously.

In accepting the Stalwarts' nomination, Joe once again assumed a humble tone. "I don't claim to be more brilliant than the next man," he said, "but I have always claimed that I have worked harder. I am going to work even harder now. That's a promise." Then he gave the crowd a glimpse of his innermost feelings. "I have looked forward to this nomination for days and nights, weeks and months—yes, years!" Those listening gave him a standing ovation.

Joe didn't waste any time mobilizing his campaign against La Follette. He assembled a team that included old friends like Urban Van Susteren and new ones like Ray Kiermas, a businessman from the small town of Stephensville, Wisconsin. Kiermas was assigned to head up a greatly expanded version of McCarthy's old favorite campaign activity, the sending of "personally written" postcards to potential voters.

Kiermas began by collecting telephone books and city and county directories from all over Wisconsin. Next, he recruited help from the Appleton area, offering half a cent for each card written. It was a dull, repetitive job, but scores of retirees, homemakers, and college students applied. Kiermas hired more than a hundred workers and opened an office in Appleton to house the operation. On one side of each postcard was a photograph of McCarthy. On the other side was the handwritten message "Your vote will be greatly appreciated by Joe McCarthy," and space for the recipient's name and address. All of the messages were to be signed "Joe." One woman managed to write and sign 1,000 cards a day.

Meanwhile, Joe himself was putting in one fourteen-hour day after another on the campaign trail. He was determined to meet and chat with as many Wisconsin residents as possible before the primary election, which was set for August 13.

A day of campaigning in the northern part of the state saw Joe waking up in the town of Marinette after just a few hours of sleep. His ultimate destination for the day was the town of Superior, a 300-mile drive from Marinette. In Superior, he was scheduled to give a radio speech at five-thirty p.m. and make an appearance at a rally at eight-thirty. Those weren't the only items on his itinerary. He planned to stop in many towns along the way, meeting people and giving impromptu sidewalk talks.

Accompanied by a young assistant to help with the driving, he set out after an early breakfast. But the poor condition of the roads, and three blown tires in the first hundred miles, slowed him down. At Rhinelander, he and his assistant left the car and got seats on a small plane headed for Superior. However, the plane developed an oil leak and had to make an emergency landing in a farmer's field. Joe and his helper hitchhiked to the town of Park Falls, where Joe hired a taxi to take them on to Superior. The taxi's engine sputtered to a stop in Ashland, though, so Joe had to charter a plane to take them the rest of the way. He arrived in Superior too late for the radio talk but managed to get to the rally.

Fortunately, not every day of campaigning was that hectic. Joe often ran late,

Joe McCarthy relaxes in front of a fireplace in a log cabin during his primary campaign for the Senate in 1946. *Wisconsin Historical Society*

but he kept most of his commitments. Wherever he traveled, he carried stacks of campaign literature to hand out. The most popular item was a pamphlet titled *The Newspapers Say*. The title had been Joe's idea; he told his advisors no one would read the publication if it was called *Joe McCarthy for Senator*. The booklet contained lots of photos of Joe and favorable comments about him from Wisconsin newspapers. It highlighted his youth, his willingness to work hard, and his accomplishments as a judge and a Marine. It said almost nothing about his views on the issues except for his strong support of more federal aid to veterans and their families.

Urban Van Susteren hired a polling firm to test the effectiveness of the pamphlet among voters in a number of small Wisconsin towns. Before the booklet was distributed, the better-known La Follette had enjoyed a two-to-one advantage over Joe in one town; afterward, they were running neck and neck. In another town, where La Follette's advantage had been three to one at the start, the booklet had helped reduce it to three to two. Tom Coleman was so impressed with these figures that he gave Van Susteren $30,000 to finance the printing and mailing of 700,000 more of the pamphlets to Wisconsin voters.

As the date of the primary drew closer, Joe stepped up his attacks on La Follette. He accused the sitting senator of using his position and influence to benefit a radio station he owned. Joe contended, without supporting evidence, that "Senator La Follette's radio station made a 314 percent profit by virtue of a license granted it by a federal agency that depended on the Wisconsin's senator's vote for its appropriation." He added that La Follette "fought long and hard to give the FCC [the Federal Communications Commission] a larger appropriation than anyone thought it should have."

Two days after making the accusation, Joe invited La Follette to a public debate: "I am ready to meet my opponent for the Republican nomination for the senatorship at any time, anywhere in Wisconsin." La Follette, busy with his senatorial duties in Washington, did not reply to the invitation, so Joe stepped up his attacks. This time he focused on the isolationist stand Sen. La Follette had taken before the war. "If those men who died in World War II could return," Joe said in a radio speech, "they would say, 'Forever sweep from power those of little minds, who, by their failure to see what even the blind could see, obstructed every effort to prepare us for war.'" At the end of the speech, Joe said again that he was willing to debate this, and other issues, with Sen. La Follette "anytime, anywhere."

Brushing aside pleas from his aides, La Follette continued to ignore Joe's challenge. "I don't see why I should help him draw a crowd," the senator said. Earlier, in a radio talk to Wisconsin voters, La Follette had laid out his view of the election in his usual careful, unemotional style: "With twenty years of service spelled out in detail on the public record, I think you have an ample basis for making an appraisal of my candidacy, without numerous political speeches on my part. . . . I am running on my record."

Early polls had shown the senator comfortably ahead of McCarthy, and La Follette didn't see how the relatively unknown judge from Appleton could possibly catch up. So the senator made the fateful decision not to return to Wisconsin to campaign until just eight days before the primary. He spent three of those days in Milwaukee, giving brief speeches to his supporters and distributing pamphlets. Belatedly, he realized that his campaign was in trouble, and he and his backers pleaded with the editors of the influential *Milwaukee Journal* to endorse him. But the editors, after much discussion, decided to remain neutral.

Meanwhile, Joe never let up. He continued to crisscross the state, meeting and greeting hundreds of people and asking for their support on primary day. The Young Republicans thought up a unique way to advance his cause. They enlisted 1,000 members, including many veterans, to distribute McCarthy campaign literature in every Wisconsin town with a population over 500 on the weekend before the election. Employing military terminology, the Young Republicans dubbed the effort "a statewide vote attack." Car drivers were called "flight captains," pilots "bombardiers," and local leaders "squadron commanders."

Three planes dropped bundles of campaign literature at airports all across Wisconsin. More than 200 cars, each staffed by four volunteers, picked up the bundles and handed out the four-page folders to voters in all the towns and villages in their assigned areas. The folders urged voters to cast their ballots for the "regular Republicans" on the ticket. They emphasized the importance of Joe's candidacy, and he was allotted a full-page photograph.

Joe ended his campaigning at a soldiers' home in Milwaukee, where he told the veterans stories of his wartime experiences in the Pacific. Then he drove to Urban Van Susteren's home in Appleton, where he listened to the election results with a number of close friends.

La Follette enjoyed a lead in the early returns, but the tide turned when votes started to come in from Milwaukee, Sheboygan, and other cities along the shore

McCarthy enjoys breakfast at the home of his friends Urban and Margery Van Susteren, the day after his stunning victory over incumbent Robert M. La Follette in the 1946 Republican primary election for the U.S. Senate. *Wisconsin Historical Society*

of Lake Michigan. In the 1940 election, La Follette had carried Milwaukee County by 55,000 votes; now, in 1946, he lost it to Joe by 10,000. In the end, Joe stunned many observers by defeating the well-known and widely respected La Follette, 207,935 to 202,557.

At six A.M., when any doubts about the outcome had been dispelled, Joe made a brief victory statement: "This was a contest not between men but between issues and the theories of government." La Follette responded with a single word: "Congratulations." Loyal Eddy offered his special acknowledgment to the Young Republicans: "Your last-minute blanketing of the state by 1,000 spirited volunteers . . . was the final touch in one of the most important elections of our time." Tom Coleman confided to friends that La Follette's defeat "marked the greatest night in my life."

Many of La Follette's colleagues in the Senate reacted with sadness and regret. Senator Edwin C. Johnson of Colorado wrote the senator: "You must know how bitter I feel over the mistake the people of Wisconsin have made."

For Joe, his victory in the primary, while gratifying, was just another step on the road to the Senate.

8

Newcomer in Washington

NOW JOE HAD TO PLOT his campaign against the Democratic nominee, Howard J. McMurray, a former congressman and a strong advocate of labor unions, in the general election. Because Republicans greatly outnumbered Democrats in Wisconsin, McMurray was considered the underdog in the race. But he put up a much stronger fight than La Follette had, calling Joe "Two-job Joe McCarthy" because he had continued to work as a judge while running for the Senate.

Joe defended himself in a speech: "I did give up my job and my salary for a period of nearly three years, which time I spent in the U.S. Marine Corps. Now, ladies and gentlemen, it so happens that I am not a rich man or I could and perhaps would give up that salary again. My job is my means of support." Joe failed to mention the sizable sums he had made recently in the stock market.

In one of several debates with Joe, McMurray made fun of the postcard tactic the McCarthy campaign had used successfully against La Follette. Referring to Ray Kiermas's fund-raising efforts, McMurray said sarcastically: "They need money to hire girls to address postcards and sign the name 'Joe.'" Joe dismissed McMurray's comment as "petty" and said there was a more important issue they needed to discuss, namely, the matter of McMurray's loyalty to his country.

McMurray was startled by Joe's abrupt change of subject. "I have never had a responsible citizen challenge my loyalty before," he responded. "I am sure my friends and the students in my political science classes [McMurray was a lecturer

Poster used in McCarthy's successful 1946 Senate campaign against his Democratic rival, Howard McMurray. *Marquette University Archives*

at the University of Wisconsin] will not challenge my loyalty. This statement is a little below the belt."

Joe was determined to pursue the matter. Several weeks earlier, Fred Blau, chairman of the Wisconsin Communist Party, had endorsed McMurray in a letter to the *Daily Worker,* the newspaper of the Communist Party U.S.A., which was published in New York City. Two pro-McCarthy newspapers in Wisconsin picked up on Blau's letter and asked in similar editorials: "Does Mr. McMurray repudiate the Communists who have infiltrated the New Deal political machine in this state? Or does he crave political success so deeply that he would accept any support, disregarding its origin and sinister purpose?" Now Joe asked McMurray if he had been glad to receive "the endorsement of the *Daily Worker.*"

McMurray replied firmly: "I have not seen the reported statement in the *Daily Worker* . . . [but] I certainly repudiate that paper and their whole tribe." McCarthy's charge had already registered with the audience at the debate, however, and it would get more space in the morning newspapers than McMurray's denial.

McCarthy wasn't the only Republican to raise the Communist issue in the 1946 election campaign. Voters were distressed that the end of the war—which had cost so much and to which so many lives had been sacrificed—had not brought genuine peace to the world. Instead, Stalin's territorial demands in Europe, which Winston Churchill had lamented in his "Iron Curtain" speech, made people fearful and uneasy. A new conflict seemed to be shaping up, one that journalists had begun to call the cold war.

In such a nervous climate, it was almost inevitable that people would look for a scapegoat to blame for their uneasy feelings, and many found one in Communism. From there, it was easy for Republicans to make a connection between Communism and their political opponents, the Democrats. E. Dewey Reese, the National Chairman of the Republican Party, stated the connection sharply and clearly: "Democratic party policy as enunciated by its officially chosen spokesmen . . . bears a made-in-Moscow label. That is why I believe I am justified in saying the choice which confronts Americans this year [1946] is between Communism and Republicanism."

Joe McCarthy didn't know much about Communism, except that most people thought it was bad. He had not taken part in any of the heated discussions about Communist ideology, pro and con, that were so common during his college years. Nor did he appreciate the distinctions among reformers, radicals, social-ists, and Communists. What he did know was that anti-Communist rhetoric could drown out the arguments of an opponent and resonate with voters who were looking for simple, clear-cut answers to complicated political and social problems. And so he was more than willing to employ it as a tactic, as he did with Howard McMurray.

On the eve of the election, Joe predicted he would win by a margin of around 227,000 votes. His guess was amazingly close. The actual vote was 620,380 for McCarthy, 378,722 for McMurray—a margin of 241,658 for Joe.

After a joyous postelection celebration in Appleton on Tuesday night, Joe and several men friends drove north to the resort town of Land O' Lakes on the Michigan border. Joe was exhausted. He went to bed at seven-thirty on Wednesday evening and slept until three-thirty on Thursday afternoon. After eating a meal of two thick steaks, he went back to bed at ten-thirty. He was still sleeping when a reporter phoned at noon on Friday. "Why are you calling me in the middle of the night?" Joe asked.

McCarthy arrived in Washington by train on December 1. He wouldn't be sworn in with the other new senators until January 3, 1947, but he wanted time to settle in and begin to get a feel for the nation's capital.

He had persuaded his good friend Ray Kiermas to come to Washington with him as his office manager. Kiermas and his wife, Dolores, found a two-bedroom apartment in the city, and Joe moved in with them. He took one of the bedrooms, while the Kiermases' young daughter slept on a couch in the living room. Joe's room was simply furnished, and a visitor noticed that there were no personal photographs on the bureau or desk. The only reading matter was a pile of the paperback Western stories that Joe liked to read before going to sleep.

Wisconsin's other senator, Alexander Wiley, had long since forgotten Joe's unsuccessful run against him in 1944. Now Wiley introduced Joe to several of the most influential Republicans in the Senate, including Henry Cabot Lodge of Massachusetts and Robert Taft of Ohio, who was known by many as "Mr. Republican" because of the respect he was accorded by his fellow Republicans. Joe was eager to impress the senators and told Taft he hoped to get a seat on the powerful Armed Services Committee. Taft made no promises; all senators got committee assignments, but seats on that committee were usually reserved for far more experienced senators than Joe.

As a good-looking young bachelor, Joe found himself receiving more invitations to Washington cocktail and dinner parties than he could accept. He bought a dinner jacket at a discount clothing store and started attending five or six social functions an evening. He couldn't keep up that pace for long, however, and soon accepted only those invitations he thought would help him politically. At one cocktail party, after looking over the elegant crowd, he turned to a friend and said, "I wonder what these people would think if they knew I once raised chickens."

Two railroad cars full of Joe's Wisconsin supporters had come to Washington for the senatorial swearing-in ceremony in January. Among them was Patricia Corry, a beautiful young woman from Menasha, whom several newspapers called Joe's fiancée. But she was only one of many women Joe was seen with in his first months in Washington. "McCarthy loved to squire pretty young women," a Wisconsin reporter recalled later, "and the more numerous the better." Their presence added to his image as a vital, attractive man, but he never displayed a serious interest in any of his dates. When a journalist asked him why he had never married, Joe replied jokingly, "I can't work at politics if I can't stay away from supper when I want to."

The new junior senator from Wisconsin.
Wisconsin Historical Society

The cartoonist Herblock's view of the 1946 election results, which gave Republicans a majority in both the House of Representatives and the Senate. *The Library of Congress*

The Congress that Joe entered in 1947 was controlled by Republicans for the first time since 1931. Their margin in the House of Representatives was 246 to 188, and they held 51 seats out of 96 in the Senate, giving them a majority in that body also. This meant Republicans chaired all the Senate and House committees and subcommittees. Even so, Joe, as a freshman, failed to get a seat on his first choice, the Armed Services Committee. He had to settle instead for seats on the less-prestigious Committee on Banking and Currency and the Committee on Expenditures in the Executive Departments.

Determined to make an impression in the Senate—and get his name into the newspapers—Joe looked for ways to make the most of his committee assignments. He fought for and obtained an immediate end to wartime sugar rationing when the matter came before the Banking and Currency Committee. In doing so, he earned the enmity of the committee chairman, Senator Ralph E. Flanders of Vermont, who favored a more cautious approach. McCarthy didn't care; he knew that the end of rationing would be popular with homemakers throughout the country, and he was right. However, his victory received far less space in the papers than another issue of the day: the rising fear of the Soviet Union's territorial ambitions abroad, and the actions of the Communist Party U.S.A. at home. In the eyes of many, there was no difference between a member of the Communist Party and a spy for the Soviet Union.

The Communist Party U.S.A. had never been a major political force in the United States. Even in the Depression year of 1932, the Communist candidate for president, William Z. Foster, garnered only 102,991 votes. During World War II, when the United States and the Soviet Union were allies, party membership reached a high of 75,000. It plummeted rapidly in the postwar years, as the Soviet Union changed from ally to enemy, until by the late 1940s there were only 10,000 or so active members.

Many idealistic young Communists and their sympathizers had entered government service during the 1930s and '40s, and some were still applying for government jobs. To counter any influence they might have on policy (and to answer his right-wing critics), President Truman, on March 21, 1947, signed an order requiring all civilians seeking employment in the executive branch to undergo an extensive investigation of their past activities and associations.

The investigations would be conducted by the heads of the government agencies or departments to which the job seekers were applying. The investigators would examine the applicants' school and college records and the files of local law-enforcement bodies, the Federal Bureau of Investigation, and other organizations. Meanwhile, starting immediately, the FBI would conduct similar investigations of all those already working in the executive branch.

New applicants could be rejected and longtime employees fired from their jobs if "on all the evidence, reasonable grounds exist for belief that the person involved is disloyal to the government of the United States." Disloyalty was defined as meaning, among other things, sabotage, espionage, disclosure of confidential government documents, and "membership in or sympathetic association with

President Harry S. Truman takes a stroll along a Washington street, accompanied by a Secret Service bodyguard. *The National Archives*

an organization or group declared by the Attorney General to be totalitarian, Fascist, Communist, or subversive." Soon after the order was announced, the attorney general released a list of 82 organizations the FBI labeled disloyal, and more were added later.

A loyalty board would be set up in each agency or department to process appeals. That wasn't enough to satisfy liberal critics, who believed that the order violated the individual's constitutional rights. One wrote, "Here is the doctrine of guilt by association with a vengeance." Others objected to the fact that an accused couldn't subpoena witnesses, cross-examine informants, or gain access to the confidential information used against him or her, as in a court of law.

Many conservatives, on the other hand, criticized the order for being timid and full of loopholes. They thought the loyalty issue was too important to be left

in the hands of the agencies and departments affected. They favored the formation of a bipartisan (two-party) loyalty review board that would have overall
authority in the matter, and could impose even stricter standards on everyone
involved. Joe sided with the conservatives.

Late in March 1947, McCarthy joined a minority of senators in opposing the
nomination of David E. Lilienthal, President Truman's choice to head the new
Atomic Energy Commission. Lilienthal, a moderate, had since 1941 served as
chairman of the Tennessee Valley Authority (TVA), a New Deal project to bring
electric power to the poverty-stricken Tennessee River Valley region. In 1946, he
was also appointed to chair a high-level commission to study how atomic energy
might be controlled internationally. Scientists hailed Lilienthal's nomination,
and it was accepted by a Senate committee in an eight-to-one vote. But conservative senators like Joe challenged the nomination when it came before the entire Senate. They believed the TVA was "socialistic" and filled with "subversive"
employees, and some even doubted Lilienthal's own loyalty to his country.

David E. Lilienthal.
The National Archives

Working quietly with the conservative senators was J. Edgar Hoover, director of the FBI. Hoover sent the senators confidential FBI reports that contained charges against some of Lilienthal's appointees at the TVA. One assistant, for example, was reported to have added the words "insofar as my conscience will allow me" at the end of an oath to support the Constitution. Joe had complete faith in the FBI report and told fellow senators he was deeply troubled by the added phrase. "That is not the type of reservation that I believe a man should make, especially when he is a man who has been chosen for such a job as this man," Joe said. He also expressed serious doubts about Lilienthal himself: "I'd much rather run the risk of discarding a competent man than run the risk of being stuck with a dangerous man."

Shortly before the Senate voted on the Lilienthal nomination, Joe took part in a radio debate about the Communist threat that was broadcast nationwide. On the program, Joe said he was in favor of outlawing the Communist Party. Some 61 percent of Americans agreed with him, according to a Gallup poll at that time. He went on to list a number of further measures the government should adopt "if we are to survive the Communist menace." To start with, he said, "All Communist aliens should be forced to leave the country." Moreover, "[American] Communists and members of Communist-front organizations [those that supported Communist goals] should be required to register with a federal agency and be fingerprinted."

Joe must have known that such proposals, especially the last, violated rights guaranteed by the Constitution and would never be accepted by the courts. He probably made them anyway in order to get attention from the national media. His remarks were picked up by a few newspapers, but they were soon overshadowed by other news, including the Senate confirmation on April 9 of David Lilienthal as the first chairman of the Atomic Energy Commission. Lilienthal's supporters had succeeded in beating back the opposition, and the final vote was 50 to 31 in favor of the nominee.

If Joe was disappointed by the outcome, he didn't express it. Besides, another, bigger news story was about to dominate the media. This was the House Un-American Activities Committee's investigation into Communist activities in Hollywood.

Charges of Torture

MANY COMMENTATORS LINK Joe McCarthy with the House Un-American Activities Committee, but there was no official connection. The Committee—commonly known by its acronym, HUAC—was an arm of the House of Representatives, whereas Joe's committee work was confined exclusively to the Senate.

In 1938, with the threat of war looming in Europe, Congress established HUAC to investigate the "disloyal" activities of Fascists and Communists in the United States. By 1947, the war had been over for two years, suspicion of the Soviet Union was mounting, and the committee had shifted its attention almost entirely to the doings of American Communists and their sympathizers.

HUAC's chairman in 1947 was Representative J. Parnell Thomas, an ultra-conservative Republican from New Jersey, and one of the committee members was Representative Richard M. Nixon of California, who had been elected to the House in 1946, the same year Joe was elected to the Senate. In the fall of 1947, Chairman Thomas launched an investigation into "the extent of Communist penetration in the Hollywood motion picture industry."

A group of ten accused Hollywood Communists—seven screenwriters, two directors, and a producer—was brought before the committee. One of the ten, director Edward Dmytryk, had actually left the party in 1945; another, screenwriter Alvah Bessie, had fought against the Fascist rebel forces in the Spanish Civil War.

The "Hollywood Ten," as the press dubbed them, were considered unfriendly witnesses because they refused to cooperate with the committee's investigation. When asked, "Are you now, or have you ever been, a member of the Communist Party?" most of the Ten refused to answer, invoking their Fifth Amendment right to remain silent. Along with others who were summoned to testify before Congressional committees, they disputed the members' right to question them about their associations in the first place, regardless of whether or not they actually belonged to the suspect organizations. One of the Ten who did respond to the question in his own way was Academy Award–winning screenwriter Ring Lardner, Jr., who said, "I could answer the question exactly the way you want, but if I did, I would hate myself in the morning." On November 24, 1947, the Hollywood Ten were cited for contempt of Congress, and each was sentenced to no more than one year in federal prison.

J. Parnell Thomas, chairman of the House Un-American Activities Committee (right), and Robert E. Stripling, a committee investigator, closely examine a Hollywood movie suspected of promoting Communist ideas and beliefs. *The Library of Congress*

Chairman J. Parnell Thomas (second from left) in front of his home with visiting members of his House Un-American Activities Committee, including Representative Richard M. Nixon (far right). *The Library of Congress*

Fifty top Hollywood executives, worried about the negative effect the investigation might have on the movie business, met to discuss how the industry should respond. They decided that the Ten would be suspended without pay until their cases went through the appeals courts. The executives also stated firmly that thereafter no Communists or other subversives would knowingly be employed in Hollywood. This policy soon led to the compilation of so-called blacklists that listed the names of entertainment-industry personnel who were suspected of being disloyal. The blacklists affected hundreds if not thousands of men and women, not just in the movies but also in the fledgling television industry and to a lesser extent in the Broadway theater. These actors, writers, directors, and technical people soon lost their jobs.

Joe was no doubt aware of the impact the House investigation had made in the press and among the general public. For now, though, he had to be content with spearheading a Senate inquiry into the postwar housing problem. The country faced a severe housing shortage, because there had been very little new construction in the Depression years and virtually none during the war, when building materials such as lumber and metal were needed for the war effort. President Truman, expressing the Democratic view, proposed that Congress enact a federal housing program that would include sizable sums for slum clearance in the cities and the construction of more than 500,000 units of affordable public housing.

Most Republicans, including Joe, were suspicious of public housing, thinking it just another example of big-government bureaucracy and waste—or worse. After visiting one troubled project in Queens, New York, Joe called it "a deliberately created slum area" and a "breeding ground for Communism." Senator Robert Taft took a different position. While Taft believed housing should remain largely in the hands of private developers, he also saw a place for public housing. However, he felt it should be modest in scope and available only to those in genuine need, and should not be allowed to infringe upon the private housing industry.

This difference would lead to clashes between Taft and Joe when the latter took charge of a joint Senate-House committee established to study the entire

Senator Robert Taft. *The National Archives*

housing field. In early February 1948, the committee issued its final report, and two weeks later Joe introduced the draft of a comprehensive housing bill in the Senate Banking and Currency Committee. It included tax exemptions for builders of low-rent housing, assistance to cities for slum clearance, and the extension of federal mortgage insurance. There was no provision for the construction of any public housing units.

Sen. Taft was not pleased. He announced that he would introduce a public-housing amendment to the bill when it reached the full Senate for discussion. The dispute went back and forth, with neither Taft nor McCarthy backing down, and was still not resolved when the 1947–48 Congressional session came to an end. As a consequence, and to Joe's regret, no major housing legislation would be possible until after the election that fall.

One positive development in Joe's life occurred as he was struggling to pass the comprehensive housing bill. In July 1948, he hired a recent journalism graduate of Northwestern University, Jean Kerr, as a research assistant. Miss Kerr—known as Jeannie to her friends—was a tall, beautiful, intelligent, and highly ambitious young woman. At Northwestern, she was named the prettiest girl in her journalism class. She also won an award for writing the best essay on the topic "The Promotion of Peace Among the Nations of the World."

Miss Kerr had first stopped by Joe's office in the late spring of 1947 to visit his secretary, who was an old friend. Jean hoped to find a summer job in Washington between her junior and senior years at the university. Joe glimpsed her as she left his office and told his secretary, "Whoever that girl is, hire her." Jean declined the offer, having found another job in the meantime with a Senate special investigation committee. Joe kept in touch with her, though, and a year later she joined his staff.

The presidential election of 1948 did not go as expected. Republicans thought their candidate, Governor Thomas E. Dewey of New York, would be a shoo-in, and many political commentators and much of the press agreed. On election night, the *Chicago Tribune* rushed out a special edition with the headline "Dewey Defeats Truman!" But he didn't. When the final votes were counted, Truman emerged the victor by a comfortable margin.

The Republicans suffered another major defeat in the 1948 election: They lost control of the Senate. This directly affected Joe's hopes of making an impression on the Banking and Currency Committee. The newly appointed Democratic

McCarthy makes a point in one of his many speeches. *Wisconsin Historical Society*

chairman of that committee, Senator Burnet R. Maybank of South Carolina, refused to accept the position if McCarthy remained a member. Maybank, who had served on the committee as minority leader, had no use for Joe's brashness and his disregard of Senate rules and traditions.

Joe appealed to Sen. Taft for help in retaining his membership, but Taft chose not to intervene. He was still smarting from Joe's refusal to defer to him on the question of public housing. This meant that Joe was left with only his membership on the Committee on Expenditures in the Executive Departments, considered the Senate's least prestigious.

Joe wasn't ready to let his Senate career sink into obscurity. Although he was no longer directly involved, he maintained a keen interest in housing legislation. In January 1949, President Truman, still savoring his election victory, introduced a greatly expanded housing bill in the Senate. Among other things, it called for the construction of 1,500,000 public housing units over the next seven years, and a five-year slum clearance and urban redevelopment program costing 1.5 billion dollars.

Realizing that some sort of housing legislation was bound to pass, the Republican minority in the Senate, led by Sen. Taft, sought to moderate the president's figures. Joe entered into the discussion, and a compromise was eventually reached, reducing the number of public housing units to 810,000, to be constructed over a six-year period. This was still a much larger figure than the one proposed in 1948, when the Republicans were in control. The compromise measure passed in the Senate, 57–13, with Joe among those voting in favor. Despite intense efforts by the real estate lobby to defeat it, a similar bill was passed in the House, 227–186.

President Truman happily signed the measure into law, saying he knew his satisfaction was shared by members of Congress from both political parties "and by the many private groups and individuals who have supported this legislation over the past four years against ill-founded opposition."

Meanwhile, Joe had made some money from his involvement with the housing problem. In February 1949, he called a press conference to announce the publication of a paperback book, *How to Own Your Own Home,* which he said he had edited, and to which he had contributed a thirty-seven-page article titled "Wanted: A Dollar's Worth of Housing for Every Dollar Spent." The publisher was the Lustron Corporation, a manufacturer of prefabricated housing that could be assembled quickly and economically. Joe said the ninety-six-page book was designed to inform readers of federal aid available to both war veterans and nonveterans who wanted to build or buy their own homes.

What Joe didn't say was that it was Jean Kerr who had actually edited the book, including Joe's contribution, as one of her first staff assignments. Nor did he mention that the Lustron Corporation had paid him $10,000—a much larger sum then than now in terms of buying power—for his work on the project. His fee was only revealed in 1950, when Lustron was in the midst of bankruptcy proceedings. At that time, the federal receiver in charge commented, "I'll bet he [Joe] wouldn't have gotten it [the $10,000] if he hadn't been a United States senator."

The housing problem wasn't the only thing that concerned Joe in 1949. Early in the year, he heard of a case he found hard to believe at first. It arose from a charge by German prisoners of war that American Army personnel had tortured them while they were in captivity. According to the Germans, the Americans had kept them in solitary confinement for six months at near-starvation rations, had driven burning matches under their fingernails, and had given them beatings that resulted in broken jaws and permanently damaged testicles. The charges were made public by the National Council for Prevention of War, a Quaker organization dedicated to "bringing food and hope" to the war-torn countries of Europe, including Germany.

A firestorm of outrage followed the revelation of the charges. Everyone knew the Nazis had practiced torture, but could American soldiers have committed such atrocities? Individuals and organizations across the country called for a federal investigation into the matter. This was the point at which Joe got involved. He may have become interested in the case initially for political reasons, thinking his involvement would be hailed by Wisconsin's large German American population. Close friends were convinced he took up the case because he believed the charges, thought they put the United States in a terrible light, and wanted to see justice done.

The background to the case was complicated. It had its beginnings in December 1944, when the German army, driven by the advancing Allied forces into Belgium, had launched a desperate counterattack. During the course of the fighting, known as the Battle of the Bulge, a German regiment overpowered and captured an American troop convoy near the village of Malmédy. The Germans herded the disarmed Americans into an open field and fired into the group with eight machine guns. Moments later, eighty-three American fighting men lay dead in what came to be called "the Malmédy Massacre."

After the war, in December 1945, American Army personnel transported four hundred members of the German regiment in question to a prison near the city of Stuttgart, Germany, for intensive questioning. It was during this interrogation that the incidents of torture allegedly occurred. When the questioning ended in May 1946, seventy-four of the soldiers most closely involved in the massacre were brought to trial. At the end of the eight-week proceeding, all the accused but one were found guilty and forty-three were sentenced to death.

General Lucius D. Clay, the American military commissioner for Germany, reduced thirty-one of the forty-three death sentences to life imprisonment, reflecting a sharp change in the political atmosphere. The desire for revenge on Germany, so heated immediately after the war, had dwindled as fear of the Soviet Union's long-range intentions mounted. When the charges of torture emerged in late 1948, the accusations that American soldiers were responsible for the atrocities reverberated throughout America and in newspaper headlines around the world.

Whatever Joe's motivation for becoming involved, he took immediate action. He began by persuading the Special Investigations Subcommittee of the Executive Expenditures Committee to launch an investigation into the matter. Before work could begin, however, the Senate Armed Services Committee, chaired by Senator Millard E. Tydings of Maryland, claimed jurisdiction over the case. Without telling Joe, Tydings appointed a subcommittee of his own, headed by Senator Raymond E. Baldwin of Connecticut, to be in charge of the investigation.

Joe was justifiably angry and told reporters the Armed Services Committee was planning a "whitewash" of the soldiers' actions. To mollify him and keep peace with the Executive Expenditures Committee, Sen. Baldwin invited McCarthy to attend the hearings as an observer. He also agreed to share with Joe all information and documentation regarding the case. Joe accepted Baldwin's offer, and told associates he did not intend to be a silent observer.

And he wasn't. Almost from the moment they began, he dominated the proceedings, frequently drowning out Chairman Baldwin. "We have been accusing the Russians of using force, physical violence, and have accused them of using mock trials in [prison] cells in the dark of night," McCarthy said, "and now we have an Army report that says we have done all the things the Russians were accused of doing. But they are all right because it created the right psychological effect to get the necessary confessions." Joe delivered the last sentence with withering sarcasm, so listeners understood that he meant the opposite.

In his questioning of witnesses, McCarthy displayed none of the humor he had often shown when conducting hearings as a judge. Instead, he badgered and belittled the witnesses without mercy. He mocked Lieutenant Colonel Burton F. Ellis, who had been the chief prosecutor at the Malmédy trial and who testified that none of the accused German soldiers had been tortured. "I have been a judge so long," McCarthy said at one point, "that it makes me rather sick inside to hear you testify what you think is proper or improper [in the way the prisoners were treated]."

In another exchange, Joe asked Ellis loaded questions and then wouldn't let him answer. "If you won't talk when I am talking," McCarthy muttered, "then I won't talk when you are talking." In many ways, Joe's bullying tactics anticipated those he would employ a few years later in his anti-Communist hearings.

As the investigation continued, the Army's evidence gradually refuted most of the German charges. McCarthy refused to concede that the charges might be false, however. He had made up his mind about what had happened at Malmédy, and nothing anyone said could get him to change it. Instead, he tried to bluff his way through, as he often had when playing poker. His tricky moves failed to prevent the subcommittee, in its final report, from dismissing almost all the German claims of torture.

Joe was still trying to get a word in edgewise as Chairman Baldwin delivered the report in mid-October 1949. At last Baldwin had had enough. He put the report aside for the moment and addressed McCarthy in the formal language often used in Senate debates. "Let me say to my distinguished friend [meaning Joe] that I am not going to let him incorporate misstatements of fact in this case, because sometimes, in his exuberance, he is a little reckless in his statements."

This was not the first—nor would it be the last—time Joe was criticized for misstating facts. But as before, he seemed to shrug it off, and he continued to accuse the Baldwin subcommittee of a "whitewash" even after its final report was accepted by the Armed Services Committee. The committee responded by passing a resolution expressing its "full confidence" in Senator Raymond Baldwin.

Joe emerged from the Malmédy investigation bruised but not crushed. He may have failed in the effort to present himself as a fighter for justice to German American voters back home in Wisconsin, and he certainly had made some new enemies in Washington, notably Sen. Baldwin. He got his name in a few newspaper headlines, however, and for Joe that sort of attention often seemed to be what counted most.

The media spotlight didn't linger long on the Malmédy investigation. Two other events stunned the world and dominated the news in the late summer and early fall of 1949. The first happened on August 29, when the Soviet Union tested its first atomic bomb, called by Russian scientists "First Lightning." It was widely known that the Russians had been trying to develop a nuclear bomb, but no one expected they would achieve success so soon. In seeking an explanation, many people in the United States jumped to the conclusion that spies must have passed America's atomic secrets to the Soviets.

The second shock occurred little more than a month later. On October 1, 1949, Mao Zedong, leader of the Chinese Communist Party, declared victory over Chiang Kai-shek's Nationalist army in the civil war that had wracked China for more than twenty years. Mao declared in a speech that "the Chinese people

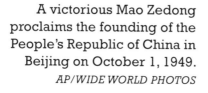

A victorious Mao Zedong proclaims the founding of the People's Republic of China in Beijing on October 1, 1949.
AP/WIDE WORLD PHOTOS

have stood up." Chiang, with his remaining troops and more than 2 million refugees associated with his regime, fled the Chinese mainland and settled on the large Chinese-owned island of Taiwan.

Like the Soviet atomic bomb test, the victory by the Chinese Communists was not entirely unexpected. After the Japanese defeat in World War II, President Truman had sent General George Marshall to China to try to arrange a truce between Mao's Communists and Chiang's Nationalists. Neither side was willing to compromise, however, and Marshall ultimately left China in 1947, his mission a failure.

The Chinese civil war blazed more hotly than ever, and the United States, banking on a Nationalist victory, sent millions of dollars in military aid to bolster Chiang's forces. Many Chinese experts in the State Department, including

John Stewart Service, and other Chinese scholars like Owen Lattimore warned that Chiang's government was riddled with corruption and lacked broad support among the Chinese people. They urged the United States to adopt a more neutral position in its relations with China.

These experts were overshadowed by American supporters of Chiang, who composed what was known as the "China Lobby" because they constantly pressed for more U.S. aid to the Nationalists. Outspoken members of the lobby included Henry Luce, the powerful and influential publisher of *Time* and *Life* magazines; Lieutenant General Claire Chennault, who had flown supplies to Chiang's forces during the war; and Chennault's Chinese-born wife, Anna. They and their fellows argued that Chiang's government was a loyal ally of the United States in its fight against the spread of Communism, and should be backed unconditionally. They found a sympathetic ear in President Truman, who had vowed to resist the expansion of Communist rule whenever and wherever he could.

And so, in 1949, after the Chinese Communists won control of a country of more than 600,000,000 people and Chiang's Nationalists experienced a humbling defeat, many Americans were perplexed and enraged. First the Soviets had tested an atomic bomb, and now China had been taken over by Communists. How could such a thing have happened? It wasn't long before the cry "Who lost China?" went up, and attention focused on the State Department experts who had advocated a more realistic policy toward the world's most populous nation.

In this climate of fear and paranoia, Joe McCarthy found the perfect environment to launch the next stage of his political career. But first he had to deal with some unfinished business back home in Wisconsin.

10

The Speech That
Started It All

THE *MADISON CAPITAL TIMES,* one of the leading newspapers in Wisconsin's capital, had been opposed to McCarthy since his campaign against Sen. La Follette. Joe's trickery and his down-the-line Republican position on the issues angered the *Capital Times*'s liberal owner. Now, in 1949, the newspaper spurred the state tax department to audit, or investigate, McCarthy's income tax returns for the past five years.

Joe anxiously awaited the results of the audit, because he knew his tax records were messy. He was elated when state tax officials not only gave him a "clean bill of health," as he put it, but also issued him a refund check for $1,100. Joe wasn't content to let the matter end there, however. As Urban Van Susteren recalled later, McCarthy loved to get revenge when he felt someone had treated him unjustly.

His revenge this time took the form of a fiery attack on the *Capital Times*'s city editor, Cedric Parker. Joe claimed that Parker had been a member of the Communist Party in the 1930s, had joined many other subversive organizations in the 1930s and '40s, and, according to Joe, still held extreme left-wing views. Parker, he said, was a perfect example of the kind of journalist J. Edgar Hoover had warned against: those who were planted by the Communists in important positions on college town newspapers "so that the young people who will take over control of the nation someday will be getting daily doses of Communist party-line propaganda."

McCarthy got more publicity in Wisconsin for questioning Parker's loyalty than for anything he had done so far in the Senate. *Time* magazine gave the story national attention, calling Joe's charges "blistering" and "well documented." Actually, the charges contained several unidentified quotations and many examples of guilt by association—accusing someone of being a Communist, for example, if the person had friends or colleagues who were members of the party. Once again, as Joe was quick to note, the response revealed that the media were more interested in accusations than in their accuracy.

Joe reached another conclusion in the wake of the Cedric Parker affair: If charges of disloyalty and subversion could get so much attention, most of it favorable, why not make more of them? On November 11, 1949, in a speech to the Shriners Club in Madison, he roused the crowd when he said, "We cannot blind our eyes to the fact that we are engaged in a showdown fight . . . a final, all-out battle between Communist atheism and Christian democracy." He went on to say he was still convinced that David Lilienthal, chairman of the Atomic Energy Commission, was disloyal and should be replaced. In the aftermath, pressured by Republican senators like Joe and ultraconservative Bourke Hickenlooper of Iowa, Lilienthal resigned his chairmanship on November 23.

Meanwhile, Joe had identified other targets. At a meeting of Young Republicans in Kenosha, Wisconsin, on November 15, he condemned the loss of China to the Communists, blamed "pinkos" (individuals with Communist leanings) like John Stewart Service for the defeat of Chiang Kai-shek, and claimed the State Department was "honeycombed with Reds. [Communists]." In his new role of anti-Communist crusader, Joe came to rely heavily on Jean Kerr. She was even more conservative than he, and had long been an ardent opponent of Communism. By the fall of 1949, she and Joe had become very close, and insiders believed she had helped turn him toward the far right of the Republican Party.

One surprise after another dominated the news in the first months of 1950, and each fed into the rising tide of anti-Communism. First, on January 21, Alger Hiss, a high official in the State Department from 1936 to 1946 and a participant in the Yalta Conference, was convicted on two charges of perjury. In 1948, a former Communist, Whittaker Chambers, had accused Hiss of being a member of the Communist Party and a Soviet spy. Hiss denied the charges, but after two years of hearings by the House Un-American Activities Committee and two court trials, a jury determined that Hiss had lied.

To the chagrin of those who believed in his innocence, the former State

Department official was sentenced to five years in prison. But others, while satisfied by the verdict, thought the revelations about Alger Hiss were just the tip of the iceberg. Richard Nixon, a member of HUAC, called the Hiss case "a small part of the whole shocking story of Communist espionage in the United States."

On January 31, President Truman announced that the United States would develop an even more powerful weapon, the hydrogen bomb. This second surprise heartened those who had been dismayed when the Soviet Union tested an atomic bomb the previous fall. Not everyone was pleased by the president's disclosure, however. World-renowned scientist Dr. Albert Einstein warned that all life on earth could be wiped out by a hydrogen bomb, and another scientist, Dr. Vannevar Bush, declared that no defense could be mounted against it.

The third surprising bit of news overshadowed Truman's announcement and revived the feelings of anger and fear aroused by the Soviet atomic test. On February 3, it was reported that Dr. Klaus Fuchs, a noted physicist, had been arrested in London as a Soviet spy. Fuchs, an exile from Hitler's Germany and a longtime Communist sympathizer, had fled first to England and then to America, where he had worked on the development of the atomic bomb at Los Alamos,

Alger Hiss. *The National Archives*

New Mexico. After the war, Fuchs had returned to England and continued his research on atomic energy. He also, according to the British police, passed along atomic and hydrogen bomb secrets to Soviet agents.

The U.S. reaction to Fuchs's treachery was quick and strong. The *Chicago Tribune,* one of the nation's most conservative newspapers, ran a huge front-page headline, "Reds Get Our Bomb Plans!" After expressing his shock at the news, Senator George W. Malone, Republican of Nevada, said, "Every move the State Department has made since 1934, when we recognized Russia, has been toward strengthening the Communists."

Meanwhile, the Republicans were busy organizing Lincoln's Day speeches around the country. The speeches would be given during the week of Lincoln's birthday. In the talks, party leaders would lay out their themes for the midterm elections that fall. Prominent among the themes, of course, would be the need to fight Communism wherever it raised its ugly head. Because of anti-Communist talks he had given recently in Washington and Wisconsin, Joe was one of the Republican senators chosen to deliver Lincoln's Day speeches.

Joe would not be speaking in big cities, where he might expect to get the most publicity. Sen. Taft and other senior Republican leaders hadn't forgotten the way McCarthy had offended them with his brashness and lack of respect. Consequently, he was handed a list of smaller cities. The tour began in Wheeling, West Virginia, on February 9, and went from there to Salt Lake City, Utah, and Reno and Las Vegas, Nevada, before winding up on February 15 in Huron, South Dakota.

If Joe was annoyed with this rather out-of-the-way itinerary, he didn't show it. Instead, he prepared for the tour with the same energy and enthusiasm he'd displayed when campaigning in Wisconsin. He had his speechwriters draft two different talks, one on the nation's housing problems, the other on Communists in government. During the cab ride into Wheeling, the first stop on his tour, he asked the Republican politician who had met his plane which of the talks he thought would be more appropriate. Without hesitation, the politician chose the one on Communists in high places, and Joe agreed.

That evening, more than 275 people gathered in the ballroom of a Wheeling hotel for the Lincoln Day celebration, sponsored by the Ohio County Republican Women's Club. A local radio station planned to broadcast Joe's talk, and reporters from Wheeling newspapers were present. No journalists from the major

Joe McCarthy attends a dinner before his Lincoln Day speech on February 8, 1950, to a women's Republican club in Wheeling, West Virginia. This was the speech in which McCarthy claimed that 205 members of the Communist Party were working in the State Department. *Marquette University Archives*

radio networks or big city newspapers attended the event. As far as they were concerned, it would be just another political speech by a little-known junior senator, and not worth the attention of a wider audience.

They were right about most of Joe's remarks, which were a rehash of the Alger Hiss case and other examples of Communists allegedly working in the State Department. But then—in what would become a recurring gesture of Joe's—he reached into his briefcase and pulled out a sheet of paper. He waved it dramatically in front of the audience and said: "Ladies and gentlemen, while I cannot take the time to name all the men in the State Department who have been named as active members of the Communist Party and members of a spy ring, I have here in my hand a list of 205—a list of names that were made known to the Secretary of State [Dean Acheson at the time] as being members of the Communist Party and who nevertheless are still working and shaping policy in the State Department."

This was not a new charge. In fact, Joe later admitted it came from a letter that the previous secretary of state, James F. Byrnes, had written to a congressman in Illinois four years earlier. The letter was in response to the congressman's inquiry into the backgrounds of 4,000 federal employees who had recently been transferred to the State Department from wartime agencies that were being shut down.

In the letter, Byrnes responded that case histories of more than 3,000 transfers had already been examined, and it was recommended that 285 of these people not be given permanent employment. Further examinations led to 79 being let go, many of them aliens—that is, not American citizens—who were ineligible for postwar government employment. That left 206 (not 205) still employed by the State Department—in 1946, not 1950, when Joe delivered his speech. And Byrnes never said that any of those involved were members of the Communist Party.

Not knowing these background facts, the Wheeling audience that night reacted to Joe's words with shock and dismay. The major local paper, the *Wheeling Intelligencer,* gave his talk front-page coverage with banner headlines, and a part-time Associated Press reporter in Wheeling phoned in a couple of paragraphs from the story to his boss in Charleston, the state capital.

The boss was astonished by Joe's claim that there were 205 known Communists working in the State Department, and asked his reporter to double-check the figure with McCarthy. Joe confirmed its accuracy, and later that day, February 10, the reporter's 110-word story went out on AP newswires to papers all across the country.

At first not that many newspapers picked it up. Then, after the State Department issued a denial on February 11, the story received much wider coverage. When Joe's plane landed in Denver on its way to Salt Lake City, reporters gathered at the airport asked for his comments on the denial. One wanted to see the list of Communists Joe had referred to in his talk.

Joe didn't have the copy of Byrnes's letter to the Illinois congressman with him; it was in his Washington office. The piece of paper he'd displayed to the Wheeling audience was just a page from his speech. But as he so often did when cornered, Joe decided to bluff. It had worked in the past; why not now? He would be glad to show the reporter the list, he said, but unfortunately he had left it on the plane. "If Dean Acheson calls me in Salt Lake City," Joe said, "I'll be glad to read the list to him."

When he got to Salt Lake City, Joe, in a radio interview, said he had the names of 57 "card-carrying members of the Communist Party" who were currently at work in the State Department. If the interviewer noticed the discrepancy between this figure and the 205 Joe had cited in Wheeling, he didn't comment on it.

This lower number came from another report that Joe's researchers had dug up. It concerned a 1947–48 House investigation into the State Department's personnel security procedures. After examining hundreds of employee files, the investigators, led by Representative Robert Lee, concluded that the loyalties of 57 men and women were "suspect."

Spokesmen for the State Department had responded quickly when the Lee

Secretary of State Dean Acheson.
The National Archives

report was issued. In early March 1948, they stated that out of the 57 men and women whose loyalty had been questioned, 35 had been cleared for employment by the FBI, and the remaining 22 were still being probed. Moreover, none of the 57 had been accused of being Communists. And, in fact, no American Communist was still carrying a party membership card in 1950, when Joe issued his charge. The Party had recalled the cards several years earlier.

If Joe was aware of these facts, he chose to ignore them. At the end of the radio interview in Salt Lake City, he repeated the offer to Dean Acheson that he had made in Denver. "Now, I want to tell the Secretary of State this, if he wants to call me tonight at the Hotel Utah, I will be glad to give him the names of those 57 card-carrying Communists." This time Joe said he would give the secretary the names only if Acheson agreed to provide "all information as to their Communistic activities" to a congressional investigating committee.

Once again, Joe was bluffing. He knew perfectly well that Acheson could not release that information because President Truman had issued an executive order in 1948 sealing all the personnel files of federal employees. The president had acted because he felt HUAC and other such committees often misused the files in the course of their investigations. In Truman's opinion, expressed during the 1948 presidential campaign, "HUAC is more un-American than the activities it investigates."

Joe was bluffing in another, more significant way. Neither the Byrnes letter to the congressman in 1946 nor Lee's report on the 1948 House investigation contained any names. The House report used numbers rather than names to identify individuals, and only the chairman of the subcommittee and one other member of Congress had names to match the numbers. This was a problem Joe would have to deal with later.

On February 11, Joe flew on to Reno, where he was greeted with a telegram from a State Department official requesting the names of the 205 Communists who Joe alleged were working in the department. Instead of being rattled, Joe sensed an opportunity for some fresh publicity. He fired off a letter to President Truman that was released to the press by the senator's Washington office at the same time. In the letter, McCarthy said he had obtained the names of 57 Communists in the State Department. "But you can obtain a much longer list by ordering Secretary Acheson to give you a list of those whom your board listed as being disloyal [back in 1946] and who are still working in the State Department."

He ended the letter with a warning. If the president didn't demand that Secretary Acheson reveal "all the available information" on the State Department suspects, and if he didn't revoke his order sealing the department's personnel files, he [Truman] would be acknowledging that the Democratic Party was "the bedfellow of international Communism."

Writing to the president in this fashion was an unusually arrogant move on McCarthy's part. He followed it up with an even bolder one that evening, in his speech to a crowd of more than 500 dedicated Republicans in Reno. For the first time, Joe offered the names of four suspects that he must have obtained from one of the congressmen who had been briefed on the 1948 House investigation. Two of the four men named were little known, but the others—Harlow Shapley, professor of astronomy at Harvard, and China expert John Stewart Service—were prominent figures in their respective fields.

The response was swift and firm. A high State Department official said that only one of the four men named by McCarthy, John Stewart Service, was currently employed there. And Service's loyalty to his country had been established beyond any doubt by the department's in-house loyalty board. The official concluded by affirming his own anti-Communist credentials, declaring to the gathered reporters that if he [the official] "learned of a single Red who was presently employed by the department, the man would be fired before sundown."

But, as often happened, Joe's charges carried more weight in the press than the State Department denials. While a few papers, like the *Baltimore Sun,* adopted a cautious approach in their coverage—the *Sun*'s front-page headline read "McCarthy Names Names in Four 'Cases'; Senator, However, Calls None 'Communist' or 'Traitor'"—many others blared Joe's charges as if they were accepted facts. The *Boston Herald* said, in a banner headline, "Senator Lists Shapley as Among Four Pro-Reds Tied to State Dept." and the *San Francisco Chronicle* headline read "4 in State Department Named as Reds."

Joe attracted a large, enthusiastic crowd for his speech in Las Vegas, and more than 300 people jammed into the First Presbyterian Church in Huron, South Dakota, to hear him speak. A local newspaper gave Joe's talk glowing coverage, and one of those who heard it wrote, in a letter to the editor, "He [Joe] left us feeling proud we were Republicans. . . . McCarthy is a thinking, acting leader, not just a politician."

His speaking tour finished, Joe flew to Milwaukee on his way to Appleton for a short visit with friends and family before returning to Washington. At the Milwaukee airport, he learned that President Truman had told reporters at a news conference that there was "not a word of truth in any of McCarthy's charges."

Milwaukee newsmen gathered around Joe, asking for his reactions to the president's comment. Once again Joe assumed a cocky attitude, saying, "President Truman should refresh his memory about certain things." He went on to repeat his claim that he had in his possession the names of 57 Communists in the State Department, and said again that he would hand the list over to the president as soon as the State Department's loyalty files were opened. Joe ended on a serious note. "I want to be sure they aren't hiding these Communists anymore."

Joe must have been delighted that his bluffs and exaggerations were paying off so handsomely. In little more than a week, he had gone from being a freshman senator from Wisconsin, little known beyond his home state, to a political celebrity whose words made headlines all across the country.

11

Where's the Evidence?

BACK IN WASHINGTON, Joe was eager to sustain the momentum his
Lincoln Day tour had generated. He requested four or five hours of speaking time on the floor of the Senate to present fresh charges of subversion in the
State Department. This so-called new information came from the 1947 Lee report on the House's investigation into the Department that Joe had already used
in his Lincoln Day speeches. McCarthy planned to talk about many of the cases
in the report, changing their order so that any senators present who knew the
Lee report would not immediately recognize Joe's source.

The Senate granted Joe's request and scheduled his presentation for the evening of February 20, 1950. Joe arrived early, carrying a briefcase bulging with
papers, some of which poked out at the top. Only a few Democrats and a dozen
or so Republicans were present for the evening session, but Joe noted a sizable
number of reporters in the gallery.

McCarthy began on a serious note. "I wish to discuss tonight a subject which
concerns me more than does any other subject I have ever discussed before this
body," he said, "and perhaps more than any other subject I shall ever have the
good fortune to discuss in the future." Then he went on the attack. His target
was Scott Lucas, a Democrat from Illinois who was serving as Senate majority
leader.

A few days earlier, Lucas had given a speech in Chicago in which he had commented negatively on Joe's Lincoln Day speeches. "If I had said the nasty things
that McCarthy has about the State Department, I would be ashamed all my life,"
Lucas was quoted as saying. Now Joe had his chance to get back at the Illinois

Sen. McCarthy reads some of the thousands of letters he received from supporters of his crusade against security risks in the State Department. *The Library of Congress*

senator, mocking him as "the Democratic leader of the Senate—at least, the alleged leader. Actually, I do not feel the Democratic Party has control of the executive branch of the government any more."

Lucas, who was present, bristled at Joe's remarks. He frequently interrupted Joe to ask loaded questions and make sarcastic comments. Lucas believed it would be easy to expose McCarthy's bluffs and contradictions, but he underestimated the wily senator from Wisconsin. When he asked Joe about the 205 supposed Communists in the State Department he had cited in Wheeling, Joe replied, "I do not believe I mentioned the figure 205. I believe I said 'over 200.'" Unfortunately, the tape recording of the Wheeling speech had been erased after it was broadcast, so there was no way of checking what McCarthy had said.

Irritated by Joe's vagueness, Lucas pressed on, asking if he had said 205, as reported in the press, or 57, as he had said later in Salt Lake City. Joe responded angrily, dismissing the question as "silly." Then he went on to claim that he had used both figures in Wheeling, saying 57 were Communists and 205 "unsafe risks." To complicate matters, he added that some of the 57 were from "this group of 205."

While Lucas pondered this confusing batch of figures, Joe held up his brief-case and said it contained photostats of information about "the Communist character of 81 State Department employees." He had obtained it, he said, "from some good loyal Americans whose identities will forever remain confidential." Joe said he had the names of all 81 suspects but felt it was "improper to make them public" until an appropriate Senate committee had a chance to study them. "If we should label one man a Communist when he is not a Communist, I think it would be too bad," he said with apparent sincerity.

Joe then reached into the briefcase, pulled out a batch of papers, and began to present his "evidence." For the next hour or more, he described case after case from the Lee report, often changing the wording as he went. He freely omit-ted sentences, added phrases, and exaggerated points, all in an attempt to make the cases seem more sinister and threatening. Where the Lee report described someone as being "inclined toward Communism," Joe described him as being an "active Communist." An applicant who in the end was rejected for a job was said by McCarthy to have received "top secret clearance."

At seven-thirty P.M., after Joe had gone through fourteen cases, Senator Lucas moved to adjourn the hearing because a quorum of senators—the minimum number required to conduct business—was not present. Joe's Republican sup-porters argued instead that the sergeant-at-arms should "compel" the missing senators to come to the Senate at once for what they described as an "urgent ses-sion." Lucas's motion was defeated on a party-line vote, with all the Democrats present voting yes and all the Republicans voting no, and the sergeant-at-arms set about calling the 72 absent senators. One by one they entered the Senate chamber; Senator Brien McMahon, reached at a party, arrived in white tie and tails. Forty minutes later a quorum had been rounded up, and Joe continued his presentation. He rambled on until eleven-forty-five when the senators—some nodding from fatigue—finally voted to adjourn the session.

The next day, the *New York Times,* in an editorial, criticized "the campaign of indiscriminate character assassination on which the senator [McCarthy] has embarked." But other newspapers were less critical in their coverage, and many Americans—still unsettled by the fall of China to the Communists and the Soviet Union's acquisition of an atomic bomb—were convinced that Joe had uncovered a nest of spies and traitors in the State Department.

The Senate, too, took McCarthy seriously. The next day, February 21, the

Democratic leaders voted for an immediate investigation into Joe's charges. They also agreed to Republican demands to hold open hearings and to subpoena the State Department's loyalty and employment files. Joe was especially eager to gain access to the files. Without them, he said, "the investigation will be completely useless, it will be a complete farce, and nothing but a whitewash."

President Truman, in a news conference, said that McCarthy's charges were entirely false and refused again to hand over the State Department's files. An angry Joe told reporters, "I don't think the Senate will allow the president to get away with his boyish thumbing of his nose at all the senators who represent the forty-eight states."

A few days later, State Department security officers made public the connection they had discovered between Joe's charges and Lee's 1947 report. Secretary of State Acheson, commenting on the link, told a news conference that "similar—perhaps identical—charges have been aired and thoroughly investigated before." Political columnist Drew Pearson, never an admirer of Joe's, recounted the story in greater detail, revealing to the public how the Wisconsin senator had twisted and distorted the Lee report in his Senate speech.

In light of these revelations, Senate Democrats thought they could quickly dismiss Joe's allegations. Majority Leader Thomas T. Connally of Texas downgraded the investigation by turning it over to a subcommittee to be chaired by Senator Millard E. Tydings of Maryland. As Connally told reporters, "I have more important things to do than to go on a skunk hunt."

Sen. Tydings disliked Joe personally, and had clashed with him earlier over the Malmédy investigation. But Tydings promised "a full, fair, and complete investigation." He went on to tell reporters, "We will let the chips fall where they may. This is neither a witchhunt on the one hand nor a whitewash on the other."

Senate Republican leaders knew how weak Joe's claims were, and how little evidence he had to back them. Worried that he would perform poorly under questioning by the Tydings subcommittee, they organized a group of prominent anti-Communists to help him prepare for the investigation. Their main goal wasn't to aid a fellow Republican in trouble but to prevent the Democrats on the subcommittee from exposing the trumped-up nature of McCarthy's charges. If that happened, the American people might begin to think the Communist menace had been exaggerated, and the Republicans might lose an issue they were counting on to win future elections.

Joe, too, realized he needed help, and welcomed the advice he got from conservative fellow senators like William F. Knowland of California, Styles Bridges of New Hampshire, and Kenneth S. Wherry of Nebraska. Representative Richard Nixon was especially helpful. When Joe requested materials from the House Un-American Activities Committee, on which Nixon served, Nixon was glad to lend Joe some of his files. He also met privately with Joe on several occasions to educate him in the politics of anti-Communism, an area in which Nixon was considered something of an expert.

J. Edgar Hoover, the FBI director, was probably Joe's most valuable advisor at this time. The two men had become friendly soon after McCarthy arrived in Washington, a friendship that was furthered by their mutual love of gambling. When Hoover was out of town, he offered Joe the use of his private box at the racetrack. But the FBI director didn't take Joe all that seriously as a senator until after the Wheeling speech. That was when he realized Joe might play an important role in the struggle against Communist influence in government, a cause that was dear to Hoover's heart.

Soon after Joe's return from the Lincoln Day speaking tour, he phoned Hoover

J. Edgar Hoover, Director of the FBI, (left), and his associate and close friend Clyde Tolson testify before a congressional committee in 1950. *The National Archives*

to say he needed some evidence to back up the charges he had made in the Wheeling speech. Hoover responded sympathetically, and he ordered his staff to go through the relevant FBI files and pass along any information they thought might be useful to Joe. This was nothing new; Hoover and his top aides often leaked classified FBI data to "friendly" members of Congress, right-wing journalists and political commentators, and conservative patriotic organizations.

Hoover also urged Joe to hire a former FBI agent, Donald Surine, as an investigator. Joe followed up on Hoover's recommendation and assigned Surine to gather incriminating material on suspected left-wingers in the State Department. Surine quickly became a key member of McCarthy's staff. Almost once a week he and Joe had lunch with Hoover and Clyde Tolson, the FBI's second in command and Hoover's close friend. Over drinks and steaks, the men exchanged information and gossip about key players on the Washington political stage.

The Tydings subcommittee opened its hearings into McCarthy's charges on March 8, 1950. The Senate caucus room, where the hearings were held, was crowded to capacity with newspaper, newsreel, and television journalists and photographers, as well as interested spectators. Smiling broadly and seeming completely self-confident, Joe swore to tell the truth, the whole truth, and nothing but the truth.

Chairman Tydings was well aware of where McCarthy had gotten the 81 names he had cited in his marathon Senate speech. But he wanted to pin Joe down and make him reveal the evidence—or lack of it—concerning their connections to Communism. At the first hearing, Tydings promised, "You are going to get one of the most complete investigations ever given in the history of this republic, so far as my abilities will permit."

In response, Joe claimed that his evidence on the 81 suspects had been "gathered over painstaking months of work," although Donald Surine was still trying to assemble it. To stall for time, Joe went on to say, "Let me make my position clear. I personally do not favor presenting names, no matter how conclusive the evidence is." McCarthy knew, though, that he would have to come up with some specifics in order to feed the media's appetite for news, and to keep Tydings and the other Democrats on the subcommittee from embarrassing him. And so he announced that he was prepared to discuss a sampling of cases as examples of what he and his researchers had unearthed.

In the next few days of hearings, Joe introduced the names of nine men and women who, he claimed, were known Communist sympathizers. Among them was Dorothy Kenyon, a sixty-two-year-old New York lawyer. Standing before the subcommittee, Joe pulled a bunch of copies of documents and newspaper clippings from his briefcase and charged that Miss Kenyon was in a "high State Department position" and "belongs to twenty-eight organizations cited by the Attorney General and House and Senate committees as subversive or disloyal."

He held up a copy of a full-page 1940 advertisement in the *Daily Worker*. It showed a petition to President Roosevelt and the attorney general protesting attacks on the veterans of the Abraham Lincoln Brigade, who had fought on the side of the republicans in the Spanish Civil War. Dorothy Kenyon had signed the petition, along with dozens of other prominent Americans whose loyalty to their country was undeniable. However, in the late 1940s, the House Un-American Activities Committee had labeled the Lincoln Brigade "subversive," and that was enough for Joe.

As he proceeded, McCarthy's case against Miss Kenyon grew weaker and weaker. He treated all of HUAC's judgments as proven facts, even when some of them were obviously questionable. He also revealed his ignorance of certain historical situations, such as the fact that the Spanish Civil War had brought liberals and Communists together in the 1930s. He concluded by saying that, in his opinion, Miss Kenyon was "an extremely bad security risk" who should be removed immediately from any connection with the State Department.

That afternoon, Dorothy Kenyon spoke to reporters in New York. She told them, "Senator McCarthy is a liar," and requested an opportunity to state her case before the Tydings subcommittee. At the same time, the State Department issued a statement defending her. It began by saying Miss Kenyon was not, and had never been, an employee of the State Department. Her only connection with it was a three-year term she had served as an American representative on a United Nations commission, a term that had ended the previous December.

Much of the press—especially the newspapers owned by longtime right-winger William Randolph Hearst—followed the usual pattern in covering the hearings. They played up Joe's charges against Miss Kenyon in bold headlines— "New York Lawyer Linked to Reds"—and played down her subsequent denial and that of the State Department spokesman. But the *New York Times* and the *Washington Post,* among others, observed that Joe was off to a thin start if he intended to prove there were Communists in the State Department.

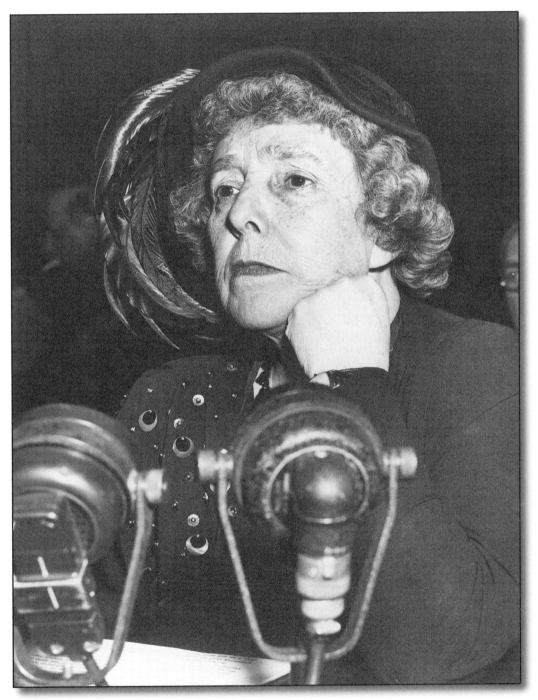

New York lawyer Dorothy Kenyon answers McCarthy's charges that she lent her name to many left-wing organizations that supported Communism.
The Library of Congress

Former First Lady Eleanor Roosevelt, a friend of Miss Kenyon's, adopted a gently mocking tone in her column, "My Day," which appeared in many newspapers. Mrs. Roosevelt wrote that Joe's charges were "very ill-informed" and even humorous. "If all of the honorable senator's 'subversives' are as subversive as Miss Kenyon, I think the State Department is entirely safe and the nation will continue on an even keel."

Despite Mrs. Roosevelt's criticism, *New York Times* editorials, and relentless questioning about his sources by Sen. Tydings and the other Democrats on the subcommittee, Joe proceeded with the other eight names on his preliminary list. He enumerated their supposed links to Communist-front organizations but refrained from calling any of them Communists. In his closing remarks, he said he had other important materials to present to the subcommittee, and Sen. Tydings invited him to return at any time to testify further. Then the subcommittee members voted to honor requests by the accused to respond in person to McCarthy's charges.

Dorothy Kenyon appeared on March 14, 1950. Joe stayed away from the hearing that day but left his papers regarding the Kenyon case with his fellow conservative Senator Bourke Hickenlooper. Miss Kenyon made a convincing witness on her own behalf. "I am, and have always been, an independent, liberal Rooseveltian Democrat," she stated, "devoted to and actively working for such causes as the improvement of the living and working conditions of labor, and the preservation of civil liberties."

She told the subcommittee she was an active member of such liberal organizations as the American Civil Liberties Union, Americans for Democratic Action, and the League of Women Voters. But she denied having ever been a member of the Communist Party, and said she had never joined or aided any organization known by her to be "even slightly subversive." As a delegate to the United Nations Commission on the Status of Women from 1947 to 1949, she had clashed many times with representatives from the Soviet Union and had been sharply criticized in the Soviet media.

Democratic senators on the subcommittee were uniformly sympathetic to Miss Kenyon. Even Bourke Hickenlooper, Joe's stand-in, had to admit that he did not consider her disloyal or "subversive in any way." Nor did the *Washington Post* editorial page. It stated, "In truth, Case No. 1 turned out to be not only an outraged and innocent American, but also a woman of spirit."

McCarthy conducts one of his many hastily called press conferences with reporters. *The Library of Congress*

Other newspapers questioned the truth of McCarthy's claims, not only against Dorothy Kenyon but also against the other eight individuals he had charged with being dangerous subversives. Joe fought back with a barrage of press releases, all of them timed to meet the deadlines of the major morning and afternoon newspapers—a way of making sure that his statements would get maximum coverage without giving his opponents a chance to respond in the same edition.

Midway through the hearings, Chairman Tydings called a news conference to report on his subcommittee's progress. When Tydings reminded the assembled reporters that to date Sen. McCarthy had not provided the subcommittee with the name of a single State Department employee accused of being a Communist, it appeared that he had shot down Joe's claims once and for all. But the Wisconsin senator wasn't through yet. He upstaged Tydings—and earned a fresh batch of headlines—by telling reporters that he was going to give Senate investigators "the name of the man, connected with the State Department, whom I consider the top Russian espionage agent in this country."

The Top Russian Spy

AS JOE HAD ANTICIPATED, his accusation became the big news story of the day. Everyone in Washington wondered who the top Russian spy might be. When the curiosity was at its height, McCarthy called Chairman Tydings and asked to appear before an executive session of the subcommittee. There, away from the popping flashbulbs of the news photographers' cameras, Joe told the senators that the man in question was China expert Owen Lattimore.

Lattimore's name had come up before in House and Senate inquiries into who had "lost" China; McCarthy had invoked it himself. But never before had Lattimore been accused of being a master spy. Now Joe said, "I think he was the chief of the whole ring of which Alger Hiss was a part. . . . If you crack this case, it will be the biggest espionage case in the history of the country."

Under questioning by Tydings and others, Joe admitted he had no fresh information about Lattimore. But he claimed—as he had in the past—that it could be found in the State Department's loyalty and security files, if only President Truman would authorize their release.

Some thoughtful Republicans, like former Secretary of State and Secretary of War Henry L. Stimson, were troubled by Joe's continuing attacks on the State Department and its secretary, Dean Acheson. In a letter to the *New York Times,* Stimson praised Acheson and, without naming McCarthy, went on to say, "The man who seeks to gain political advantage from personal attacks on a secretary of state is a man who seeks political advantage from damage to his country."

Owen Lattimore. *The National Archives*

The Republican leaders in the Senate made it clear that Joe's claims were "not a matter of party policy." But other prominent Republicans played to the right-wingers in their party. Senator Robert Taft encouraged McCarthy and reportedly urged him "to keep talking, and if one case doesn't work out, proceed with another."

And that's what Joe did. He revealed in a news conference that he had given the Tydings subcommittee the name of the "top Russian espionage agent," and pressed on with his demand that President Truman order the State Department to open its security files. Adopting a tough-guy tone, Joe said, "It is up to the President to put up or shut up. Unless the President is afraid of what the files would disclose, he should hand them over now." He applied further pressure in a telegram he sent the president the next day and simultaneously released to the press: "I feel that your delay of this investigation by your arrogant refusal to release all necessary files is inexcusable and is endangering the security of the nation."

Worried about the impact of McCarthy's charges, Sen. Tydings asked President Truman to grant his subcommittee access to the files on Lattimore and the others Joe had named. The president acknowledged the bind Tydings was in but didn't want to set a precedent for other "fishing expeditions" by McCarthy and his fellow Republicans. Instead, Truman ordered J. Edgar Hoover to prepare an analysis of Lattimore's file for private examination by the members of the Tydings subcommittee.

After studying Hoover's report, all the subcommittee members (except for Sen. Hickenlooper, who was absent that day) concluded that there was nothing in the file that showed Lattimore had ever been a Communist or a member of a spy ring.

With these findings in hand, Sen. Tydings told a news conference that Joe's unnamed "top" agent had been employed by the State Department for only a brief period five years earlier, and since then had given only one speech to State Department employees. Joe was predictably disdainful of Tydings's statement. It was, he said, "a deliberate misstatement of the facts" and "another one of those obvious attempts to twist and distort the truth." He went on to charge that the accused "has a desk in the State Department, or at least he did until three or four months ago. He is one of their top advisers on Far Eastern affairs, or at least he was until three or four weeks ago."

Next, McCarthy deliberately leaked Lattimore's name to Jack Anderson, a newspaper reporter who worked for columnist Drew Pearson. When Anderson asked if the information was on or off the record, Joe said "on." During his next weekly radio broadcast, Pearson identified Lattimore but went on to defend him and to reveal his own animosity toward McCarthy. "I happen to know Owen Lattimore personally," Pearson said, "and I only wish this country had more patriots like him."

Lattimore himself was in Afghanistan on a mission for the United Nations when Pearson revealed his name. Asked for his reaction to Joe's charge that he was a Soviet agent, Lattimore called it "pure moonshine" and made arrangements to fly back to Washington as soon as possible.

Four Democratic senators—including Theodore F. Green of Rhode Island, who was serving on the Tydings subcommittee—denounced McCarthy's tactics on a network radio program hosted by Eleanor Roosevelt. Sen. Green said Joe's attacks on respected figures like Owen Lattimore were "reckless and unfair, and did irreparable damage to America's image abroad." On a lighter note, when asked about Joe's claim that Lattimore had a desk in the State Department, Sen. Tydings laughed and said no one in the department could find it.

A few days later, the *Washington Post* ran a cartoon by Herblock (pen name of Herbert Block) publicizing a new term that would come to define Joe's tactics and those of others who followed in his wake. The cartoon showed an elephant, symbol of the Republican Party, being dragged by its right-wing members toward an overflowing barrel of tar labeled "McCarthyism." "You mean I'm supposed to stand on that?" the anxious-looking elephant asks.

Privately, according to his associates, Joe hated the new word. In public, though, he laughed off its negative implications and claimed that as far as he was concerned, McCarthyism meant the same thing as Americanism. In a speech later on, he expanded on this idea. "In my state," he said, "McCarthyism means fighting Communism. People write me all the time saying they wish there was more McCarthyism."

Meanwhile, in late March 1950, Joe and his staff were busy assembling all the information they could find on Owen Lattimore for a speech Joe planned to give to the entire Senate. They worked until two in the morning on the day McCarthy was to deliver the speech, and were back at their desks at seven o'clock after just a few hours of sleep.

When Joe walked into the Senate chamber on the afternoon of March 30, the balcony was crowded with journalists and cheering supporters. But only thirty-six of the ninety-six senators, including eight Democrats, were in their assigned seats on the ground floor. Joe repeated his by now familiar charge that "Owen Lattimore is or was a Soviet agent" and went on to say that "he either is, or at least has been, a member of the Communist Party."

He asserted that Lattimore had "a dominant influence over the formation and implementation of the policy which has delivered China to the Communists." Beyond that, Joe claimed that two State Department operations, the Far Eastern division and the Voice of America radio broadcasts, were "almost completely controlled and dominated by individuals [like Lattimore] who are more loyal to the ideals and designs of Communism than to those of the free, God-fearing half of the world."

Angry Democrats frequently interrupted the speech to raise objections. Senator Herbert H. Lehman of New York said Joe was "making a spectacle to the galleries here and to the public where a man accused has no chance to answer." Joe responded quickly and heatedly to Lehman's attack. "Crocodile tears are being shed for traitorous individuals," he intoned, "but forgotten are the 400,000,000 people [referring to China's population, which was actually more than 600,000,000 at the time] who have been sold into slavery by these people."

What with McCarthy's lengthy list of charges and all the interruptions, the speech went on for more than four hours. Midway through, Joe removed a small bottle from his breast pocket and took a long swallow from it. To quell any suspicions that the bottle contained liquor, Joe smiled and told the crowd that it was just cough syrup. Which it was. His old sinus problem had returned, and with it a cough, as Joe told reporters the next day when he entered a Washington hospital for treatment. McCarthy's friend and ally Senator Kenneth Wherry explained to the Senate the reason for Joe's absence. Majority Leader Tom Connally asked how long McCarthy expected to be out. "Just today," Sen. Wherry replied. "Is that all?" Connally said dryly.

Meanwhile, President Truman, on vacation in Key West, Florida, had called a news conference even before Joe had finished his speech. Making no effort to conceal his anger, Truman charged that McCarthy and other right-wing senators were playing politics with American foreign policy. He went on to call Joe "the greatest asset that the Kremlin [the seat of Soviet power] has."

Sen. Taft, now one of Joe's strongest backers, denounced the president's news conference statement as a "bitter and prejudiced attack on Republicans." Reversing Truman's comment about Joe, Taft said, "The greatest Kremlin asset in our history has been the pro-Communist group in the State Department." The Ohio senator concluded his remarks by hailing Joe as "a fighting Marine who risked his life to preserve the liberties of the United States."

Even Sen. Wiley, Joe's moderate senatorial colleague from Wisconsin, joined Taft and other Republicans in loudly criticizing the president's words. "The nation wants to get the facts," Wiley said, "and it does not want to see Senator McCarthy or any member of the Senate smeared merely because he has the guts to seek those facts on behalf of the American people."

By now it was early April, and the Tydings subcommittee was getting ready to hear Owen Lattimore's side of the story. The beleaguered China expert had returned to the United States from Afghanistan a few days earlier. At the airport, he assured reporters that he was neither a Communist nor a fellow traveler [someone who usually followed the Soviet political line]. He called Joe a "base and miserable creature."

The thin forty-nine-year-old Lattimore looked more like the college professor he was than the stereotypical image of a dangerous spy. He had been director of the Walter Page School of International Relations at Johns Hopkins University from 1938 until 1950 and was a lecturer at the school after that. Born in the United States, Lattimore was raised in China, where both of his parents were teachers of English at a university in the port city of Tientsin.

Lattimore, who spoke Chinese like a native, became the editor of *Pacific Affairs* magazine in the 1930s. He sought articles written from different perspectives and was later accused of publishing too many pieces that presented the Chinese Communists in a favorable light. In 1944, President Roosevelt had asked Lattimore to accompany Vice-President Henry Wallace on a fact-finding mission to China for the U.S. Office of War Information. After the war, Lattimore occasionally served as a consultant to the State Department on Far Eastern matters.

Joe was at home, recuperating from the sinus attack, when Lattimore flew back to Washington. Stung by Lattimore's harsh words at the airport, McCarthy contacted Sen. Tydings and asked for the right to cross-examine the professor when he appeared before Tydings's subcommittee. Tydings denied Joe's request but invited him to submit any questions he had through a subcommittee member. McCarthy rejected that idea.

On April 6, 1950, surrounded by photographers armed with flashbulbs, Owen Lattimore entered the packed Senate caucus room and was sworn as a witness before the subcommittee. Tom Connally, the Senate majority leader, sat with Tydings and the other subcommittee members. Behind them sat a group of conservative Republican lawmakers, Joe among them. As Lattimore, who faced the senators, looked at Tydings, he couldn't help but see Joe's face, too. Later, the China expert wrote, "I soon found out something interesting. Joe McCarthy couldn't look you straight in the eye."

Lattimore began his testimony by reading a lengthy prepared statement. Employing the same direct, uncompromising tone he had used in his airport remarks, he denounced McCarthy, calling his behavior "unworthy of a senator or an American" and saying his charges were "base and contemptible lies." He went on to assert that Joe had become a "willing tool" of the right-wing China Lobby, "the simple and willing dupe of a group of fanatical persons who have been thoroughly discredited."

Many of the spectators in the caucus room cheered Lattimore's comments. Others, like Joe and his fellow Republicans, remained silent. They were among the conservative Americans who sided with the China Lobby and believed that Chiang Kai-shek could have won his struggle with the Chinese Communists if only the United States had continued to back him.

Lattimore wasn't through yet. He accused McCarthy of using secret government documents, like the Lee report, without permission; of destroying the reputations of American citizens without giving them a chance to defend themselves; and of launching a "reign of terror" among federal employees. He claimed that McCarthy was making the U.S. government "an object of suspicion in the eyes of the anti-Communist world, and undoubtedly the laughingstock of the Communist governments."

Responding to Joe's assertion that he had "a desk in the State Department," Lattimore said that he had had "only three brief associations" with the department over a period of more than five years. He had served on a postwar mission to Japan in 1945, had offered his views on the Far Eastern situation in a requested memo to the department in 1947, and had taken part in a two-day panel discussion on China at the department the previous October. "I think I can fairly claim, with great regret," Lattimore said, "that I am the least consulted man of all those who have a public reputation in this country as specialists on the Far East."

Democrats on the subcommittee responded favorably to Lattimore and had few questions for him. Sen. Hickenlooper, however, asked one question after another, most of them concerning the fall of China. In response, Lattimore blamed Chiang Kai-shek and his Nationalists for losing the support of the Chinese people, and expressed the then highly controversial opinion that the new Communist government of China should be recognized by the United States. Throughout the questioning, Lattimore revealed a broad knowledge of China and the Far East that Sen. Hickenlooper obviously could not match.

Joe remained surprisingly quiet and expressionless during Lattimore's appearance. His anger emerged only later, when he told reporters, "I am not retracting anything. I intend to prove everything I have said." The next day, in another meeting with reporters, he announced that he had given Senate investigators the name of a witness who would swear that Lattimore either was or had been a Communist.

The mystery witness turned out to be Louis F. Budenz, a former Communist who had joined the party in 1935 and had been managing editor of its newspaper, the *Daily Worker*, from 1941 until 1945. Budenz resigned from the party that year, saying he had become disillusioned with Communism and the policies of the Soviet Union. In 1946, he gave a full confession to the FBI, and after that he became a key government witness at trials and congressional investigations.

Before the Tydings subcommittee, Budenz testified that he had been told by Communist leaders in 1937 that Lattimore was part of a group of Communists associated with the Institute of Pacific Relations. He also said that, while editing the *Daily Worker*, he had seen highly confidential Communist reports with the code name "L" or "XL" written on them. Party officials had told Budenz, he said, that the reports came from Lattimore. But under questioning by Democratic members of the subcommittee, Budenz admitted that he had no direct, personal knowledge that Lattimore was a party member.

In a follow-up question, the former Communist editor was asked whether, as McCarthy did, he believed Lattimore was the top Soviet agent in the United States. Budenz paused for a moment, then said, "Well, to my knowledge, that statement is not accurate. I do not know, of course, the whole story, what other evidence there is, but from my own knowledge I would not say he was a top Soviet agent."

Although Budenz's testimony had seriously weakened Joe's case against Lattimore, Joe was not about to acknowledge it. Instead, he fought back fiercely that evening in a speech before the American Society of Newspaper Editors. "I knew it would be thus," he said, "that vilification, smear, and falsehoods would follow [Joe's charges about Communists in the State Department]." Using wildly inflated language, he continued. These falsehoods were "peddled by the Reds, their minions, and the egg-sucking phony liberals who . . . clutter up American thinking with their simple-minded arguments. Some write columns for your newspapers. It is your privilege to buy them; mine to ignore them." He had nothing but scorn, Joe said, "for the pitiful squealing of those who would hold sacrosanct those Communists and queers who have sold 400 million Asiatic people into atheistic slavery and have the American people in a hypnotic trance, headed blindly toward the same precipice."

As the Tydings hearings continued, a number of Communists and former Communists testified that they had heard this and that about Lattimore's affiliations. But none of them provided solid evidence that he was a member of the party, let alone that the China expert had also been a Soviet spy.

An objective evaluation of the Lattimore case, and Joe's overall campaign, would have to conclude that, almost three months after Joe's Wheeling speech, not one of his charges of Communist subversion in the State Department had been proved. But Congress and the nation weren't in an objective frame of mind in the late spring of 1950. A poll of Minnesota residents revealed that 41 percent believed Joe's claims that Communists were active in the State Department, while 29 percent did not and 30 percent were undecided. On the national level, a Gallup poll showed that 39 percent of those interviewed believed McCarthy's accusations were "a good thing," while 29 percent thought they were "doing harm" and 32 percent were undecided.

With figures like those in hand, a majority of Republican leaders was convinced that Communist infiltration of the U.S. government would be a key issue in the coming midterm election of 1950, midway between the presidential election of 1948 and the next presidential contest in 1952.

13

War Breaks Out in Korea

A S THE TYDINGS HEARINGS dragged on, Democrats claimed that there was no basis to the charges Joe had first voiced in his Wheeling speech. "The time has now come to call a spade a spade," Senator Matthew Neely of West Virginia said in early May 1950. "If there is no foundation to this charge of 205 Communists in the State Department, I think the senator [McCarthy] will have destroyed himself in the Senate and will have destroyed his usefulness to the country."

Joe erupted in rage. "Let's be done with this silly numbers game. If a word I said is not true, the President has only to open the loyalty files to show it!"

In response, several Democrats went so far as to suggest that Joe himself should be the subject of an investigation as to whether his claims "constituted a hoax, a deceit, or a fraud . . . upon the American people." To which Joe's ally Sen. Wherry retorted, "The American people want an investigation not of Mr. McCarthy but of subversives in the State Department!"

Late the next day, pressured by Sen. Tydings and other Democrats who were eager to disprove Joe's case once and for all, President Truman agreed to open the loyalty files. But only those of the 71 cases McCarthy had introduced in his speech to the Senate on February 20 would be opened—and only to the members of the Tydings subcommittee. Sen. Tydings announced that the members would examine the files at the White House, and would not be allowed to take notes. These precautions were intended to ensure that the contents of the files would not be leaked to the press.

Now that Joe had gotten what he had so often demanded, he had to figure out what to do next. He knew what Truman and Tydings knew—that he had obtained the names from the Lee report, which summarized the information in the State Department loyalty files. All three also knew there was no additional evidence in the files that would support his wild assertions. So as he always did when he found himself in a tight spot, Joe bluffed. In a speech to the Midwest Council of Young Republicans on May 7, he claimed that the files the senators would be looking at were "phony," that they had been tampered with—"raped," according to Joe—since he had learned about them.

Meanwhile, the Tydings subcommittee had begun to go through the 71 files. In the end, Chairman Tydings and the three other Democrats on the subcommittee would read all of them. The two Republican members, Senator Henry Cabot Lodge and Senator Bourke Hickenlooper, would not be so thorough. Lodge examined only twelve of the files, Hickenlooper only nine. Perhaps they believed what Joe had said—that the contents had been altered.

At the same time, the subcommittee began closed hearings on the case of John Stewart Service, another of the people in the Lee report whom McCarthy had accused of having ties to the Communist Party. Service, the son of American missionaries for the YMCA, was born and grew up in China, becoming fluent in the Chinese language. His parents returned briefly to the United States in the 1920s, and John graduated from high school in Berkeley, California. From there, he went on to Oberlin College in Ohio and upon graduation entered the Foreign Service. Because of his background, Service was assigned to the U.S. diplomatic corps in China. In a few years he rose from a clerk's position to the post of second secretary at the American Embassy in Chungking, the Chinese capital during World War II.

Service gradually became disillusioned with Chiang Kai-shek's Nationalist government, calling it "fascist" and "undemocratic" in reports he wrote for his superiors. In 1944, Service accompanied a U.S. Army observation group that traveled to Yenan, where the Chinese Communists had their headquarters. He was the first State Department official to visit this remote region in western China. While in Yenan, Service met and interviewed many of the Communist leaders, including Mao Zedong and Zhou Enlai (spelled Chou En-lai at that time). He was favorably impressed by much of what he saw and heard, writing in one memorandum that "the Communists are in China to stay, and China's destiny is not Chiang's but theirs."

John Stewart Service in 1948.
AP/WIDE WORLD PHOTOS

Back in Chungking, Service came to believe that all-out civil war was inevitable in China once Japan had been defeated. He urged the State Department to adopt an evenhanded policy toward the Nationalists and the Communists rather than continue to endorse Chiang's government exclusively. The new U.S. ambassador at that time, Patrick Hurley, a staunch supporter of Chiang, totally rejected Service's recommendations. Going further, Hurley asked that Service and others in the embassy who shared his views be recalled at once to Washington.

John Service returned to Washington and the State Department in the spring of 1945. Shortly thereafter, he met and befriended Philip Jaffe, editor of *Amerasia* magazine, which focused on U.S. relations with Asian nations. He agreed to share with Jaffe some of the memos about Chiang's forces and the Communists that he had written while stationed in China. Service said later that he believed Jaffe was simply an interested journalist, and that he did not know that Jaffe was under surveillance by the FBI as a suspected Communist.

On June 6, 1945, to his great surprise, Service was arrested and charged with "conspiracy to violate the Espionage Act" by passing confidential State Department documents to Philip Jaffe. The Justice Department submitted its evidence against him to a federal grand jury. After studying the material carefully, the jury members voted 23–0 not to indict Service. They stated that none of the papers Service had given Jaffe were classified. J. Edgar Hoover, joined by conservatives in the House and Senate and the right-wing media, refused to accept the grand jury's verdict, then or later. They called it a "whitewash," and five years later Joe McCarthy used the Service case as a prime example of Communist influence in the State Department.

This fresh charge led to Service's being called upon to defend himself once again, this time before the Tydings subcommittee. At his request, the hearing was open to the press and public. Service recounted in detail his friendly relations with Philip Jaffe and said he had lent the *Amerasia* editor nine or ten personal copies of memos he had written while in China. He emphasized that they were "factual in nature and did not contain discussions of United States political or military policy." While he admitted to the subcommittee that he was probably guilty of "indiscretion," he insisted that he was innocent of the charge of treason. And he heatedly denied that he was a Communist or a Communist sympathizer.

The Democrats on the subcommittee responded favorably to Service's candid, straightforward manner, but Joe did not. In a speech in Janesville, Wisconsin, McCarthy said: "Service was arrested by the FBI in connection with the theft of hundreds of secret government documents. . . . At the time Service and his five codefendants were arrested, J. Edgar Hoover, according to a Washington newspaper, said, 'This is a 100 percent airtight case of espionage.' But Service did not go to jail." Joe summarized his charges against Service with a question to his audience. "Do you want on your payroll a man who admits turning government secrets over to a Communist, and who was caught by the FBI giving secret military information to a convicted Communist thief of government secrets?"

The audience greeted McCarthy's remarks with loud applause. Most of them probably had no means of judging whether he had conveyed the facts of the Service case or doctored them to suit his own partisan purposes. A majority of those present had voted enthusiastically to send Joe to the Senate. Now, like many other Americans across the country, they were proud that he had dedicated himself to getting rid of all the "Commies" in the government. As a woman in St. Paul, Minnesota, put it, "If it wasn't for courage like McCarthy's, we'd be run like Stalin runs Russia."

Not all the members of his own party marched in step with Joe, however. Senator Margaret Chase Smith of Maine surprised colleagues, the press, and the public when she rose in the Senate on June 1, 1950, to deliver a speech lamenting the wild accusations and personal attacks that had marked so many recent Senate debates. Although she never mentioned Sen. McCarthy by name, it was clear that he was the chief target of her attack.

Margaret Chase Smith had long been recognized for her firm principles and independent thinking. She came to Washington in 1940 as a replacement for her late husband, Clyde H. Smith, in the House of Representatives. Smith served eight years in that body, then decided in 1948 to run for the U.S. Senate. Upon her election, after a hard-fought campaign, she became the first woman in the nation's history to serve in both houses of Congress, and the first woman to be elected to the Senate in her own right. At the time, she was also the only female senator.

A moderate Republican, Smith was at first impressed by Joe's disclosures of Communist activity in the State Department. "It looks as if he is onto something disturbing and frightening," she remarked to a Senate colleague. But after she'd examined some of the documents Joe had cited as evidence, and listened to more of his vehement speeches, she came to question the accuracy, credibility, and fairness of his charges, and she felt compelled to voice her feelings in what she hoped would be a constructive way. Smith drafted a "Declaration of Conscience" that she planned to introduce in a Senate speech. She circulated the draft among six other moderate Republican senators, all of whom agreed to endorse it, and a seventh senator later added his name to the list.

When Smith entered the Senate on June 1 to give the speech, she saw Joe in his usual seat two rows behind hers. They did not exchange greetings.

Smith began by saying, "I speak as briefly as possible because too much harm has already been done with irresponsible words of bitterness and selfish political opportunism." Soon she reached the heart of her speech. "Those of us who shout the loudest about Americanism in making character assassinations are all too frequently those who, by our own words and acts, ignore some of the basic principles of Americanism." She went on to list those principles: "The right to criticize; the right to hold unpopular beliefs; the right to protest; the right of independent thought."

Emphasizing their importance, she said, "The exercise of these rights should

Senator Margaret Chase Smith discusses a Senate matter with an aide.
The National Archives

not cost one single American citizen his reputation or his right to a livelihood, nor should he be in danger of losing his reputation or livelihood merely because he happens to know someone who holds unpopular beliefs. Who of us doesn't? Otherwise, none of us could call our souls our own. Otherwise thought control would have set in."

When she'd finished, Smith braced herself for Joe to respond in his usual sharp-tongued way. He surprised her by leaving the chamber without saying anything. A few senators rose to praise her remarks, but most remained silent.

Perhaps they were afraid—especially the Republicans—of saying something that would arouse Joe's ire. Later, Sen. Tydings called Smith's speech "temperate and fair" and complimented the senator from Maine on her "stateswomanship." The next time President Truman came to the Capitol for lunch, he invited Sen. Smith to join him. Over sandwiches and coffee, he told her, "Mrs. Smith, your 'Declaration of Conscience' was one of the finest things that has happened here in Washington in all my years in the Senate and the White House."

The reaction from Sen. McCarthy's camp was slow in coming but predictably mean-spirited when it finally did. First, one of Joe's chief aides, Don Surine, labeled Sen. Smith "Moscow Maggie" in a meeting with reporters. Then Joe himself demeaned Mrs. Smith and the seven Republican moderates who had signed or endorsed her declaration by calling them "Snow White and the Seven Dwarfs."

McCarthy's mocking comment seemed to intimidate Smith's Republican supporters. Less than a week after Smith's speech, Senator Irving M. Ives of New York switched his allegiance back to Joe and accused the Tydings subcommittee of "trying to whitewash the State Department." Within a short time, all the Republican senators except one, Senator Wayne Morse of Oregon, had backed away from Smith's strong stand on civil rights.

Sen. Smith may have been disappointed by her colleagues' defections, but she took them in stride. As she later recalled in an interview, "Joe had the Senate paralyzed with fear. The political risk of taking issue with him was too great a hazard to the political security of senators." No one, Republican or Democrat, wanted to be labeled by Joe as "soft on Communism," especially in an election year.

Even so, Margaret Chase Smith's declaration would go down as one of the earliest and most powerful challenges to the undemocratic methods Joe employed throughout his anti-Communist campaign. She herself summed up its importance in these words: "If I am to be remembered in history, it will not be because of legislative accomplishments, but for an act I took as a legislator in the U.S. Senate when on June 1, 1950, I spoke out in condemnation of McCarthyism."

For a week or so after she delivered it, Sen. Smith's speech, and the various reactions to it, occupied center stage in the U.S. press. All that changed on June 25, when North Korea shocked America and the world by invading South Korea.

Just the week before, on June 20, Secretary of State Dean Acheson had told Congress that U.S. intelligence agencies believed war between North and South Korea was highly unlikely. Acheson had felt compelled to speak because of

General Douglas MacArthur, supreme commander of U.N. forces, arrives at the South Korean port of Inchon aboard the U.S.S. *Mount McKinley* on September 1, 1950. *AP/WIDE WORLD PHOTOS*

reports that tensions between the two Koreas were steadily mounting. At the end of World War II, Korea was divided between a Soviet occupation zone in the North and an American occupation zone in the South. The two zones were divided at the 38th Parallel above the equator. In the North, the Russians installed a Soviet-style regime under the leadership of Kim Il Sung, a Korean Communist who had spent the war years in the Soviet Union. Meanwhile, in the South, the United States supported the government of President Syngman Rhee, an ardent anti-Communist.

In 1948, the Russians and the Americans agreed to withdraw their respective occupation armies. The North became known as the People's Democratic Republic of Korea while the South claimed the name Republic of Korea. The stated goal of all parties concerned was the eventual reunification of the two Koreas. But Kim Il Sung and Syngman Rhee had very different ideas for a reunified Korea: Kim envisioned a Soviet-type state, while Rhee imagined a dictatorship with some democratic features.

Their views of government were so far apart that any compromise through diplomacy seemed impossible. If either leader was to achieve his vision, force would probably be required. In 1949 and the early months of 1950, a number of armed skirmishes between North and South broke out along the 38th Parallel.

But no Western leader—including Dean Acheson—expected the full-scale civil war that Kim Il Sung launched in the predawn hours of June 25, 1950.

As the North Korean army, equipped with tanks and aircraft the Russians had left behind, drove south, President Truman acted quickly. On the day the North invaded, Truman asked the United Nations Security Council to authorize a police action against the aggressors. The Security Council responded immediately by passing a resolution that called for all hostilities in Korea to end and for North Korea to withdraw to the 38th Parallel.

President Truman went further to support South Korea in its struggle for survival. On June 27, he authorized the use of American land, sea, and air forces, at that time stationed in Japan. The American forces were eventually joined, in what was officially a "police action" rather than a war, by troops and supplies from fifteen other U.N. members, including Britain, France, Canada, Australia, the Netherlands, and New Zealand. General Douglas MacArthur, the World War II hero who was in charge of the American armed forces in Japan, was named supreme commander of the U.N. effort.

In the meantime, North Korea ignored the U.N. resolution and advanced farther south, meeting only limited resistance from the less well equipped South Korean army. Seoul, the South Korean capital, fell to the North on June 28, just three days after the war began. The first American troops to reach Korea—a task force from the Army's 24th Infantry Division—entered the fray on July 5. Outnumbered by the North Koreans, they suffered heavy losses and were forced to retreat.

The Republicans in Congress did not admire President Truman's swift response to North Korea's invasion of the South. Sen. Taft declared that the Administration's "weak" Far Eastern policy had encouraged the Communist aggression. Joe McCarthy took an even tougher stand. A few days after the invasion, he charged that Truman's decision was further evidence of Communist infiltration into the highest levels of the administration. Speaking in the Senate on July 6, he accused Secretary of State Acheson of harboring "highly placed Red counselors" who were "far more deadly than Red machine gunners in Korea."

As McCarthy spoke, the Tydings subcommittee was winding up its lengthy hearings and getting ready to write its final report. People who had contact with the committee members and Chairman Tydings spread the word around Washington that the report would come down hard on Joe.

14

Revenge

JOE MCCARTHY'S CHARGES against supposed Communists in the State Department, and the methods he had used to expose them, represented "perhaps the most nefarious campaign of half-truths and untruths in the history of the Republic." This was just one of the damning statements in the report that the Tydings subcommittee issued on July 17, 1950.

All three Democrats on the subcommittee signed the report. The two Republicans did not. Senator Bourke Hickenlooper claimed he had not been invited to the meeting at which the report was voted on. The other Republican, Senator Henry Cabot Lodge, issued a minority report of his own, criticizing the Democrats for conducting a "superficial and inconclusive" investigation.

In fact, the subcommittee's report was unusually thorough. A careful study of the State Department loyalty files found no Communists on the roster of employees. All the individuals Joe had accused by name, including Dorothy Kenyon, Owen Lattimore, and John Stewart Service, were completely cleared of the charges against them. The report was especially critical of McCarthy's attack on Lattimore: "We have seen a distortion of the facts of such a magnitude as to be truly alarming."

Joe's reaction to the report was angry and immediate. He issued a statement to the press, saying: "It is a signal to the traitors, Communists, and fellow travelers in our Government that they have no fear of exposure from this Administration. . . . The most loyal stooges of the Kremlin could not have done a better job of giving a clean bill of health to Stalin's fifth column [network of spies and secret agents] in this country."

Joe's Republican supporters in the Senate echoed his denunciation of the report. Senator William Jenner of Indiana called it "the most scandalous and brazen whitewash of treasonable conspiracy in our history." But no amount of frantic Republican maneuvering could prevent the report from being brought to the full Senate for consideration. There followed much heated oratory on both sides, some of it colored by the war in Korea, which American troops had just entered. Sen. Jenner asked, "Considering the fact that we are now at war . . . how can we get the Reds out of Korea if we cannot get them out of Washington?"

Despite such comments, and other delaying tactics, the Republicans failed to bring any Democratic senators over to their side. The Tydings report was finally approved in the Senate on a straight party-line vote, all Democrats for, all Republicans against. Joe refused to concede that he had suffered a setback. In a speech delivered in Wisconsin in late July, he called the report "dishonest." He went on to describe its Democratic authors as "men without the mental or moral capacity to rise above politics in this hour of the nation's gravest danger." The crowd of more than 4,500 broke into cheers and loud applause. McCarthy was still their man.

Because of his anti-Communist crusade, Joe was now one of the best-known politicians in the United States. When he voiced a new charge of subversion in government, it would almost always make the front pages of the next day's newspapers. Joe reveled in the publicity he was getting—and all the things that came with it. These included thousands of fan letters from supporters; invitations to speak to groups all across the country; and unsolicited contributions—most of them in small amounts, five to fifty dollars—from ordinary Americans who wanted to join him in the fight against Communism. Joe used much of the money to hire more investigators, but some of it went to help pay his personal expenses.

Not that Joe lived extravagantly, except for occasional nights of gambling. He still roomed with Ray Kiermas and his family in Washington, and he worked closely with longtime associates like Don Surine, Jean Kerr, and Ed Nellor. At some point, Joe's professional relationship with Jean had developed into a romantic one. Neither of them talked about it, but it was obvious from Jean's outbursts of jealous anger when she discovered Joe flirting with other women. On one occasion, she persuaded J. Edgar Hoover to have an FBI agent, the husband of a secretary in Joe's office, transferred to Alaska so Joe would no longer have contact with the attractive young wife.

McCarthy and his chief assistant, Jean Kerr, look over a compilation of Communist attacks on the senator that she assembled. *The Library of Congress*

Joe and Jean frequently quarreled, broke up, then came back together. Whatever the state of their romantic involvement, they needed each other. Joe relied on Jean's quick mind, her writing and organizational abilities, and her unwavering faith in his anti-Communist investigations. She, in turn, depended on him to put her own long-held conservative beliefs into action. They made a formidable team, and their partnership was never more effective than in the campaign they launched in the fall of 1950 to defeat Millard Tydings's bid for reelection to the Senate.

Joe had a long history of seeking revenge on anyone who stood in his way, most notably Cedric Parker, the Madison, Wisconsin, newspaper editor. But he went all out in the effort to "get" Tydings, who had badgered him in the Senate subcommittee hearings. McCarthy had plenty of time to devote to the anti-Tydings campaign, since he himself was not up for reelection in 1950. He began by helping to enlist a Republican opponent for Tydings, a tall, good-looking, and conservative Baltimore attorney named John Marshall Butler. Jean arranged for Butler to meet her close friend Ruth McCormick Miller, the influential editor of the *Washington Times-Herald,* and Mrs. Miller seemed to be impressed.

Once Butler was in place, Joe, Jean, and other members of his staff met in Baltimore with the candidate's public relations advisor to plot strategy for Butler's primary campaign. Joe suggested Butler use the postcard tactic that had worked so well for McCarthy in his Wisconsin races. Butler's advisor agreed, and more than 200,000 handwritten cards, supposedly bearing Butler's signature, were mailed to prospective Republican voters in the weeks before the primary. Jean provided Butler's speechwriters with anti-Tydings information she had researched, and they wove it into the candidate's speeches.

Butler faced strong opposition in the Republican primary but ultimately won by a thin margin. At that point, McCarthy and Jean met again with Ruth McCormick Miller, who told them she was ready to announce her editorial support for Butler. This was a major coup, since her newspaper circulated widely in the Baltimore suburbs where many Republican voters lived.

Now Joe, Jean, and other members of his staff planned Butler's campaign against Tydings in the general election. Joe got on the phone and persuaded wealthy Texas oilmen like Clint Murchison and H. L. Hunt to donate large sums of money to the effort. As a result, Butler was able to outspend Tydings three to one. Joe also made two speeches in Maryland, one in Baltimore and another in Hyattsville, in support of Butler. Otherwise, he tried to keep a low profile so as not to arouse Tydings's suspicions. He put Jean Kerr in charge of most campaign operations, assigning her to the job full-time.

One of Jean's chief contributions was a four-page, large-format brochure titled *From the Record,* which she saw through from manuscript to publication. The brochure accused Tydings of, among other things, "sponsoring Owen Lattimore in a series of lectures on Communist Russia," blocking appropriations to arm South Korea in the Senate Armed Forces Committee, and, as chairman of the subcommittee investigating Joe McCarthy's statements, "refusing to carry out Senate instructions to investigate disloyalty in the State Department." The majority of these accusations were either lies, exaggerations, or half-truths.

The most controversial part of the brochure was a photograph of Tydings in a friendly conversation with Earl Browder, a leader of the Communist Party U.S.A. The caption admitted that the photo was a "composite." Close examination revealed that it had been doctored to give the impression that the two men were in the same room when actually they were not.

Up till then, Tydings, a four-term senator, had run a rather complacent campaign, assuming he would easily defeat the relatively unknown Butler. But when he saw the doctored photograph, he exploded. "That picture," he said, "brings into clear focus the intent of the conspirators [Joe and staff] to deceive the people of the State of Maryland in the selection of a candidate for one of the highest offices in the land."

Jean Kerr, when questioned later, saw nothing wrong in doctoring the photo. "I think it did him [Tydings] a favor," she said. The kid-glove treatment the senator had given Browder when the Communist leader appeared as a witness before Tydings's subcommittee was "a hundred times more damaging than the photo," Kerr added.

Joe McCarthy sounded a more cautious note when asked to comment on the photo. "In the main, composite photos are wrong," he said. "They should not be used." But then he cleverly shifted his position to echo what Jean Kerr had said. "Luckily, it [the photo] didn't do any injustice to Tydings," McCarthy continued, "because if they had taken the testimony, the statements made between Tydings and Browder [in the subcommittee hearings], it would have shown their

Senator Millard Tydings.
The National Archives

relationship to be much closer and much more cooperative [than the photo indicated]."

Such comments only served to fuel Tydings's anger. In the days just before the election, he went on Maryland radio and the new medium, television, to denounce the brochure as a whole and the altered photograph in particular. But by then it was too late. The brochure had already been distributed to hundreds of thousands of Maryland homes and had created its own strong impression.

Many in Maryland were stunned when, on election night, Millard Tydings lost his Senate seat to newcomer John Marshall Butler by more than 40,000 votes. But not Joe. He had seen how successfully tactics like the use of "personally signed" postcards and boldly stated lies had worked in his own campaigns against Judge Werner and Sen. La Follette in Wisconsin. Now the Tydings defeat showed that such tactics were equally effective when used on another candidate's behalf.

Joe had other reasons to celebrate the outcome of the 1950 midterm elections. He had campaigned actively on behalf of many conservative Republican candidates, and all of them had either retained or won their House and Senate seats. In Ohio, Senator Robert Taft triumphed over his Democratic opponent by taking more than 57 percent of the vote and now seemed poised to make a run for the White House in 1952. And in California, Representative Richard Nixon, running for the Senate, trounced his Democratic opponent, Helen Gahagan Douglas, in a hard-fought contest, during which Douglas was the first to call Nixon "Tricky Dick."

Joe was disappointed, however, with the overall outcome of the election. Although the Republicans had gained twenty-eight seats in the House and five in the Senate, control of both bodies still remained in the hands of the Democrats. Even so, McCarthy's influence in the Senate had been greatly enhanced. All the successful Republican candidates had claimed to be his allies in the fight against Communism. That fight seemed even more urgent in light of recent developments in the Korean War.

By September 1950, two months before the midterm elections, the North Koreans had driven the forces of the United Nations all the way down to Pusan, a city in the southeastern corner of South Korea. The beleaguered allies then launched a massive air offensive using B-29 bombers based in Japan. The air raids knocked out North Korean supply dumps along with bridges, roads, and railroad tracks used to transport food and equipment to the North Korean troops.

The North Koreans, with only a limited number of planes at their disposal, were unable to slow or halt the U.N. air assault.

The American people were deeply troubled by the fighting in Korea. A letter to Senator Theodore Green, Democrat of Rhode Island, was typical of those received by lawmakers in Washington. "There is something wrong in the government," the letter said. "How else do you account for the tragedy in Korea?"

President Truman responded quickly to the criticism that the country was unprepared for the North Korean invasion. He fired the man with overall responsibility, Secretary of Defense Louis A. Johnson, and replaced him with one of the greatest heroes to emerge from World War II, General George Marshall.

But Truman's moves failed to satisfy Joe McCarthy. In his campaign speeches, Joe capitalized on the anxious mood of the country: "The government is again playing politics with the lives of other people's sons." He went on to warn, "If you want more of that, keep them [the Democrats] in office. But if you vote for them, remember this: When the Communist trap to conquer this nation is sprung, it will be your vote that pulled the trigger."

The nation's mood brightened noticeably when Gen. MacArthur launched a successful landing at the city of Inchon, on the western side of South Korea. Caught by surprise, the North Koreans retreated, and the U.N. forces advanced. Their fellow fighters in the southeast were finally able to break out of the area around Pusan, where they had been under siege since the summer.

Heartened by these initial victories, the U.N. troops marched steadily northward. MacArthur recaptured Seoul in late September and drove the North Koreans back past the 38th Parallel. Then the Truman government reached a fateful decision. Before, Truman's policy had been to contain the Communists' movement and prevent them from acquiring more territory. Now, spurred on by MacArthur, the president saw an opportunity not only to contain but to roll back the Communists and, in the process, reunite North and South Korea under the auspices of the United Nations.

The U.N. gave its assent to this change in U.S. policy, and MacArthur pressed on into North Korea, seizing control of its capital, Pyongyang, on October 19. By late October, a week before the midterm elections in the U.S., the North Korean army was reeling under constant air attacks and the U.N. forces had taken more than 135,000 prisoners. As the American troops and their allies marched farther and farther north, they got ever closer to the Yalu River, North Korea's border

U.S. Marines take a break along a North Korean road during the bitterly cold winter of 1950–51.
AP/WIDE WORLD PHOTOS

with China. Now the question became: How will China's Communist leaders respond?

Many in the United States, including Joe McCarthy and his fellow conservatives in the Republican Party, believed it would be necessary to go on into China in order to destroy the fuel and equipment depots that were supplying the North Korean army. But Truman and his chief advisors hesitated to make any hasty moves that might bring China—and possibly even the Soviet Union—into the conflict. Consequently, they urged General MacArthur to be extremely cautious as he neared the Chinese border. But what if the Chinese attacked first?

In mid-October, China had warned the U.S. through a third-party diplomat (since the U.S. had no direct diplomatic communication with China) that it would use "all means necessary" to protect its national security. Neither Truman nor MacArthur took the warning seriously, thinking, as Truman said, that it was just "a bold attempt to blackmail the U.N." MacArthur was so confident that he boasted to his men, "The war is over. The Chinese are not coming. . . . The Third Division will be back in Fort Benning [Georgia] for Christmas dinner."

MacArthur's and Truman's high spirits were based on reports from the CIA. The intelligence agency had informed Truman that, after evaluating all the evidence, agents believed it highly unlikely that China would enter the war. So the president and Gen. MacArthur were caught off-guard when, in late November, 270,000 Chinese troops crossed the Yalu River under cover of darkness and attacked a large U.N. force gathered on the other side. The unprepared U.S. and U.N. soldiers beat a hasty retreat as the Chinese and North Koreans moved swiftly forward. The retreat continued through December 1950 and on into January

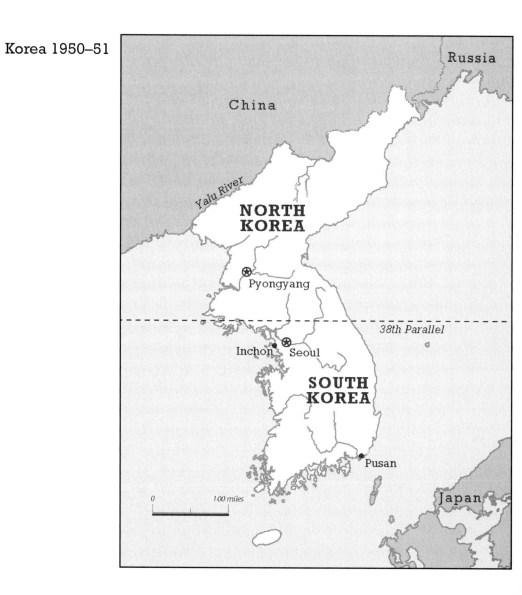

Korea 1950–51

1951, with heavy casualties on both sides. The Chinese and North Koreans recaptured Seoul on January 4 and drove the allied troops farther south.

Back in the United States, the public was distressed by the losses, and especially by the mounting death toll of American soldiers. Conservative Republicans, sensing the rising dissatisfaction with President Truman and other Democratic leaders, stepped up their attacks on the administration. Led by Joe McCarthy, Robert Taft, and Richard Nixon, the Republicans called for the resignation or impeachment (formal accusation) of Secretary of State Dean Acheson. They also aimed sharp criticisms at President Truman and George Marshall, the new secretary of defense.

In Korea, the U.N. troops halted their retreat in late January when they realized that the Chinese and North Korean forces were no longer advancing. The Communists had outrun their supply lines and had to pause until more food and ammunition reached them from China.

Gen. MacArthur and his second in command, General Matthew B. Ridgway, seized the moment to go on the offensive once more. The American and U.N. troops under their command, bolstered by American air support, forced the Communist armies to fall back before they could be resupplied. On March 14, after fierce fighting, U.N. forces recaptured Seoul, which by now was in almost complete ruin. This was the fourth time in a year the city had changed hands, and its prewar population of 1,500,000 had dwindled to fewer than 200,000.

As Americans and their allies continued to advance and approached the 38th Parallel, Gen. MacArthur called the situation in Korea "an entirely new war" that should be fought to a successful conclusion. He repeatedly asked President Truman for authorization to strike the bases in northeastern China that were supporting the Communist armies. According to insiders, the general also wanted permission to use nuclear weapons if he felt they were necessary to achieve victory.

Truman was not ready to grant the general's requests. The president feared that if the U.N. troops attacked China, with or without nuclear weapons, the Soviet Union would almost inevitably enter the conflict, and that could precipitate World War III. In Korea, the situation on the ground had settled into a sort of stalemate. Each side launched attacks on the other in the area north of Seoul and just below the 38th Parallel, but neither side gained much territory.

General MacArthur seemed to have accepted President Truman's decision.

That was only to be expected; according to the Constitution, the president is commander-in-chief of the armed forces and has the final word on all military matters. But MacArthur, a man with a strong ego whom many called arrogant, was not used to having his plans questioned. He wrote a letter to Joseph Martin, a Republican representative from Massachusetts and minority leader in the House of Representatives, disagreeing strongly with the president's policies in Korea.

When Truman heard of the letter and of other statements MacArthur had made about his leadership, he saw it as a challenge to his authority as president that had to be met swiftly and decisively. On April 11, 1951, Truman fired Gen. MacArthur for insubordination and replaced him with Gen. Ridgway.

The president's action set off a firestorm of protest around the country. It was loudest among those who regarded MacArthur as one of the nation's great heroes. Senator Richard Nixon condemned the general's firing as "appeasement of the Reds," and urged the Senate to censure President Truman. Joe McCarthy went even further. Speaking with a reporter in Milwaukee, the enraged senator called MacArthur "the greatest American I know" and said of President Truman, "The son of a bitch should be impeached!" Joe went on to add that MacArthur's dismissal was "a victory for the Communists, homemade and foreign made."

McCarthy was expressing in his own crude terms what many Americans were feeling. According to a Gallup poll, more than two thirds of those questioned disapproved of MacArthur's firing. At the same time, President Truman's approval rating had fallen to 30 percent, a new low.

The Republicans exploited the national mood by sponsoring MacArthur's return to the U.S. and inviting him to speak before a joint session of Congress on April 19, 1951. More than 60 million Americans watched on television as the seventy-one-year-old general offered a spirited defense of his motivations and actions in Korea. The speech was interrupted by more than thirty ovations and concluded with an emotional farewell, delivered in MacArthur's deep, preacher-like voice. "Old soldiers never die; they just fade away," the general intoned. "And like the old soldier of that ballad, I now close my military career and just fade away—an old soldier who tried to do his duty as God gave him the light to see that duty. Goodbye."

Joe was profoundly moved by MacArthur's oratory. "It was actually the greatest speech I have ever heard or ever hope to hear," he told a Washington, D.C., audience a few days later. He went on to praise MacArthur as "the greatest military leader and strategist since even before the days of Genghis Khan [the ruthless Mongol general of the 1200s whose armies conquered a vast territory extending from what is today northern China in the east to European Russia in the west]."

In the wake of MacArthur's speech, Joe remarked to close associates that, despite his age, the general would be his choice for the Republican candidate in the 1952 presidential election. Joe also laid the groundwork for an attack on another revered World War II general, George Marshall, who, he believed, had encouraged President Truman to fire MacArthur. Once again Joe sought revenge on someone who had opposed him—or, in this case, who had opposed one of his heroes.

15

"We Like Ike!"

WHEN JOE ROSE FROM his Senate seat on June 14, 1951, and launched his attack on General George Marshall, he was targeting one of the most respected public servants America had ever known.

A 1902 graduate of the Virginia Military Institute, Marshall had devoted his entire adult life to the Army. He had risen to the rank of general when he was nominated by President Franklin D. Roosevelt to be Army chief of staff. Marshall was sworn in on September 1, 1939, the same day that World War II began in Europe. As chief of staff, he oversaw the largest military expansion in U.S. history. He inherited a poorly equipped Army of 200,000 men and expanded it into a well-trained force of more than 8 million by the summer of 1942, six months after America entered the conflict.

During the war, Marshall chose General Dwight D. Eisenhower to be supreme commander of the Allied armies in Europe, and Marshall was the man who planned Operation Overlord, the Allied invasion of France, which began on June 6, 1944, now known as D-Day. In December of that year, with the Allies advancing swiftly toward the border of Hitler's Germany, Marshall became the first American general to be promoted to 5-star rank. *Time* magazine named him Man of the Year for 1944, and the British prime minister, Winston Churchill, hailed him as "the true organizer of victory" after first Germany and then Japan surrendered to the Allies in 1945.

His wartime job done, Marshall resigned his post as chief of staff. But his service to the nation didn't end with the war. In December 1945, as noted earlier,

Brigadier General George Marshall in 1938. *AP/WIDE WORLD PHOTOS*

President Truman sent him to China to try to get the warring Nationalists and Communists to sign a truce and form a coalition government. Unfortunately, both sides rejected Marshall's proposals, and he returned to the U.S. empty-handed in 1947.

Marshall may have failed in China, but his next assignment more than made up for it. Soon after the general's return from the Far East, President Truman appointed him secretary of state. The devastated European economy had barely begun to recover from the war and was a fertile field for the spread of Communism. To guard against this, Marshall suggested that the U.S. invest vast amounts of money to help the nations of Western Europe—including a former enemy, West Germany—to rebuild their shaky economies as swiftly as possible. This policy, which came to be known as the Marshall Plan, proved a great success. In recognition, *Time* magazine in 1948 once again selected Marshall as Man of the Year.

The general's reputation suffered a setback when the Chinese Communists defeated the Nationalists in 1949 and established the People's Republic of China under Mao Zedong. Conservative Republicans in the U.S. were quick to respond. Their leaders, including Joe McCarthy, accused Marshall of being among those responsible for "losing China." The charge did not affect his job, however, since Marshall had left the State Department in January 1949.

His government service resumed when the U.S. was caught unprepared by the outbreak of the Korean War, and President Truman turned to him to replace Louis Johnson as secretary of defense. Marshall's chief role was to help restore confidence in the Defense Department, which had been badly shaken by the intelligence failure in Korea. As he set about his new assignment, it was almost inevitable that Secretary Marshall would be subjected to fresh criticism by the Republican right. But no one expected the savage attack that Joe McCarthy aimed at him on June 14, 1951.

McCarthy began his Senate speech by recapping what had happened in China before the Communists emerged victorious from their civil war with the Nationalists. He charged that Marshall, in his role as President Truman's envoy, was directly responsible for "the loss of China." According to McCarthy, the general had "sabotaged" a plan prepared by another American leader, General Albert Wedemeyer—a "wise plan that would have kept China a valued ally" in the fight against Communism.

Why would Marshall have done such a thing? In answering that question, McCarthy went further than he ever had in his anti-Communist campaign. The reason, he claimed, why the U.S. "fell from our position as the most powerful nation on earth at the end of World War II to a position of declared weakness by our leadership" was because of "a conspiracy so immense as to dwarf any such venture in the history of man. A conspiracy of infamy so black that, when it is finally exposed, its principals shall be forever deserving of the maledictions of all honest men." McCarthy did not name Marshall as one of the principals in this conspiracy and never used the word "treason" in his lengthy speech. But it was clear that Marshall was the chief target of the senator's accusation, and that the "infamy" of which he spoke—the so-called loss of China—was, in his opinion, a treasonable act.

Liberal newspapers and spokesmen were outraged by Joe's denunciation of Marshall. Adlai Stevenson, the Democratic governor of Illinois, called the speech "a hysterical form of putrid slander." In a full-page editorial, *Collier's* magazine told its more than 3 million readers that McCarthy's words set "a new high for irresponsibility," and it called on Republican leaders to disassociate themselves from his "senseless and vicious charges."

Predictably, though, the right-wing press hailed the speech. Political columnist John O'Donnell, writing in the *New York Daily News,* judged it "a coldly documented, carefully edited, and restrained indictment in which damning evidence [concerning Marshall] marched steadily on the heels of accusation."

Marshall himself refused to comment on McCarthy's attack, believing that any fair-minded student of postwar American foreign policy would dismiss it as unworthy of serious consideration. President Truman and other Democratic leaders ignored the speech also. Stewart Alsop, a moderate political commentator, had a different take on the matter. "His [McCarthy's] charge that Marshall is implicated in 'infamy so immense as to dwarf any previous such venture in the history of man' is so ridiculous that it may seem silly to discuss it seriously. Yet a man [Joe] who has proved that he can use demonstrable falsehoods to devastating political effect cannot be entirely laughed off."

Many Americans in government and elsewhere were by no means ready to laugh Joe off in 1951. Despite the fear that he inspired in Congress, a number of senators did their best to challenge his arrogant and underhanded methods. A Senate subcommittee began an investigation into Millard Tydings's claim that Joe and his staff had used unfair tactics against Tydings in the 1950 election. Joe himself did not respond to three invitations to appear before the subcommittee. Jean Kerr agreed to appear, but she deflected most questions about her activities by saying she couldn't remember.

The subcommittee's final report was a tame affair. It contrasted the "front street," or positive, campaign Tydings had waged with the "back-street effort conducted by non-Maryland outsiders." The report condemned the latter group's tactics, but it made no specific reference to McCarthy's key role.

Despite its mildness, Joe took exception to the report, labeling it "an attempt to whitewash Tydings." He was particularly upset by the subcommittee's treatment of Jean. Using the kind of sexist language that was common at the time, Joe said, "What I most resent in this report is the reference to a little girl [Jean] who works in my office. There are a lot of small, evil-minded people in this town [Washington] who are trying to smear this girl just because she works for me. I'm not going to stand for that."

Another, stronger attempt to weaken McCarthy's power in the Senate arose later in 1951, after McCarthy's denunciation of George Marshall. Senator William F. Benton, Democrat of Connecticut, decided that Joe had become a national menace because of his frequent and unwarranted attacks on high officials. Benton introduced a resolution on the Senate floor requesting an investigation of McCarthy's activities by the Rules Committee's Subcommittee on Privileges and Elections. The aim of the investigation: to determine whether or not Joe should be expelled from the Senate.

McCarthy meets and greets supporters in Platteville, Wisconsin, in 1951.
Marquette University Archives

Joe responded with quick anger to this request. He referred to Benton as "Connecticut's mental midget" and went on to add that Benton, by introducing the resolution against him, had "established himself as the hero of every Communist and crook in and out of government."

At first no senator spoke out in defense of Benton. Joseph A. Harsch, a Washington reporter for the *Christian Science Monitor,* wrote that many Washington insiders thought Benton "went into this thing as an innocent, walking blithely to his doom." If Joe had kept quiet, Benton's resolution might well have been filed and forgotten. But McCarthy, on August 9, 1951, once again accused the State Department of harboring 26 employees "charged with Communist activities."

This was too much for the Senate majority leader, Ernest W. McFarland, Democrat of Arizona, who publicly condemned Joe as a "character assassin." The Arizona senator's courage was catching. Other senators voiced support for Benton, and the Subcommittee on Privileges and Elections, chaired by Iowa Democrat Guy M. Gillette, voted on September 24 to hear William Benton present his case.

Benton appeared before the subcommittee on September 28, 1951, and read a statement accusing McCarthy of "practicing deceit and falsehood on both the U.S. Senate and the American people." After hearing Benton lay out ten examples of such falsehoods, the subcommittee voted unanimously to have its staff conduct a thorough investigation into Benton's charges.

In October, the subcommittee's investigators conducted interviews about Joe in Washington, Wheeling, and several towns and cities in Wisconsin. Joe attempted to block the investigation, claiming in a letter to Guy Gillette—with copies to the newspapers, as usual—that the subcommittee was "stealing from the pockets of the American taxpayer tens of thousands of dollars and then using the money to protect the Democrat [sic] party from the political effect of the exposure of Communists in government." Gillette dismissed Joe's claim as "of course, erroneous," and the investigators went on with their work.

The frustrating stalemate in Korea had continued through the summer months. Both sides in the conflict had dug into positions just north of the 38th Parallel, and negotiations aimed at reaching a truce had begun on July 10. At the same time, the U.N. troops kept on bombing Communist military positions in North Korea, and the Communists launched raids on U.N. forces in South

Korea. Both sides were determined to gain as much territory as they could before a truce was signed.

Back in Washington, the media in the fall of 1951 started to focus on the upcoming presidential election. After twenty years with Democrats in control of the White House, Republicans believed they had an excellent chance of winning it back in 1952. Voters were deeply troubled by the lack of progress in the Korean War and the rising number of American combat deaths. In February 1952, President Truman's approval rating sank to its lowest level yet, 22 percent, and he abruptly canceled plans to campaign for a second full term.

The Republican Party was divided into two wings: the conservatives led by Robert Taft and other senators like Joe McCarthy, and the moderates represented by such senators as Henry Cabot Lodge and Margaret Chase Smith. Joe himself was up for reelection in 1952. His friend Taft gave McCarthy's campaign a boost when he arranged for him to give one of the evening speeches at the Republican nominating convention, ensuring that Joe would get major media attention.

Taft and Gen. MacArthur were the leading conservative contenders for the Republican nomination, and MacArthur was scheduled to deliver the keynote speech at the convention. The earlier enthusiastic support for the general had cooled, though, after a Senate investigation of his removal from command largely vindicated President Truman's decision. The Republican moderates hadn't settled on their contender yet. But they were looking beyond the party for someone who might appeal to conservative Democrats and independents as well as the Republican base. Many thought they had found their man in another military hero: General Dwight D. Eisenhower.

Eisenhower had earned the nation's admiration as supreme commander of the Allied armies that had helped to defeat Nazi Germany in World War II. He was serving as commander of North Atlantic Treaty Organization (NATO) forces in Europe when both the Democrats and the Republicans sounded him out as a possible candidate for president. Eisenhower had never registered with either party, but in the spring of 1952 he made it known that he had always voted Republican. He resigned from active duty, returned to the United States, and entered the race for the Republican nomination.

Sen. Taft, the conservative favorite, had already lined up 40 percent of the delegates prior to the convention and appeared to have a lock on the nomination. But Eisenhower defeated him in a write-in campaign in the New Hampshire

Dwight D. Eisenhower in his four-star general's uniform. *AP/WIDE WORLD PHOTOS*

primary, and polled more than a 100,000 votes in another write-in campaign in Minnesota. MacArthur was no longer a serious contender, but Joe continued to endorse him anyway. It was a good way to stay out of the developing conflict between Taft and Eisenhower.

Joe was under a lot of stress in the spring of 1952. Besides the upcoming convention—it was set to take place in Chicago in early July—he and Jean and the other members of his staff were hard at work laying the groundwork for his reelection campaign in Wisconsin. At the same time, the Gillette subcommittee labored on, trying to find something criminal in McCarthy's past that would justify his expulsion from the Senate, or at least derail his reelection.

In the face of these pressures, Joe began to drink heavily. Before speaking to the Republican state convention in Milwaukee that spring, he darted into a men's room, pulled out a bottle of Scotch from his briefcase, and swallowed a large amount in one long gulp. On another occasion, an Associated Press reporter was startled when Joe ordered nothing for breakfast except a glass of whiskey, into which he poured a tablespoon of orange juice. His old problem with sinusitis had returned, and his doctors said an operation would be necessary. But first Joe was determined to attend the Republican convention and deliver his important evening speech.

The convention opened on July 6. Taft came into the gathering with 530 committed delegates; Eisenhower had amassed 427; Harold Stassen, a "favorite son" candidate from Minnesota, had 100 or so; and a number of delegates still supported General MacArthur. The latter's keynote speech at the convention, in which he condemned "those reckless men [President Truman and those close to him] who, yielding to international intrigue, set the stage for Soviet ascendancy as a world power and our own relative decline," was received enthusiastically.

Joe agreed completely with the thrust of MacArthur's speech but sensed that the tide of the convention was going against the former commander of U.N. forces in Korea. He told reporters he would not campaign for MacArthur during the convention because "both Senator Taft and General Eisenhower are honorable men." But he refused to discuss which of the two he favored.

Introduced as "that fighting Marine from Wisconsin," McCarthy spoke to convention delegates and a nationwide television audience on the evening of July 9. He repeated his familiar charges about Communists in high places, then roused the crowd in the convention hall with four stirring statements, delivered in his deep, almost menacing voice.

> My good friends, I say one Communist in a defense plant is one Communist too many.
>
> One Communist on the faculty of one university is one Communist too many.
>
> One Communist among the American advisors at Yalta was one Communist too many.
>
> And even if there were only one Communist in the State Department, that would be one Communist too many.

Cheers greeted each of the statements, and loud, sustained applause resounded through the hall when Joe had finished.

The next day, the right-wing Hearst newspaper chain hailed his speech, but the *New York Times,* in an editorial, said that McCarthy's remarks "reached rock bottom." A Wisconsin reporter called it a "middle-of-the-gutter speech." When President Truman was asked for his reaction, he said he had not seen or heard Joe but doubted he had missed "an enriching experience." The reporter pressed on, asking the president what he thought of Joe's mention of "the mistakes of the Acheson-Truman-Lattimore party." "I don't know anything about that," Truman replied, "but if McCarthy said it, it's a damned lie, you can be sure of that."

The media had predicted that the nominating process would be a long-drawn-out fight. Thus, many were surprised when Harold Stassen threw his support (and delegates) to Eisenhower, and the general eked out a victory over Taft on the first ballot. But the general paid a high price for his triumph. To please conservative Republicans, he had to accept Senator Richard Nixon as his vice-presidential running mate. He also had to endorse a Republican platform that blamed Democratic leaders for the Korean War, charged that they had abandoned Eastern Europe to Communism, and accused them of letting China fall to the Communists. The platform went on to assure voters that "there are no Communists in the Republican party" and that "a Republican President will appoint only persons of unquestioned loyalty."

Most convention delegates were enthusiastic about the Eisenhower nomination. "Ike" had been Eisenhower's nickname from his early youth, and buttons proclaiming "I like Ike!" and "We like Ike!" blossomed throughout the hall. Joe joined the chorus of praise for the general. "I think that Eisenhower will make a great President," he told reporters. "One of the finest things I've seen is Eisenhower going to Taft's headquarters [after winning the nomination] and accepting Taft's offer of cooperation."

Eisenhower didn't have as rosy a view of Joe. He kept his opinion to himself in public, but in private he expressed a strong dislike of McCarthy. The general had been deeply offended by what he considered Joe's totally unjustified attack on his friend and close wartime associate George Marshall.

There were other important differences between the two that Henry S. Reuss, a Wisconsin Democrat and former junior officer on Eisenhower's staff, laid out for reporters. "General Eisenhower and Senator McCarthy are at opposite poles of the G.O.P. [Republican] scale," Reuss said. "Where one is honest, the other is

Dwight D. Eisenhower, the Republican Party's candidate for president, confers with his vice-presidential running mate, Senator Richard M. Nixon, in the summer of 1952. *The National Archives*

devious. Where one is well advised in foreign affairs, the other is ignorant. The two are utterly opposed on issues and principles. Therefore," Reuss concluded, "it is obvious that Eisenhower will find it impossible to campaign in Wisconsin. For if he does, he will have to either ignore our junior senator [Joe] or repudiate him."

If Joe was aware of Reuss's statement, he probably dismissed it. His sinuses were bothering him more than ever, and the day after the convention ended, he flew back to Washington for surgery.

16

The Missing Paragraph

THE OPERATION TO CLEAR Joe's sinuses went well, but then another problem arose. For some time, the senator had complained of sharp stomach pains, and his doctors discovered that he was suffering from a herniated diaphragm. Another operation was required, a complicated one that involved the removal of a rib. It left Joe with a long scar that began on his belly, then ran under his right arm and on up his back to his right shoulder. Later, he delighted in showing the scar to children and watching their astonished expressions.

Joe's doctors urged him to take two months off to recover from the surgeries, but he was impatient to get back into the election campaign. The Democrats, meeting in Chicago in late July, had chosen Illinois's Governor Adlai E. Stevenson as their candidate for president. Gifted with a fine mind and guided by strong principles, Stevenson intended to carry forward the liberal policies of Franklin Roosevelt and Harry Truman. He had no patience with the methods employed by Joe in his anti-Communist campaign, and had criticized them openly on more than one occasion.

Soon after accepting the Democratic nomination, Stevenson gave a speech at the convention of the American Legion, an ultraconservative organization. Without naming McCarthy, he said, "There are those among us who use 'patriotism' as a club for attacking other Americans." He went on to cite as a "shocking example" of such false patriotism "the attacks which have been made on the loyalty and the motives of our great wartime Chief of Staff, General George Marshall." The Democratic nominee concluded his remarks by stating, "The tragedy of our day is the climate of fear in which we live, and fear breeds repression. Too often sinister threats to the Bill of Rights, to freedom of the mind . . . are concealed under the patriotic cloak of anti-Communism."

Joe could not let such a speech go unchallenged. Although less than three weeks had passed since his abdominal surgery, he called reporters to his bedside to denounce Stevenson's remarks and hint that the governor was a supporter of accused Communist spy Alger Hiss. Three weeks after that impromptu press conference, Joe ignored his doctors' orders to rest and flew to Wisconsin to preside over his Senate reelection campaign.

In his absence, Jean Kerr and his other staffers had been hard at work. Jean had prepared a 104-page paperback book called *McCarthyism: The Fight for America*. It chronicled Joe's struggle against Communists in the government and was filled with photographs of documents and clippings that seemed to prove his case. Thousands of copies of the book were printed, and it sold briskly for fifty cents a copy wherever McCarthy appeared on the campaign trail. Long lines of purchasers waited to get his autograph, and Joe willingly stayed to sign every last one of their books.

Governor Adlai E. Stevenson accepts the Democratic Party's nomination for president at the party's convention on July 25, 1952. *AP/WIDE WORLD PHOTOS*

Joe's sole opponent in the Republican primary was Len Schmitt, a progressive lawyer. He had the backing of William T. Evjue, editor of the *Madison Capital Times* and McCarthy's longtime foe. Schmitt launched a series of stinging attacks on Joe, but he lacked the funds to promote his campaign, and the media, except for Evjue's newspaper, paid little attention to him. Meanwhile, conservative national newsmen like Fulton Lewis, Jr., and Westbrook Pegler urged their readers and listeners to contribute to Joe's campaign. And on the West Coast, a "Hollywood Committee for McCarthy," under the leadership of cowboy movie star John Wayne, raised large amounts of money for Joe.

On September 3, 1952, McCarthy gave his first and only speech prior to the primary election, which was set for September 9. The senator made no mention of his opponent, Schmitt. Instead, he concentrated his fire on Adlai Stevenson. "Mr. Stevenson, in three of the speeches which you made since you were nominated on the Democrat ticket, you went out of your way to viciously berate me. Why, Mr. Stevenson?" Then McCarthy went on to make one of his typical vague, unsupported charges. "Could you be disturbed, Mr. Stevenson," he said, "because I am checking your record since the day you entered government service at about the same time and in the same department as [Alger] Hiss . . . ? Are you getting worried about what we are finding?"

Joe's speech was greeted with repeated cheers by an audience of more than 2,000 gathered in a suburban Milwaukee high school auditorium. A thirty-one-station radio hookup carried his words to thousands of listeners throughout Wisconsin. In the meantime, Adlai Stevenson denied that he had ever had a close association with Alger Hiss. His statement received less coverage in the media than Joe's original intimation that the Democratic candidate had been involved in something shady.

On primary day, Joe defeated Schmitt by a margin of almost two and a half to one (515,581 votes to 213,701). The size of McCarthy's victory startled political commentators nationally as well as locally. *Time* magazine said, "McCarthy has grown in power because millions of Americans think he is 'the only one' really against the internal Communist threat."

Right-wing newspaper magnate William Randolph Hearst was jubilant. He wrote in an editorial: "While Communist apologists and others, including the Democratic Presidential candidate, keep acting as if the [Communist] conspiracy never existed, Fighting Joe has appealed to the conscience of a people aroused

The mud leaking from a vehicle driven by Sen. McCarthy attracts three neat and clean children carrying signboards saying they're against McCarthyism BUT—
Cartoon by Herblock, The Library of Congress

by the treachery of the Hisses and the other proven associates of the Kremlin."

Others were far less enthusiastic. The *St. Louis Post-Dispatch* said, "McCarthy is what he is, not because he opposes Communism but because he exploits the fear of it for his own political gain." *U.S. News and World Report* sounded a warning: "McCarthyism, as a result [of Joe's primary victory], emerges as a political force to be reckoned with, not just in Wisconsin but in other states where others in politics will be tempted to exploit its vote-getting possibilities."

One Wisconsin politician, Thomas Fairchild, had just won the Democratic primary for U.S. senator and would be facing Joe in the general election. Because of the effective way Joe employed the issue of Communists in government, Fairchild decided to avoid the Communist theme as much as possible and focus instead on the continuing investigation in Washington of Joe's alleged ethical misconduct.

That investigation, triggered by Senator William Benton, had suffered one blow after another. First, a key investigator for the subcommittee resigned. Then

PAY DIRT

An elephant, symbol of the Republican Party, runs gleefully toward an overturned garbage can labeled "McCarthyism."
Cartoon by Fitzpatrick, The Library of Congress

a Republican member, Herman Welker, quit, charging that the subcommittee was being used as a "political vehicle by the Democratic Party." When the chairman, Guy Gillette, submitted his resignation also, many Washington observers thought the investigation of McCarthy's activities was dead.

Carl Hayden, the seventy-six-year-old chairman of the parent Rules Committee, was determined on principle that the subcommittee continue its investigation. He appointed a new chairman, Senator Thomas Hennings, and Hennings and the remaining members went back to work. It wasn't likely, though, that their findings, if any, would come in time to affect Joe's reelection campaign. Election Day, November 4, was less than two months away.

Back in Wisconsin, Thomas Fairchild pursued a thoughtful, intelligent, but unexciting campaign against Joe. Fairchild occasionally attacked McCarthy for "destroying the rights of free speech and free thought," but he mainly tried to revive voters' interest in the old, unproved charges that Joe had been guilty of income tax evasion while serving as a judge. As a result, Joe didn't take Fairchild seriously. In speeches on the campaign trail, he often ignored his opponent and focused his scorn instead on Adlai Stevenson. He drew big laughs whenever, in a seeming slip of the tongue, he called the Democratic presidential candidate "Alger Stevenson."

McCarthy was so confident of victory that he volunteered to tour the country and speak on behalf of other Republican candidates. Party officials jumped at the offer; Joe's reputation as a fighter against Communism carried tremendous weight with the Republican base. McCarthy was stung, however, when a political columnist reported a rumor that Gen. Eisenhower did not intend to campaign with him in Wisconsin. McCarthy was aware Ike didn't like him, but he still expected to be included in the general's plans because of his home-state popularity.

Joe shouldn't have been surprised. In a news conference in late August, Eisenhower had declared that he would back McCarthy as "a member of the Republican organization." But the general went on to say, "I am not going to campaign for or give blanket endorsement to any man who does anything that I believe to be un-American in its methods and procedures."

Everyone at the conference realized Eisenhower was referring to McCarthy. When a reporter brought up Joe's speech attacking George Marshall, Ike got angry. He rose from his desk and began to pace back and forth. "There is nothing of disloyalty in General Marshall's soul," he asserted, adding that Marshall was "a patriot and a man of real selflessness. I have no patience with anyone," he concluded, "who can find in his record of service to his country anything to criticize."

After Joe's overwhelming primary victory in September, Eisenhower's aides urged him to reconsider his decision not to campaign with McCarthy when his whistle-stop train tour of the Midwest reached Wisconsin. Much back-and-forth discussion ensued, and in the end Eisenhower gave in reluctantly. But he insisted that his speechwriter, Emmett John Hughes, include a passage defending George Marshall in the speech Ike was scheduled to give in Milwaukee on October 3. Hughes came up with the following paragraph:

Let me be quite specific. I know that charges of disloyalty have, in the past, been leveled against General George C. Marshall. I have been privileged for thirty-five years to know General Marshall personally. I know him, as a man and as a soldier, to be dedicated with singular selflessness and the profoundest patriotism to the service of America. And this episode is a sobering lesson in the way freedom must not defend itself.

The paragraph seems like quite a mild rebuke, given the strength of Eisenhower's feelings about Marshall. However, the general's aides were still debating whether it should be included in the Milwaukee speech as Ike's campaign train moved slowly across central Illinois. Some of the aides thought it would be taken as an unfair attack on McCarthy. Others feared it might hurt the chances of the entire slate of Republican candidates in Wisconsin.

Word reached Joe of what Ike intended to say, and he and Wisconsin governor Walter Kohler decided to fly to Illinois and confront Eisenhower in person. Their mission: to get the general to agree to change the speech before he reached Wisconsin. Ike was not pleased to see them, and, according to witnesses, even less pleased when Joe said straight out that he didn't want him to include the passage about Marshall in his Milwaukee speech.

The general responded with what one aide described as "red-hot anger." He began by telling Joe exactly what he thought of the way he had conducted his anti-Communist crusade. Then he defended Marshall and reaffirmed his determination to include the words of praise for his old friend in his talk. The meeting lasted half an hour. At its end, Eisenhower issued no statement but McCarthy, smiling broadly, told waiting reporters that his conversation with Ike had been "very, very pleasant." Joe added that he and Governor Kohler would be traveling on the general's train when it entered Wisconsin. The reporters wanted to get a shot of Ike and Joe together, but they were turned down.

The discussion among Eisenhower, Joe, and Governor Kohler continued the next day as the train headed toward Green Bay, the candidate's first stop in Wisconsin. The men gathered in Ike's private car, and he restated his opposition to what he called "un-American methods in combating Communism." Addressing Joe directly, he said, "I'm going to say that I disagree with you."

"If you say that, you'll be booed," Joe warned.

"I've been booed before," Eisenhower replied, "and being booed doesn't bother me."

A crowd of more than 3,000 awaited the candidate at the Green Bay station. Ike and Joe were introduced together, but Joe stood back as Eisenhower addressed the crowd. The general began by calling for the election of all the Republican candidates in the state, but he didn't single out Joe for special mention.

When Eisenhower discussed the issue of Communists in the government, he said he believed weeding them out was the responsibility of the executive branch, implying that it was not the responsibility of senators like Joe. He added, "We can do it with absolute assurance that American principles of trial by jury, of innocence until proof of guilt, are all observed, and I expect to do [just that]."

At the conclusion of his remarks, the crowd did not boo as Joe had predicted; instead, they cheered. One of Ike's aides noted that Joe was scowling as he left the candidate's car.

The next stop on the tour was Appleton, where Joe had served as a judge, and which he thought of as his hometown. He expressed a desire to introduce Ike there. Only after local politicians argued strenuously on Joe's behalf did Eisenhower agree to the idea. As it turned out, Joe's introduction of Ike to the crowd of 5,000 was just one sentence. He said, "I wish to present to the people of my home city the next president of the United States—General Dwight Eisenhower." Then he stood aside as Ike began his stump speech, the one he usually gave at these train stops. Later, a longtime friend of Joe's said it was the only time he could remember McCarthy apparently at a loss for words.

As the train moved on toward Milwaukee, where Eisenhower was scheduled to deliver his major speech, Governor Kohler approached the general's chief aide, Sherman Adams, to make a final plea on Joe's behalf. Kohler began by reminding Adams how strongly the American people felt about Communist subversion in government, and how they looked to the Republican Party to deal forcefully with the problem. In light of that, he said, including the paragraph in defense of George Marshall, who some believed had been "soft on Communism," could jeopardize Republican candidates' chances for success, nationally as well as locally.

Adams was impressed by Kohler's argument and took him to Eisenhower's private car. Accompanying them was another trusted aide of Ike's, Major General Wilton B. Persons, who also agreed with Kohler. At first Ike stood his ground, but after hearing the trio press their case for deleting the paragraph, he reluctantly accepted the political realities of the situation. "Take it out," he growled.

That evening a crowd of 8,500 filled the Milwaukee Arena to hear Eisenhower speak. Many of them wore "I like Ike!" buttons on their lapels, and some had two.

Much of what Eisenhower said could have been lifted from speeches Joe had made about the Communist menace. The general raised the alarm that Communism had "poisoned two whole decades of our national life" and had "insinuated itself into our schools, public forums, news channels, labor unions, and—most terrifyingly—into our government itself." He continued in the same vein, blaming Communists and Communist sympathizers in the government for the "fall of China and the surrender of whole nations in Eastern Europe to the Soviet Union."

At the end, the standing-room-only crowd applauded and cheered Ike just as similar crowds had so often cheered Joe. A few listeners may have wondered why Eisenhower never mentioned McCarthy in his remarks. They had no way of knowing of the clash of wills that had so recently taken place between the general and Joe.

But many reporters knew. Advance copies of the original speech had leaked to the press, and the reporters were waiting to hear Eisenhower defend George Marshall. When he didn't, they assumed—rightly—that Joe and his supporters had put pressure on Ike to delete the paragraph in question, and had succeeded. After news stories to that effect appeared in the *New York Times* and other papers, Eisenhower, Sherman Adams, Governor Kohler, and Joe all said it wasn't so. A top aide of Ike's, who asked not to be identified, went so far as to claim that McCarthy had not seen the general's speech until it was in its final form.

Adlai Stevenson made much of the story. In a speech before an enthusiastic crowd in Waukesha, Wisconsin, the Democratic candidate accused Eisenhower of deliberately changing his views on George Marshall in "an opportunistic grasping for votes." He called the Republican Party's right wing "the most accomplished wrecking crew in this country's history," and charged that Ike had given it "a first, second, and third mortgage on every principle he once held."

Eventually, though, the story of the deleted paragraph left the front pages, replaced by fresh incidents in the ongoing presidential campaign. Eisenhower traveled on to Minnesota while Joe resumed campaigning in Wisconsin. Some reporters had heard rumors that Eisenhower treated Joe disdainfully in their meetings. They confronted Joe about it, hoping to evoke an angry response that could lead to a hot new story. Joe laughed off any suggestion that he and Ike didn't get along, calling the notion completely false. Why shouldn't he put a good face on things? After all, Joe had set out to persuade a determined Ike to change his mind about defending George Marshall. And he had gotten exactly what he wanted.

"I Can Investigate Anybody"

JOE STILL HADN'T RECOVERED completely from his surgeries, but that didn't stop him from keeping his promise to campaign for other conservative Republicans around the country. In the month before the November 4 election, he traveled to Arizona, Nevada, Wyoming, Montana, and Washington state in the West, and to Missouri, Michigan, and Indiana in the Midwest. Sometimes he made as many as four speeches a day, warning his audiences of the internal Communist threat and urging them to vote for staunch anti-Communist candidates.

One Republican McCarthy didn't campaign for was Henry Cabot Lodge, the moderate senator from Massachusetts. Lodge, a man of wealth and high social position, had tended to look down on the upstart McCarthy. But that wasn't the main reason Joe chose not to support him. Lodge was running for reelection against Representative John F. Kennedy, a bright young man with tremendous personal appeal. And Joe had a long-standing special relationship with the Kennedy family, especially its patriarch, Joseph P. Kennedy.

The elder Kennedy had made a fortune in the bootleg liquor business when alcoholic beverages were outlawed during the 1920s and early 1930s. He was a conservative Irish American Catholic with strong right-wing views. Although a lifelong Democrat, he had often warned of the Communist menace and had expressed his support for McCarthy's position on the matter even before the senator's Wheeling speech. After McCarthy came to Washington and met Joe Kennedy's eldest living son, John, he was a frequent guest at the Kennedy family compound on Cape Cod. He dated John's sister Patricia and was also fond of another sister, Eunice. He once joked to his friend Ray Kiermas that if worse came to worst, he could always marry a Kennedy girl.

Rumors circulated in Washington that Joe Kennedy had persuaded McCarthy not to involve himself in the contest between Lodge and John Kennedy. Joe Kennedy was known to have contributed $10,000 to McCarthy's own reelection campaign. McCarthy may not have needed much persuading, since he and John Kennedy, a Democrat like his father, shared many political views. As far back as 1949, the young Kennedy had attacked the policies of Owen Lattimore, the agreements with the Soviet Union that President Roosevelt had reached at the Yalta Conference, and the role George Marshall had played in the Chinese civil war.

Now, in 1952, the fall election campaign was heating up. In Wisconsin, Joe's Democratic opponent, Thomas Fairchild, had received strong support from the state's labor unions. The unions affiliated with the two large union coalitions, the American Federation of Labor (AFL) and the Congress of Industrial Organizations (CIO), spent almost $100,000 on the 1952 election, a very large sum at the time. Most of the unions' money went to the Fairchild organization to bolster its efforts to defeat McCarthy. The AFL also published a brochure, *Inside McCarthy,* that contained a slashing attack on the senator. Not to be outdone, the CIO issued its own pamphlet titled *Smear Incorporated: The Record of Joe McCarthy's One-Man Mob Operations.*

Both publications were mailed to thousands of voters throughout Wisconsin. However, they lacked the impact they might have had because they focused mainly on Joe's conservative voting record, steering clear of any serious discussion of his anti-Communist tactics. Like candidate Fairchild, the unions feared that such a discussion would stir up an unwanted controversy. While Wisconsin voters might have doubts about McCarthy the man, a majority of them favored his campaign to get the Communists out of Washington.

The Republicans, on the other hand, didn't hesitate to exploit the Communist issue for all it was worth. A main theme of their national campaign was "Korea, Communism, and Corruption." In Maryland, a Republican candidate for the U.S. Senate, J. Glenn Beall, said, "We have got to slug it out, toe to toe, with the parlor pinks and so-called 'liberals,' who call themselves Democrats." Beall went on to challenge his Democratic opponent "to identify one charge that Joe McCarthy made that he's ever been wrong on."

Senator William Jenner, engaged in a tight race in Indiana, picked up on the Korean part of the Republican theme. "If the Democrats win in November," Jenner warned, "the bodies of thousands more American boys will be tossed on Truman's funeral pyre in Asia." Should Stevenson become president, he said, "the Red network will continue to work secretly and safely for the destruction of the United States."

In Connecticut, William F. Buckley, Jr., a recent graduate of Yale and an ambitious young conservative, headed a committee to drive Communists out of government. Buckley's immediate target was Senator William Benton, who had inspired the ongoing Senate investigation of Joe and was running for reelection. Buckley used his considerable wealth to run a series of anti-Benton ads in Connecticut newspapers. The ads, which Benton denounced as "scurrilous," were intended to prove that the senator held "Communistic" views.

But no Republican outdid the vice-presidential candidate, Richard Nixon, in milking the anti-Communist issue. In one speech, Nixon called President Truman "spineless" and "soft on the Reds." In another, he described Adlai Stevenson as "Adlai the Appeaser" who boasts "a Ph.D. from Dean Acheson's Cowardly College of Communist Containment." He told a Minnesota audience that he would rather have a "khaki-clad President" like Eisenhower than "one clad in State Department pinks." And in Superior, Wisconsin, Nixon made a point of endorsing the reelection of "my good friend Joe McCarthy."

After leaving Wisconsin and Joe's unwelcome company, Gen. Eisenhower sounded more like himself. In his speeches on the campaign trail, Ike often mentioned his dislike of "witch-hunts" and those who indulged in "character assassination." He told a friendly crowd in Salt Lake City, Utah, "We cannot pretend to defend freedom with weapons suited only to the arsenals of tyrants." At the same time, he took pains to avoid any suggestion that he wasn't solidly anti-Communist. In Billings, Montana, he vowed, "We will find the men and women who may fail to live up to our standards [of patriotism]; we will find the pinks; we will find the Communists; we will find the disloyal."

When polls showed that the Korean War was the main concern of more than half of registered voters, Eisenhower addressed that issue. In speech after speech, he charged that the Truman administration had left South Korea "wide open to Communist aggression." He often cited the rising toll of American casualties and condemned the stalemate in the fighting that had persisted since the previous summer. As the campaign progressed, Ike promised voters that he would go to Korea to survey the situation in person as soon as he was elected.

On the Democratic side, Adlai Stevenson tried to fend off Republican accusations that he was soft on Communism by asserting his own firm belief in the anti-Communist cause. "The Communist conspiracy within the United States deserves the attention of every American citizen and the sleepless concern of the responsible government agencies," he stated in a New York City speech. Stevenson went on to praise J. Edgar Hoover's FBI: "In all this effort we have had the faithful and resourceful work in national protection of the Federal Bureau of Investigation."

Stevenson was careful to emphasize, however, that his support of the fight against Communism did not imply an endorsement of McCarthy and his methods. In one of his final campaign appearances, at a rally in Cleveland, Ohio, the Democratic candidate offered an implied criticism of McCarthy: "I believe with all my heart that those who would beguile the voters by lies or half-truths, or corrupt them by fear and falsehood, are committing spiritual treason against our institutions. They are doing the work of our enemies."

Stevenson's eloquence and clear thinking were not enough to turn the tide of the election. On November 4, Eisenhower defeated him in 39 of the 48 states, including Wisconsin, and won the presidency by a decisive 10-percent margin, 55 percent to 45 percent. Ike's victory returned a Republican to the White House for the first time since 1933, when Franklin Roosevelt was inaugurated. The Republicans also regained control of both houses of Congress. The margin in the Senate was a razor-thin 48–47 (there was one Independent), the margin in the House of Representatives a slightly wider 221–213.

Joe rode the Republican tide to victory, winning reelection with 54 percent of the votes, 870,444 to Thomas Fairchild's 731,402. After celebrating with friends and backers in Appleton, Joe spoke with reporters around one in the morning. "The election of Eisenhower and a Republican Senate and House more than justifies my faith in the intelligence of the American people," he said. "This is a new day for America."

In Connecticut, William F. Benton, Joe's nemesis, was soundly defeated in his bid for reelection. Later, McCarthy couldn't resist gloating a little. "How do you like what happened to my friend Benton?" he asked an interviewer. Benton's defeat, coupled with the earlier departure of Millard Tydings, meant that two of

McCarthy's most vocal and influential Senate foes would no longer be around to challenge him. No wonder Joe felt confident as he looked forward to his second term.

Several important political developments took place before that term began. The first affected Joe directly. Senator Carl Hayden, outgoing chairman of the Rules Committee, knew that the incoming Eisenhower administration was likely to drop the investigation of McCarthy that was under way. So Hayden pressed the members of the subcommittee to issue a report on its findings before the Truman administration came to an end.

The bipartisan subcommittee submitted the report with only twenty-four hours to spare. It was not the bombshell some had predicted. In their haste, the subcommittee members had sidestepped the serious questions about the methods Joe had used in his campaign against Communists in government, and had focused instead on his questionable financial dealings. The 328-page report laid out in detail all the old charges—the tax problems in Wisconsin, the Lustron fee in Washington—but in the end failed to prove McCarthy guilty of any illegal conduct.

Although the document was little more than a slap on the wrist, Joe still reacted angrily when he got his copy. He claimed the Privileges and Elections Subcommittee had sunk to "a new low in dishonesty and smear," and called its chairman, Thomas Hennings, and the chair of the parent Rules Committee, Carl Hayden, "lackeys of this [Truman's] corrupt administration." Then, buoyed by his reelection victory, he added, "They should know by this time that they cannot scare me, or turn me aside."

The other development began to clear the way for at least a partial resolution of the Korean War. On November 29, 1952, a little more than three weeks after the election, Dwight Eisenhower fulfilled a campaign promise by flying to Korea to find out what could be done to end the conflict. Sometime later, India offered a proposal for a Korean armistice that was accepted by the United Nations. The parties involved finally signed a cease-fire on July 27, 1953. At the same time, the border between North and South Korea was established along the 38th Parallel, with a demilitarized zone (DMZ) around it. The zone was defended by North Korean soldiers to the north and South Korean and American forces to the south.

While the Eisenhower administration was taking shape, Joe had his pick of

Senate committee assignments because of his seniority. He chose to be chair of the Committee on Government Operations and told reporters he would also serve as chairman of that committee's Permanent Subcommittee on Investigations. "Some people don't realize it," he told a friend, "but that committee [and subcommittee] could be the most powerful in the Senate. I can investigate anybody who ever received money from the government, and that covers a lot of ground."

Most of the Republican members of the committee were conservative friends of his, like Karl E. Mundt of South Dakota, so it looked as though Joe would have few challenges as chairman. The Democratic members weren't likely to present any major problems, either. The Democratic minority leader, Lyndon B. Johnson of Texas, appointed moderates and conservatives like John F. Kennedy, who had won his race against Henry Cabot Lodge in Massachusetts.

Johnson didn't particularly like McCarthy or his methods, but he had an instinct for what would be good for the Democratic party in the long run. He was well aware that Joe's anti-Communist crusade was popular with a majority of the American people, including many Democrats, and he did not want to arouse Joe's ire unnecessarily. Johnson told a confidant, "I will not commit my party to some high-school debate on the subject, 'Resolved that Communism is good for the United States,' with my party taking the affirmative."

Joe expressed great optimism about what the new administration could accomplish in the next four years. "I don't think we'll run into any whitewashes or coverups after Eisenhower takes over," he told reporters. He also affirmed his support of the new secretary of state, John Foster Dulles. "I think he's a good American," Joe said, and he promised to hand over to Dulles "every particle of evidence I've collected."

McCarthy was delighted when his friend Scott McLeod, a former FBI agent, was chosen as chief security officer of Dulles's State Department. McLeod would be responsible for confirming the loyalty of the department's personnel. Right-wingers cheered his choice. Many liberal commentators feared what would happen when McLeod gave Joe and his committee access to the State Department's files.

Meanwhile, Joe was busy planning new investigations for his committee. He announced that three senators, whom he didn't name, had asked that he inquire into Communist influence at the Federal Communications Commission (FCC). Several weeks later, he said he planned to "root out Communist thinkers from

Senator Lyndon B. Johnson. *The National Archives*

the nation's colleges." He admitted the latter would be "an awfully unpleasant task," and predicted that "all hell will break loose, and there will be screaming of interference with academic freedom." But he told an interviewer he was determined to proceed anyway.

To support his ambitious plans, Joe set about building a strong backup staff for the committee's work. Joseph P. Kennedy suggested that McCarthy consider his younger son, Robert, for the post of chief legal counsel. Robert Kennedy had graduated from the University of Virginia Law School the year before, and had helped run his brother John's Senate campaign. Robert, called Bobby by his friends, shared many of McCarthy's views and was known to be extremely ambitious. He hadn't had time to build much of a resumé, though.

Joe wanted someone with an established reputation for the job in question, but at the same time he didn't want to offend the elder Kennedy. So he offered Robert a position as assistant to the committee's general counsel, Francis Flanagan, instead. The younger Kennedy accepted the lesser job after Joe promised that in time he would succeed Flanagan.

Now McCarthy focused his efforts on finding a chief counsel. J. Edgar Hoover recommended twenty-five-year-old Roy Marcus Cohn, an assistant U.S. attorney in New York City. Cohn was the only child of Albert Cohn, a respected New York State judge, and Dora Marcus Cohn, from the well-to-do Marcus family. Doted on by his parents, the young Cohn was a prodigy of sorts. He graduated from Columbia College at nineteen and from Columbia Law School a year later. After being admitted to the bar at twenty-one, Cohn used family connections to help him obtain the position of assistant U.S. attorney.

Like Joe, Roy Cohn had a knack for getting publicity. He first attracted notice for his participation in a number of important anti-Communist cases. But it was the prominent role he played in the 1951 espionage trial of Julius Rosenberg and his wife, Ethel, that brought Cohn to the attention of J. Edgar Hoover. The Rosenbergs, both natives of New York City, had met when they joined the Young Communist League in 1936 to support the republican cause in the Spanish Civil War. They married three years later and had two young sons. In March 1951, the Rosenbergs were put on trial, charged with being spies for the Soviet Union. Julius, an electrical engineer, was accused of obtaining atomic secrets from his brother-in-law, David Greenglass, a machinist at Los Alamos where the first bombs were developed, and of passing on the highly classified information to

Ethel and Julius Rosenberg during their trial for espionage in New York City in 1951. Note that Julius is handcuffed. *AP/WIDE WORLD PHOTOS*

Soviet agents. Ethel was charged with aiding her husband in his spying efforts.

Roy Cohn conducted much of the questioning at the Rosenbergs' trial. His relentless cross-examination of David Greenglass produced the testimony that many said had the most impact on the jury. Its members found Julius and Ethel Rosenberg guilty of all charges on March 29, less than three weeks after their trial began.

Moving swiftly, Judge Irving Kaufman on April 5 sentenced them both to death in the electric chair and went on to explain why he had settled on such a severe penalty. "I consider your crime worse than murder," he said, looking straight at the Rosenbergs. "I believe your conduct in putting into the hands of the Russians the A-bomb years before our best scientists predicted Russia would perfect the bomb has already caused, in my opinion, the Communist aggression in Korea, with the resultant casualties exceeding 50,000, and who knows but that millions more innocent people may pay the price of your treason." Later, Roy

Cohn would claim that he had persuaded Judge Kaufman to impose the death penalty on both Rosenbergs.

The case went through several appeals, and the sentence still had not been carried out in December 1952, when Cohn met Joe McCarthy to discuss the job of chief counsel for the senator's committee. The meeting took place during a crowded party for Joe's supporters in his suite at the Hotel Astor in New York City. In a memoir, Cohn recalled his first impression of Joe. "Among the dozens of men and women in formal dress, the senator had removed his jacket, shirt, and tie. He wore tuxedo trousers, patent leather shoes—and suspenders over a T-shirt."

Joe made it clear he was aware of Cohn's background and accomplishments. Cohn thought the senator might be put off by the fact that—though he usually supported Republican candidates—he, Cohn, was a registered Democrat. But that didn't matter to Joe. "I couldn't care less about your politics," he said. "I'm interested only in your ability to do the job."

Joe proudly announced the hiring of Roy Cohn as his chief counsel on January 3, 1953, the same day the Senate committee investigating McCarthy issued its report. He was truly impressed with Cohn, whom he often described as "one of

McCarthy listens to his newly appointed chief counsel, Roy Cohn.
The National Archives

G. David Schine (left) with Roy Cohn and Sen. McCarthy at a hearing of
McCarthy's subcommittee. *The Library of Congress*

the most brilliant young men whom I have ever met." The hiring story overshadowed accounts of the report in many newspapers, as Joe had hoped it would.

A month or so later, Cohn persuaded Joe to take on a good friend of his,
twenty-six-year-old G. David Schine, as an unpaid "consultant" to the committee. The son of a wealthy entrepreneur who owned a chain of hotels and a string
of movie theaters, Schine had attended Harvard College, spent some time in
Hollywood, and worked as a press agent in the music business. He had also tried
his hand at writing song lyrics. One of his efforts, a mournful ballad that he published himself, was called "Please Say Yes or It's Goodbye."

At some point along the way, David Schine had become interested in ideology and had produced a six-page pamphlet, filled with misspellings and errors of fact, titled *Definition of Communism*. Schine's father had copies of the pamphlet placed in the rooms of all Schine Hotels, and one of them came to the attention of Roy Cohn. He sought out Schine, and that was the beginning of their friendship.

The two young men couldn't have been more different in appearance. Cohn was five feet eight and dark complected, with black hair that he combed straight back. His heavy-lidded eyes made him look sleepy, but his mind was always active. He spoke quickly, rarely smiled, worked long hours, and usually seemed tense. Schine, on the other hand, was tall, slim, and fair skinned, with short blond hair. Unlike Cohn, he had a relaxed, easygoing manner. Writer Richard Rovere summed him up as "a good-looking young man in the bland style that one used to associate with male big band singers."

Some of Joe's colleagues questioned why he had hired Schine, even as an unpaid consultant. Schine seemed to be a lightweight, with almost no credentials for the job. McCarthy brushed aside their concerns, saying that as long as Schine's appointment made Roy Cohn happy, it was fine with him. Besides, he had more important things on his mind. He wanted his subcommittee to have first choice when it came to future anti-Communist investigations, and that meant a struggle with other powerful Congressional committees that conducted such investigations. Joe assured doubters he was ready for the fight.

18

Cohn and Schine Go to Europe

JOE FAILED TO ANTICIPATE how strongly the other Congressional committees would defend their turf. In the end, he had to work out a compromise with the Senate Internal Security Subcommittee; it would continue to have first crack at anti-Communist investigations but would consult on them and share information with McCarthy's subcommittee. He also agreed to exchange information with the House Un-American Activities Committee so that the two committees would not launch similar probes.

When he was questioned about these arrangements on the TV program *Meet the Press,* Joe explained that his subcommittee retained the right to look into any examples of Communist subversion that the other two committees failed to explore. When the interviewer suggested that perhaps Joe was being pushed out of the main struggle against Communism, McCarthy bristled. "No one can push me out of anything," he said.

He seemed to prove the point when budgets for the various Senate committees came up for discussion. Joe made such an eloquent plea for funds to finance his planned investigations that his subcommittee received $200,000 to cover the cost of its operations. The Internal Security Subcommittee received only $150,000.

Those sums may not sound particularly large today, but they seemed extravagant to many at the time—especially to some Senate Democrats. Allan J. Ellender of Louisiana, a fiscal conservative, believed the Senate was going "somewhat haywire" on investigations. He had especially harsh words for McCarthy's budget request. "He wants to televise all these hearings," Ellender said. "He is going

Premier Joseph Stalin (left foreground) and President Harry S. Truman meet for the first and only time at the Potsdam Conference in July 1945. Behind Stalin's right shoulder is Charles E. Bohlen, and behind Truman's left shoulder is Soviet Foreign Minister Andrei A. Gromyko. The smiling man between Bohlen and Gromyko is unidentified. *The Library of Congress*

overboard on this." But Ellender's criticism didn't prevent Joe's subcommittee from getting the full $200,000 that had been appropriated.

Before the subcommittee could begin its work, Joe's attention was claimed by a decision of President Eisenhower's that made him furious. The position of ambassador to the Soviet Union was vacant, and the president selected Charles E. Bohlen to fill it. Moderate Republicans and liberal Democrats alike thought Bohlen was an excellent choice. He had worked in the Foreign Service branch of the State Department for twenty-five years, spoke Russian fluently, and was an authority on the Soviet Union.

Joe and other right-wing Republicans saw Bohlen very differently. The experienced diplomat had been a key advisor to President Roosevelt at the Yalta Conference, which ultraconservative Republicans wanted the Eisenhower administration to repudiate. He had also worked closely at the State Department with Dean Acheson, an archvillain in the minds of the same Republicans. His nomination to such a key position seemed to Joe and his fellows like a major betrayal, and they vowed to fight it every step of the way.

The Senate Foreign Relations Committee began consideration of the nomination in late February. Charles Bohlen appeared before the committee on March 3. He impressed the members with his frank, thoughtful answers to their probing questions about Yalta and other matters, and he appeared to be headed toward a relatively quick confirmation. But right-wing newspapers ran critical accounts of Bohlen's testimony—accounts that reflected the thinking of Joe and other Republican conservatives.

Further discussion of the nomination was delayed by startling news from Moscow on March 5, 1953. Joseph Stalin, who had ruled the Soviet Union with an iron fist for almost thirty years, had died of heart failure. It wasn't immediately clear who would succeed Stalin, but most observers of the Soviet Union believed that major changes in the way the country was ruled were bound to occur no matter who took power.

Walter Bedell Smith, the undersecretary of state, gave the members of the Foreign Relations Committee a private briefing on the implications of Stalin's death. Smith urged the committee to swiftly confirm Charles Bohlen as ambassador to the Soviet Union. "The sooner we get in there, the better, because there is going to be a very unusual series of developments," Smith predicted. "And Mr. Bohlen, of course, is the best man we have . . . to go there and make reports during this critical period."

Joe and his allies didn't see it that way. They viewed the Communist-ruled Soviet Union as an immovable force, totally resistant to change, and Charles Bohlen as a weak-willed liberal who had aided in the "surrender" of Eastern Europe to Stalin at the Yalta Conference. With the help of Scott McLeod at the State Department, Joe and the others claimed they had information that Bohlen had associated with "some bad eggs" in the past. Although the information was based on an anonymous letter and several hearsay reports, it was enough to make the Foreign Relations Committee postpone action on Bohlen's nomination and schedule another hearing.

Secretary of State Dulles thought seriously about withdrawing Bohlen's name from consideration, but President Eisenhower persuaded him to continue resisting the heavy pressure from Joe and other right-wingers. When McCarthy learned of the secretary's decision, he warned Dulles that he was making "a great mistake."

Dulles and Bohlen were both invited to appear before the Foreign Relations Committee on the day of the second hearing. Dulles contacted Bohlen and suggested they not ride in the same car to Capitol Hill. That way there was no chance they could be photographed together. Bohlen later wrote, "His [Dulles's] remark made me wonder if he would have the courage to stand up to the McCarthyites."

In fact, Dulles did much more than stand up for Bohlen. The secretary had read all the FBI information on Bohlen that Scott McLeod had passed along to Joe, and he told the committee that it contained nothing that was seriously damaging: "There is not a whisper of a suggestion that I have been able to turn up throwing any doubt at all about his [Bohlen's] loyalty, or upon his security as a person." Dulles's words were so convincing that the committee members voted unanimously, 15–0, to approve Bohlen's nomination.

Joe was enraged by the committee's action. He said he was sure the president would withdraw his backing for the nominee if he saw "the entire file on Bohlen." Senator Pat McCarran echoed McCarthy and urged that Bohlen's nomination be delayed until every senator had a chance to see "the full and complete file on the nominee."

The Eisenhower administration responded swiftly to these and similar challenges from the Republican right. The president told reporters he "thoroughly approved" of Bohlen's nomination. Secretary of State Dulles held a news conference during which he said he had informed Eisenhower of all the "derogatory material" in Bohlen's file. Senator Charles Tobey, a moderate Republican from New Hampshire, was disgusted by the delaying tactics of Joe and his fellow right-wingers. "The opposition comes from a little group of willful men," Tobey said. "Instead of backing the President, they are trying to block him and put daggers in his back. . . . These critics are not worthy to unlace Bohlen's shoes."

Joe, Pat McCarran, and others made every effort to block the nomination. But Majority Leader Taft—pressured by the president—overrode their objections and scheduled a debate on the nomination by the full Senate.

Not surprisingly, the debate, which began on March 23, was unusually heated. Joe started things off by suggesting that Bohlen be given a lie-detector test about the material in the FBI files. "I think Mr. Bohlen would agree with me that if the information in the files . . . is correct, Moscow is the last place in the world to which he should be sent," McCarthy said.

No one supported the lie-detector idea. Senator Ralph E. Flanders accused Joe of undermining Secretary of State Dulles and President Eisenhower by trying to defeat their nomination of Bohlen. Flanders urged Joe to take a second look at the matter and give the new Republican administration a chance to succeed.

Joe was not about to take orders from Flanders. Stubborn as ever, he said, "I do not care whether a president is a Democrat or a Republican; when he has made a bad nomination I intend to oppose it, on the floor of the Senate or anywhere else!"

The debate remained at an impasse until Majority Leader Taft proposed that a senator from each party read the FBI file on Bohlen and report to the full Senate on their findings. Taft and Senator John J. Sparkman, Democrat of Alabama, were selected for the job, and J. Edgar Hoover assured them that the file summarized all the relevant FBI material on Bohlen. They were also told that they would be reading the same summary that Scott McLeod and Secretary Dulles had seen earlier.

The next day the senators made their report. They echoed Secretary Dulles's statement to the Foreign Relations Committee, saying they had found nothing in the summary to shake their confidence in Bohlen. Taft commented, "There was no suggestion anywhere by anyone reflecting on the loyalty of Mr. Bohlen in any way, or any association by him with Communism, or support of Communism, or even tolerance of Communism."

Joe and his cohorts were still not satisfied. They kept on trying to throw up roadblocks to the nomination, going so far as to suggest that Bohlen was not the president's personal choice. Eisenhower put a stop to that rumor at a news conference on March 26. He stated firmly that Charles Bohlen was the best-qualified man he could find for the job, and said he was deeply concerned about the fate of the nomination.

Some of Eisenhower's close associates urged him to take an even stronger stand and denounce Joe's delaying tactics. But Eisenhower refused, just as he had refused to confront Joe about George Marshall during the election campaign. He told aide Emmett John Hughes, "I just will not—I refuse—to get into the gutter with that guy."

At last Joe and his allies ran out of excuses for delaying a decision on the nomination, and Majority Leader Taft called for a vote. Most Senate Democrats joined forces with moderate Republicans to confirm Bohlen's nomination by an overwhelming margin, 74–13. The vote was a major setback for Joe and the ten other Republicans and two conservative Democrats who had voted against Bohlen. Even some of McCarthy's most loyal supporters criticized Joe's actions during the nomination fight. The *Wisconsin State Journal,* for example, said, "There are times when Joe McCarthy makes it tough to play on his team."

Joe didn't seem fazed by the Senate defeat, or the criticism of his behavior. He turned his attention to an investigation his subcommittee had launched while the Bohlen hearings were still going on. The inquiry focused on the Voice of America (VOA), a State Department agency that broadcast information on the United States in more than fifty different languages to listeners all over the world. In announcing the probe, Joe said it would look into possible instances of "kickbacks, mismanagement, and subversion" within the agency's ranks.

McCarthy was by no means alone in investigating suspected subversion in the late winter of 1953. The House Un-American Activities Committee sought evidence of Communist leanings among public school teachers in New York City and returned to Hollywood for a renewed investigation of Communist influence in the movie industry. The Senate Internal Security Subcommittee looked into the loyalty of Americans working for the United Nations in New York, then shifted its focus to charges that Communist sympathizers were active in the public schools of Washington and Boston.

A climate of caution and fear affected the entire country, influencing all aspects of the nation's life from labor unions to cultural institutions. People were afraid that someone would accuse them of saying or doing something that seemed unpatriotic, or worse yet, something that made it sound as if they held left-wing views. If that happened, they might well lose their jobs and find themselves blacklisted in their chosen professions.

The quiet urban campus of Western Reserve University in Cleveland, Ohio, was hundreds of miles from the hurly-burly of the Capitol in Washington, but the investigations taking place in the halls of Congress still had a huge impact on the individuals who taught and studied at the university.

One of those affected was a junior who signed up in the spring of 1953 for a survey course on the major world philosophies. The course sounded dull, but the student had heard that the young professor who taught it made the content exciting and meaningful. He had also heard gossip that the professor was only teaching in Cleveland because he'd lost a similar job at one of the major New York City universities. People couldn't help but wonder why, since the man had a reputation for being a brilliant teacher.

And he was, as the student discovered from the day the class first met. The professor, a wiry, energetic man with thinning black hair, led him and his classmates on a brisk, scintillating journey from the ancient Greeks to the Romans to the scholars of the Middle Ages, and on down to modern times. But he came to an abrupt halt in the middle of the nineteenth century.

"At this point, I usually introduce Karl Marx and assign readings from *Das Kapital* and his other works. But this year"—he paused and looked at the floor—"there will be no class discussion of Marx or Marxism or Communism, the ideology that grew out of Marx's ideas."

A student raised her hand to ask a question, but the professor ignored her and continued. "If you're interested in pursuing Marx on your own, I can give you a reading list of significant books by and about him. But, as I said, there won't be any discussion of his philosophy in class, and there won't be any questions about Marxism on the final exam." With that, he picked up a book from the stack on his desk. "Now let's move on to John Dewey and begin thinking about his philosophical ideas."

After class, a number of students talked together as they walked down the hall. One asked why the professor was skipping Marx. Another replied it was probably because he didn't want to get in trouble for teaching a controversial subject. A third said she knew the real reason. The professor had been fired the year before from his job in New York after he was accused of being a Communist and spreading Communist ideas.

That seemed to settle the matter. The students said their goodbyes and went their separate ways. On further reflection, they might have called the professor a coward for taking the easy way out. Or they might have decided he was merely being realistic, given what had happened to him earlier. The mood of the time did not favor those who tried to look at Communism in a calm, thoughtful manner.

At least one student felt shortchanged, then and later. It would have been helpful to have some background knowledge of Marx's basic philosophy as the cold war progressed and Communism remained in the forefront of the news. The student kept the professor's reading list and referred to it from time to time. But lively classroom discussions would probably have made more of an impression, and given the student a stronger intellectual base from which to judge future events. The stifling atmosphere that McCarthy and others generated had put a lid on the free exchange of ideas in the United States.

The effects would have been even more damaging if Joe's investigations of the Voice of America and its parent agency, the International Information Administration (IIA), had gone further than they did. As it was, the probes caused considerable damage.

McCarthy found support for his work in a directive the State Department had issued in February 1953. It banned books and musical compositions by "Communists, fellow travelers, et cetera" from broadcast over the Voice of America, and ordered librarians working in IIA libraries overseas to remove from their shelves all books by "known Communists and other controversial authors."

McCarthy and members of his staff pored over the catalogues of all the libraries maintained by the IIA, and Joe angrily proclaimed that they had found listed "more than 30,000 volumes by 418 Communist writers." Among the well-known names on the list were historian Arthur Schlesinger, Jr., poets W. H. Auden and Steven Vincent Benét, and novelists Howard Fast and Edna Ferber.

Fearing the loss of their jobs, many overseas librarians quickly removed books by these and other "controversial authors," such as mystery writer Dashiell Hammett, playwright Lillian Hellman, poet Langston Hughes, and Walter White, head of the National Association for the Advancement of Colored People (NAACP). White had written a book that explored relations between white and African American troops during World War II. Most of the books in question were simply discarded, but some were pulped or even burned.

McCarthy's aides, Roy Cohn and David Schine, had been heavily involved in the Voice of America and IIA investigations since the beginning. They had

David Schine and Roy Cohn look on as Sen. McCarthy discusses with reporters their ongoing investigation of the Voice of America. *The Library of Congress*

moved into the Schine family's suite at the Waldorf-Astoria Hotel in New York and questioned dozens of Voice of America employees in the living room. No members of Joe's subcommittee sat in on these sessions, but it was understood that Cohn and Schine had McCarthy's full approval.

Karl H. Baarslag, an American Legion official whom they interviewed, had visited a number of IIA libraries abroad. He told Cohn and Schine he had found many Communist and pro-Communist books and other publications on the shelves. "It seemed like a planned conspiracy," Baarslag said. At this point, Cohn and Schine decided to fly to Europe and personally inspect IIA libraries in major cities.

Cohn and Schine landed in Paris, the first stop on their tour, on April 4, 1953. In the next eighteen days, they flew from Paris to Bonn, Berlin, and Munich in West Germany, then on to Vienna, Austria; Belgrade, Yugoslavia; Athens, Greece; and Rome, Italy. From there, it was back to Paris, then on to London, the final stop. Their stays in the various countries were often extremely brief—they spent twenty-four hours in Rome, and only six in London—and it wasn't always clear to observers what they hoped to accomplish.

In Belgrade, they toured the American embassy and interviewed the ambassador and members of his staff. In Munich, they talked with two German ex-Communists and hired one of them as a researcher. Sometimes in the various cities they made quick visits to IIA libraries, where they said they discovered "lots of books and magazines written by Reds."

Everywhere they went, Cohn and Schine were accompanied by hordes of European reporters, who viewed their doings with a mixture of amusement and contempt. A London tabloid called them "scummy snoopers," and another labeled them "Mr. McCarthy's distempered jackals." After attending their press conference in Rome, a foreign correspondent for England's *Manchester Guardian* wrote: "Their limited vocabulary, their self-complacency, and their paucity of ideas, coupled with the immense power they wield, had the effect of drawing sympathy for all ranks of the United States diplomatic service who have to submit to this sort of thing."

Some made jokes at their expense. At the end of the day, State Department employees were said to chant, "See you tomorrow, come Cohn or Schine!" Germans were amused by a report that an angry Schine had been seen chasing Cohn around a Berlin hotel lobby and hitting him on the head with a rolled-up newspaper. In private, some Europeans whispered about the nature of their relationship, and wondered if the two young men were homosexuals. But no hint of that possibility appeared in the press. In the 1950s, homosexuality was a taboo topic, and homosexuals—the word "gay" was not in use as a synonym by the general public then—did everything they could to conceal their identity.

Word of their less-than-favorable reception reached American readers, and some questioned why the taxpayers' money was being spent on such a jaunt. Even Cohn had difficulty justifying the venture. "It turned out to be one of the most publicized trips of the decade," he wrote later. "We soon realized, although neither of us could admit to the distressing fact, that it was a colossal mistake."

Joe forgave them, though. In his eyes, the investigations of the Voice of America and the IIA had brought positive results. In response to the public outcry they had stirred up, the Eisenhower administration fired hundreds of IIA employees in the spring of 1953. The government dropped a number of the Voice of America's broadcasts and closed several of the IIA's overseas libraries. The president also endorsed a plan that removed the VOA and other information units from the State Department and placed them in a new organization, the United States Information Agency, where they could be more easily monitored.

Privately, Eisenhower regretted the removal of controversial books from library shelves and the closing of some overseas libraries. In commencement remarks at Dartmouth College in June, he told an audience of 10,000, "Don't be afraid to go in your library and read every book as long as they do not offend your own ideas of decency. That should be the only censorship."

At the same time, the president took care not to offend the powerful right wing of the Republican Party. In late May, he had signed an executive order concerning employee hiring policies in the executive branch that went far beyond the security procedures followed by the Truman administration. Instead of determining employee eligibility on the basis of loyalty alone, the new directive said employees could be rejected or fired for personal traits such as alcoholism, homosexuality, and other "infamous" (but undefined) conduct. Many interpreted the order as a sign that McCarthy and his fellow right-wingers remained extremely influential in Washington.

Joe was delighted with this new executive order. He told reporters: "I think it is a tremendous improvement over the old method. . . . It shows that the new administration was sincere in its campaign promises to clean house."

19

McCarthy Gets Married

JOE MCCARTHY AND HIS fellow Republicans seemed to be all-powerful in the early summer of 1953. The party controlled the White House and both houses of Congress, and Joe headed a subcommittee that won constant headlines and popular support for its ongoing investigations of Communist subversion in government. Commenting on Joe's position, columnist William S. White wrote, "To come down to simple reckonings of naked power, who in the Senate has more—not in terms of the legislative hierarchy but in the ability to reward and punish? No one."

Many observers wondered what ambitions McCarthy might have beyond the Senate. Publications such as *Newsweek* and the *New York Times Magazine* speculated that he might be planning to make a run for the presidency in 1956.

Joe squelched such rumors. He told reporters he was sure President Eisenhower would be renominated in 1956. "He is more popular than ever with the people . . . and on the whole Eisenhower is doing a good job," Joe said. As for his own ambitions, McCarthy said that what he wanted most was to continue representing Wisconsin in the Senate. "Over the long haul, a senator can sometimes do more than most Presidents. Don't forget that a senator can serve as much as fifty years, but a president no more than eight." Meanwhile, he added, he thought he could best serve his Wisconsin constituents and the American people generally by "kicking the Communists and pro-Communists out of Washington."

A growing number of Democrats and moderate Republicans disagreed with Joe's aims. The officers of Freedom House, a nonpartisan organization founded to honor the late Wendell Willkie, Republican candidate for president in 1940, called McCarthy "a man who is ever ready to stoop to false innuendo and commit as dangerous an assault on Democracy as any perpetrated in the propaganda of the Communists." At a news conference, Eleanor Roosevelt said that the tactics Joe employed in his hearings "look like Mr. Hitler's methods." The respected Methodist bishop G. Bromley Oxnam wrote, "The time to have stopped Hitler was when he went into the Rhineland. There is a time to stop McCarthy." Another clergyman, Dr. A. Powell Davies, minister of All Souls Episcopal Church in Washington, D.C., charged that McCarthy was "to a great extent ruling the United States" and that Secretary of State Dulles "might well be called his administrative assistant."

On July 10, 1953, Joe railroaded through a measure in his subcommittee that gave him sole authority to hire and fire staff. The vote was 4–3, with all the Republican members for the proposal, and all the Democratic members against it. Angered by McCarthy's highhanded attitude, the three Democrats resigned in protest and walked out of the room.

Their departure was big news, and not the kind Joe sought. In interviews with reporters, he tried to minimize the Democrats' action, calling it just another example of "the old Democratic policy of either rule or ruin." To change the subject, he announced that he and his staff had uncovered "tons of" evidence that Soviet agents had infiltrated the ranks of the Central Intelligence Agency (CIA). McCarthy went on to say that he planned to launch a full-scale investigation of the agency. It would begin with testimony from a high CIA official, William P. Bundy. If Bundy refused to appear before the subcommittee, Joe said, he would be subpoenaed.

McCarthy hadn't reckoned with President Eisenhower's response to such an announcement. The last thing the president wanted was to have Joe digging into the CIA files and exposing the agency's innermost secrets. He told Bundy not to submit to any subpoena from McCarthy, and at a hastily arranged meeting, the National Security Council (NSC) endorsed Eisenhower's position. Vice-President Nixon informed Joe of the NSC's action and told him point-blank that the president would not tolerate any investigation of the CIA. Later, at a private lunch with McCarthy and the Republican members of his subcommittee, Nixon spelled out Eisenhower's reasons for putting a stop to the planned inquiry. Chief among them was the president's fear that it might endanger national security.

McCarthy finally accepted Nixon's argument and agreed to issue a joint statement with CIA Director Allen Dulles (brother of Secretary of State John Foster Dulles), saying they both agreed the investigation should be suspended. The media were not fooled, however. Political columnist Joseph Alsop bluntly expressed his interpretation of what had transpired: "Sen. Joseph R. McCarthy has just suffered his first total, unmitigated, unqualified defeat by the White House."

A Visit to the China Shop

In this cartoon by B. Green, President Eisenhower and Allen Dulles, Director of the Central Intelligence Agency, look on nervously as a snorting bull labeled "McCarthy" forces open the door of the Agency, which is pictured as a china shop filled with fragile objects. *The Library of Congress*

Senator Mike Monroney, Democrat of Oklahoma, chose this moment to issue a withering attack in the Senate on Joe's entire anti-Communist campaign. He charged that, unlike the FBI, Joe had wasted the taxpayers' money on one fruitless investigation after another. He mocked Cohn and Schine's European trip, labeling it a "Keystone-Kop chase," and warned of the dangers that could have resulted from Joe's aborted inquiry into the CIA.

Joe, as one might expect, reacted angrily to Monroney's speech. During a television interview, he called the senator's criticism of Cohn and Schine, both of whom were Jewish, "the most flagrant, the most shameful example of anti-Semitism." Later, in a tense Senate discussion with Monroney, Joe asked, "Can the senator give me the name of a single Communist he has exposed during his long period in public life?"

Monroney wasn't ready to give up the fight. Although he knew it wasn't likely to pass, he introduced a resolution in the Senate that would give it the right to cut off a line of investigation by any of its committees. When questioned by reporters, Monroney admitted that the resolution was aimed directly at Joe, and said it was designed to prevent him from becoming a "one-man Senate." He explained what he meant on a television talk show: "[So far] the 83rd Congress has produced a record of molehills of legislation and mountains of McCarthy."

Monroney's resolution, as he had expected, got nowhere in the Senate, but he and his liberal colleagues weren't dejected. He had made the point that there were those in the Senate who strongly opposed McCarthy—and they would not remain silent if the senator from Wisconsin embarked on a course they disapproved of.

Meanwhile, the Eisenhower administration was distressed by the continuing absence of the three Democratic members of Joe's subcommittee. Without them, the subcommittee lost its credibility as a bipartisan body. Eisenhower and his chief advisors also feared that Joe's insistence on investigating Communist subversion in agencies like the Voice of America and the CIA would reflect badly on the Republican appointees who were now running those agencies. Once again, Vice-President Nixon was deputized to meet with McCarthy and urge him to work out some sort of compromise that would bring the Democrats back to his subcommittee. Nixon suggested also that it would be helpful to his fellow Republicans if Joe shifted the focus of his investigations from Communism to charges of corruption in the Truman administration.

Joe seemed to be enthusiastic about this new approach. The Associated Press reported that he assured Nixon he would "try to make the Democrats wince as they prepare for next year's Congressional elections." But Nixon and other leading Republicans soon discovered that it was difficult if not impossible to get McCarthy to toe the party's official line. In a Milwaukee speech in early August, Joe denounced the armistice that had ended the Korean War, saying it failed to fulfill the Republicans' campaign promise to "call to account those responsible for our tremendous defeat in Korea."

Then, in a press conference on August 10, he announced he had evidence that at least one Communist Party member had access to the military secrets of the Atomic Energy Commission. Two days later, an event occurred that stunned the American people and gave fresh impetus to Joe's latest anti-Communist campaigns. On August 12, the media were filled with alarming reports that the Soviet Union had exploded its first hydrogen bomb.

The United States had successfully tested its own hydrogen bomb nine months earlier, on November 1, 1952, but President Truman had ordered a news black-out on the test, fearing it would become an issue in the presidential election that was just a few days away. Reports inevitably leaked, however, about a new bomb that was 450 times more powerful than the atomic bomb, and Truman finally issued an official announcement about the test shortly before he left office in January 1953. The fact that the hydrogen bomb could wreak even greater destruction than the atomic bomb dismayed some Americans. But the majority welcomed the news that the nation had regained the lead in the cold war arms race.

Now, just nine months later, it was disheartening to learn that the Soviet Union had caught up—especially when four years had passed between the first American test of an atomic bomb and the first Soviet explosion of a similar weapon. How had the Russians managed to produce a hydrogen bomb so quickly? Did they have the help of American spies? In June, Julius and Ethel Rosenberg had been executed for supplying the Russians with atomic secrets. Had others aided the Soviets in making the hydrogen bomb?

The fact that such questions were being asked by a large segment of the American public gave Joe the justification he needed to continue pursuing Communist subversives in government. He set aside the search for a Communist in the Atomic Energy Commission—perhaps for lack of evidence—and focused on a hotter tip: that the Army had distributed what McCarthy called "clearcut

Communist propaganda" to thirty-seven of its commands in 1952. He displayed a document titled *Psychological and Cultural Traits of Soviet Siberia* at a press conference and said, "If you read this and believed it, you would move to Siberia."

An Army spokesman responded by saying that anyone who did read the entire document would realize that Joe's description wasn't accurate. Besides, the spokesman said, it wasn't widely distributed; only one hundred copies had been printed. The Army followed up by releasing the final pages of the publication, which clearly showed that the content was pro-American, not pro-Soviet.

The Army's dismissive attitude made Joe angry. He called General Richard C. Partridge, chief of Army Intelligence, to testify about the publication on September 21. Secretary of the Army Robert T. Stevens sat in on the session. McCarthy began by sharply criticizing Gen. Partridge for authorizing publication of the Siberia document, and then for defending it.

> McCARTHY: You come here and say it is a good, honest attempt. I wonder how much you know about the book. Do you know that the book quotes verbatim from Joe Stalin, without attributing it to him, as a stamp of approval of the U.S. Army? Are you aware of that?
>
> GEN. PARTRIDGE: I don't know that it quotes from Joe Stalin.
>
> McCARTHY: Don't you think before you testify you should take time to conduct some research to find out whether it quotes Joe Stalin and other notorious Communists? Don't you think you are incompetent to testify before you know that?
>
> GEN. PARTRIDGE: No, sir.
>
> McCARTHY: I don't want someone here who knows nothing about this document, just giving us conversation.

Joe then called another witness, a civilian consultant to Army Intelligence who had reviewed and approved the Siberian document. After Joe and Roy Cohn subjected the man to the same kind of relentless questioning, Joe dismissed the witness, calling the man "completely and hopelessly incompetent."

Secretary of the Army Stevens attempted to defend Gen. Partridge and the other witness, saying, "I think they have tried to get before you the facts, right or wrong, to the best of their ability." That only led Joe to attack Partridge more fiercely. "We need someone who has some conception of the danger of Communism!" McCarthy shouted. His attacks proved effective. A short time

Jean Kerr and Joe McCarthy on their wedding day, September 29, 1953.
The National Archives

later, Gen. Partridge was replaced as head of Army Intelligence and sent to Europe on a lesser assignment.

In late September, Joe took an unexpected break from the hearings, leaving Roy Cohn in charge. Surprising many Washington insiders, including some of his closest friends, Joe married his longtime assistant, Jean Kerr, on September 29 at St. Matthew's Cathedral in Washington.

Jean had earlier converted from Presbyterianism to Catholicism so that the marriage could go forward. She looked glowing in her long white wedding dress and veil. Joe seemed a bit uncomfortable, though, in the formal outfit Jean had probably persuaded him to wear.

Almost 900 invited guests assembled in the cathedral for the ceremony. Among those present were Vice-President Nixon and his wife, Pat; key Eisenhower aide

Sherman Adams; CIA director Allen Dulles; and many congressmen and senators, including Senator John F. Kennedy. President Eisenhower and his wife did not attend but sent their regrets in a letter of congratulation. Pope Pius XII dispatched a cablegram from the Vatican giving the bride and groom his "apostolic blessing." More than 200 of Joe's Wisconsin relatives and friends traveled to Washington for the event, and McCarthy's brother William served as best man.

Most of the friends rejoiced with the McCarthys, but a few had doubts about the marriage. After all, Joe was almost forty-five and had never seemed like "the marrying kind," as his friend Ray Kiermas said later. Willard Edwards, a reporter from the *Chicago Tribune,* put the matter more bluntly. He told friends and associates he thought McCarthy had gotten married to squelch rumors that he was homosexual. The rumors had spread because of Joe's close association with Roy Cohn, but few in Washington believed them. While it was true that McCarthy appeared to have more lasting relationships with his male buddies than with any of the women he had dated, except for Jean, no evidence had ever surfaced that he engaged in homosexual activity.

At the conclusion of the wedding ceremony, the newlyweds walked slowly up the cathedral's central aisle, both smiling broadly. Joe waved to Nixon as he passed the row in which the Vice-President was sitting. Outside, the McCarthys acknowledged the cheers of a crowd estimated at around 3,500 before they entered a waiting limousine. Later that day they flew to Spanish Cay in the British West Indies, where they planned to honeymoon for ten days.

Their stay on the island was cut short, however, when Joe received an urgent phone call from Roy Cohn. Cohn said that while Joe was away, he had been alerted that Communist subversives had infiltrated the Army Signal Corps Center at Fort Monmouth, New Jersey. The Center housed the Signal Corps' main research, development, and training facility. In one of its laboratories, scientists conducted top-secret radar research.

McCarthy agreed with Cohn that the situation at Fort Monmouth required his immediate attention. He and Jean made arrangements to return at once to Washington. On their arrival, Joe told reporters that his subcommittee had uncovered evidence of "extremely dangerous espionage" at Fort Monmouth that threatened to "envelop the whole Signal Corps." The evidence was recent, he added, and concerned "our entire defense against atomic attack."

20

The Dangerous Dentist

IMMEDIATELY AFTER HIS RETURN to Washington, McCarthy launched closed-door subcommittee hearings into the situation at the Fort Monmouth radar laboratory. The investigation centered on charges that Julius Rosenberg had set up a Communist spy ring there when he worked for the Signal Corps in the 1940s.

After each day's session, Joe invited a group of reporters to his office to give them his version of what had transpired. The hearings were supposed to be confidential, but McCarthy conducted these little press conferences to get maximum coverage of the subcommittee's activities on the front pages of the nation's major newspapers. A headline that appeared in the *New York Times* shows how well he succeeded: "Rosenberg Called Radar Spy Leader: McCarthy Says Ring He Set Up 'May Still Be in Operation at Monmouth Laboratories.'"

When the Army suspended thirty-three civilian employees at Fort Monmouth during the month after the hearings began, Joe's investigation appeared to be getting quick results. The senator had nothing but praise for Secretary of the Army Stevens and Major General Kirke B. Lawton, the commander at Fort Monmouth. Joe called the suspensions "a very important step in making sure that all government employees are the true, loyal, fine type of people that the vast majority of them are."

If Secretary Stevens thought McCarthy's compliments indicated he would ease up on the investigation, he was much mistaken. At the end of October, Roy Cohn and David Schine told reporters that McCarthy had given the subcommittee

McCarthy and Roy Cohn at a subcommittee hearing. *Wisconsin Historical Society*

the go-ahead to call as witnesses members of the Army's top screening board in Washington. Cohn said the subcommittee had learned that the board had been negligent in approving "many civilian employees suspected of Communist activities."

Secretary Stevens knew he had to act before the situation got out of hand. He called a press conference to announce that the Army had conducted its own investigation of security at Fort Monmouth and had found no evidence that any of the thirty-three recently suspended employees were spies. Nor had the Army investigators uncovered any "current cases" of subversion at the fort.

Joe was furious. He instructed Cohn to prepare for immediate public hearings and told reporters he was sure they would be "of great interest to the American people." The subcommittee held ten hearings between November 1953 and the end of the year, and five more in the early months of 1954. Forty witnesses testified during the course of the hearings, thirty-four of whom were suspected by Joe and his staff of being Communists or spies, or both. When Joe or Roy Cohn asked, "Are you now, or have you ever been, a member of the Communist Party?" twenty-five of the thirty-four declined to answer, claiming the protection of the Fifth Amendment.

"Taking the Fifth" was and is perfectly legal, but for Joe and other right-wing Republicans it was the same as an admission of guilt. In fact, McCarthy frequently called witnesses who did so "Fifth Amendment Communists." That was not a description to be dismissed lightly, for it could have serious consequences. Back in the summer of 1953, a good friend of Joe's, Senator Everett Dirksen, had proposed legislation barring government employment to any person who claimed the Fifth Amendment when called to testify by an investigating committee. Even before the legislation came to a vote, the rule was adopted voluntarily by many government agencies. The armed forces followed suit, as did President Eisenhower, who said the rule should be applied to all employees in the White House and other executive branch departments.

Witnesses who claimed the protection of the Fifth Amendment during the Fort Monmouth hearings paid a heavy price. Not only were their reputations ruined, but many were suspended from their jobs without pay pending the outcome of the investigation, or fired outright. The government covered none of their legal expenses. Their lawyers were not given the names or addresses of their accusers, so they could not interview these witnesses while preparing their cases.

As McCarthy had anticipated, the hearings received prominent newspaper, radio, and television coverage over many months. Not all of it was favorable. A newspaper in the Fort Monmouth area, the *Long Branch Daily Record,* criticized Joe for assuming "the roles of prosecutor, judge, and jury," and for treating with "callous disregard . . . American citizens who have never been accused of any crime, much less convicted." Jewish groups and publications were especially upset, because a majority of the witnesses at the public hearings, and almost all the employees suspended by the Army, were Jews.

In the midst of the Fort Monmouth investigation, McCarthy launched another inquiry, this one focused on employees at the General Electric Company plant in Schenectady, New York. Hearings began in November 1953 in Albany, the state capital. A few days later, an FBI undercover agent testified that he had discovered a number of Communist cells operating in the GE plant. Joe responded by demanding that any "Fifth Amendment Communists" working at GE be fired.

In early December, company officials gave in to Joe's demand. They agreed to suspend any employee who invoked the Fifth Amendment and to fire immediately all employees who admitted they were Communists. With these threats hanging over them, several dozen witnesses testified before Joe's subcommittee during the weeks that followed. Among those called were grinders of castings, coil winders, and drill-press operators. One sixty-four-year-old man, who had been employed by GE for thirty-one years, worked exclusively on streetlights. None of them had access to classified information.

Whenever someone took the Fifth, Joe denounced the witness. On one occasion, he bellowed, "I wish there were some way to make these conspirators testify, because the Fifth Amendment was for the purpose of protecting the individual, not for the purpose of protecting a conspiracy against this nation."

Roy Cohn later boasted that thirty-two GE employees were fired, and many others suspended, as a result of the investigation. But not a single act of subversion or espionage had been traced conclusively to any of those called before McCarthy's subcommittee. Still, the wide press coverage given the hearings convinced many Americans that Joe and his staff were exposing one traitor after another.

The public became even more aroused when the White House, in late fall, announced that 1,456 government employees had been fired from their jobs during the first months of the Eisenhower administration. Appearing on the television program *Meet the Press,* Joe claimed that 90 percent of the firings were for "a combination of Communist activities and perversion." But he added a cautionary note: "Believe me when I say 1,400 [firings] is just scratching the surface."

Later, Attorney General Herbert Brownell declared that 2,200 government employees deemed to be "security risks" had been dismissed since President Eisenhower took office. Once again Joe cheered the news, saying it proved that his investigations, along with those pursued by other Congressional committees, were effective. But many commentators believed that the Republicans were merely laying the groundwork for what would be one of their main themes in the 1954 Congressional elections: the continuing threat of Communist subversion. Whatever the explanation for the wave of dismissals, one thing was clear. Many Americans were losing their livelihoods because of unproved charges lodged against them by Joe and other Congressional investigators.

While the inquiries into alleged Communist activities at Fort Monmouth and General Electric continued, Roy Cohn was preoccupied with a personal matter. Although the Korean War had come to an end the previous summer, thousands of American troops remained on guard along the 38th Parallel, and young Americans were still being drafted into the armed forces. Cohn himself was designated 4F (unable to serve for medical reasons) because of an old injury, but his friend David Schine was likely to be called up at any time.

Starting in July 1953, Cohn began trying to get special consideration for Schine. First, he sought a commission (officer's rank) in the Air Force or Navy Reserve for his friend. When that was ruled out because Schine lacked the necessary qualifications, Cohn asked Army Secretary Stevens if Schine could be given an assignment in the New York City area. Stevens rejected the idea, saying he thought Cohn's colleague should be treated like any other Army private.

Schine was drafted on November 3 and told to report to Fort Dix, New Jersey, fifteen days later. Cohn arranged a delay, saying that Schine needed to finish an important job for the subcommittee. Joe backed up Cohn, telling Army Secretary Stevens he, too, would like to have Schine remain in New York. McCarthy suggested that Private Schine be assigned to study textbooks the Army used at West Point to see if pro-Communist ideas were expressed in them. Stevens ignored Joe's suggestion, but he made a concession to placate the senator. The Army secretary said that Schine might be permitted to leave Fort Dix on some evenings and weekends if he was urgently needed for subcommittee work.

McCarthy and Secretary of the Army Robert Stevens share a joke after a tense meeting in early 1954. *The National Archives*

Schine's basic training began on November 23 after five days of indoctrination. Almost immediately, he sought passes to leave the base in the evening and return late at night. He told the officer in charge that Secretary Stevens had personally okayed it. Schine also requested passes to go into New York almost every weekend.

General Cornelius Ryan, commander of Fort Dix, wondered about Schine's special privileges and contacted Secretary Stevens to make sure they had been authorized. Stevens was surprised to learn that Schine left the base almost every evening. The Army secretary ordered Ryan to put a stop to Schine's weekday departures, but to continue to allow his weekend passes.

While Roy Cohn kept on trying to obtain special treatment for his friend, Joe was active on many different fronts. In early January 1954, he reached a compromise with the Democratic members of his subcommittee and they returned to work, more than six months after they had walked out. As part of the compromise, the Democrats won the right to hire their own legal counsel. They chose Robert Kennedy, who had left Joe's employ on friendly terms the year before.

After much back-and-forth, Joe also got the budget he wanted for expanded subcommittee activities. Indirect support for his investigations came from the Gallup poll released in mid-January. It showed that Joe's overall popularity had soared a remarkable 16 percent since August, probably due to the publicity his Fort Monmouth and General Electric investigations had received. A whopping 62 percent of Republicans approved of his performance, 19 percent disapproved, and 19 percent had no opinion. Democrats were almost equally divided—39 percent approved of what Joe was doing, 38 percent disapproved, and 23 percent had no opinion.

Buoyed by the poll's evidence of strong public support, Joe turned his attention back to the Army. In December 1953, he had received a tip that Irving Peress, a thirty-six-year-old Army dentist stationed at Camp Kilmer, New Jersey, had received a promotion from captain to major. The promotion was approved even though shortly after entering the Army the previous January, Peress had refused to answer an Army questionnaire that asked whether he had ever been a member of a subversive organization.

McCarthy summoned Peress to testify at an executive hearing of his subcommittee on January 30, 1954. When he was asked about his membership in organizations the Army deemed subversive, including the Communist Party, Peress repeatedly took the Fifth Amendment. In return, Joe angrily charged that fellow Communists within the Army must have helped Peress get his promotion, and he vowed to hold public hearings on the matter in February.

In a meeting with reporters, McCarthy demanded that the Army court-martial Peress, who, he said, was "a major in the United States Army at this very moment." He also called upon the Army to "severely punish the officers who had failed to expose him or had played a part in his promotion." His voice rose to a shout: "This is the only way to notify every Army officer that twenty years of treason are past and that this really is a new day."

What Joe didn't know was that the Army, in response to the information that Peress had failed to address the question, had ordered in mid-January that the dentist be discharged. The officers involved with the discharge hoped to avoid publicity, so it would be an honorable one. Peress was given ninety days to select the date on which he would leave the Army. At first he planned to depart on March 31, but after testifying before McCarthy's subcommittee, he changed his mind. Fearing further pressure from Joe, the dentist asked for immediate release, and the Army granted his request on February 2.

That same day, Joe followed up on his statement to reporters and sent a letter by messenger to Army Secretary Stevens. He said he would be launching a full inquiry into the Peress case. Once again he urged that the dentist be court-martialed. He was too late; the Army had already announced Peress's honorable discharge.

Joe was outraged when he heard the news. He told Roy Cohn, "When they [the Army] want to move fast, they can shuffle those papers faster than you can see them." Later, at a news conference, he accused the Army of "highly improper conduct," and said it only made him more determined to pursue the case. Army

Dentist Irving Peress works on a patient in his pre-Army days. The original photo was altered, but why, when, and by whom are not known.
The National Archives

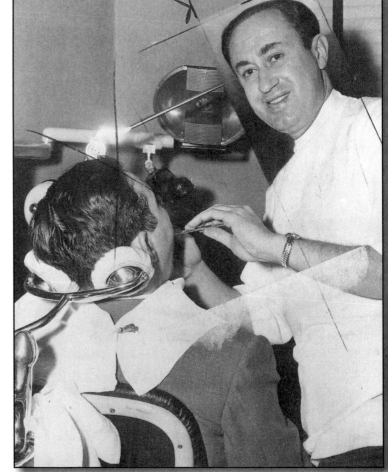

Secretary Stevens, not wanting to be upstaged, promised that he would personally investigate the circumstances surrounding Peress's honorable discharge.

In the meantime, Roy Cohn had continued to badger the Army about David Schine. By then every phone call he made to Army Secretary Stevens or Army counsel John G. Adams was being recorded. Back in January, presidential aide Sherman Adams had been informed of Cohn's relentless pressure on top Army officials. Adams summoned counsel Adams (no relation) to his office and advised him to keep a detailed chronological record of Cohn's calls and other actions on behalf of Schine. The presidential aide said such a record might prove a useful weapon against McCarthy if he persisted in his investigations of the Army and tried to expand them.

President Eisenhower's name didn't enter the conversation, but counsel Adams understood that he must have given his approval to Sherman Adams's initiative. Eisenhower had devoted his life to the Army. He wasn't about to stand by and let Joe McCarthy question the loyalty of its dedicated officers and enlisted men. At the same time, the president was well aware of the senator's favorable poll numbers and his popularity with the Republican base. He might think twice about confronting Joe directly, but he could fight McCarthy in other ways—by keeping a record of Roy Cohn's damaging phone calls, for one.

Joe, meanwhile, was more determined than ever to pursue his investigation of Irving Peress. But before launching its next phase, he and Jean embarked on an eight-day tour of the country, sponsored by the Republican National Committee. During the tour, Joe made a number of Lincoln Day speeches, starting with one in Charleston, West Virginia—the state where, four years earlier, he had given the speech on Communists in government that brought him instant fame.

Joe was greeted by enthusiastic crowds wherever he went, and he responded with fire-breathing rhetoric. "The fact is," he said in one speech, "that those who wear the label 'Democrat' wear it with the stain of historic betrayal; wear it with the corrosion of unprecedented corruption; wear it with the blood of dying men who crawled up the hills of Korea." But more immediate matters were never far from his mind. At a news conference in San Francisco, he said he wouldn't be satisfied until "each and every Army officer" who had been involved in granting an honorable discharge to Irving Peress, "a Fifth Amendment Communist," was court-martialed. After finishing the tour in Dallas, Joe and Jean vacationed briefly in Mexico with Texas oil millionaire Clint Murchison. Then they flew to

New York, where the public hearing on Irving Peress was scheduled to begin on February 18.

At about the same time, Roy Cohn was getting nowhere with his attempts to have the Army assign David Schine to duty in or near New York City after he completed basic training. First Cohn was told no, that Schine would probably be sent from Fort Dix to a school at Camp Gordon, Georgia. There the private would enter an eight-week course of study, at the end of which he would qualify as an assistant criminal investigator. Cohn asked repeatedly if Schine would be assigned to a post in New York after he graduated, but none of the officials he talked to seemed to know. Then word came that the initial information Cohn had been given was incorrect; Schine would need to spend five months in the school at Camp Gordon, not eight weeks. And after the course ended, there was a good chance he would not receive a New York assignment but would be sent abroad for a lengthy tour of duty in Europe.

At that point, Cohn lost all control. He accused the Army of double-crossing him and said he would not stand for it. Then he went further, reminding his listeners of the power he wielded as Joe McCarthy's chief deputy. He could "wreck the Army," he said, and make sure that Robert Stevens was "through as Army Secretary."

This was risky business, since Joe had not expressed any strong feelings about David Schine in his conversations with Stevens and other military personnel. McCarthy had supported Cohn's request that Schine be given an assignment in New York so that he could contribute to the work of the subcommittee, but he had not made it seem like an urgent issue.

Certainly not as urgent as the charges pending against Dr. Irving Peress.

21

Grilling General Zwicker

Joe didn't spend much time questioning Irving Peress. When the dentist's public hearing began in New York's federal court on February 18, Joe turned his fire on the Army for granting Peress an honorable discharge. He summoned the officer who had signed the discharge to appear in court that afternoon and gave the Army twenty-four hours to hand over a list of all military personnel who had played a role in the case. "I think here you have the key to the deliberate Communist infiltration of our armed forces," Joe intoned. "And the men responsible for the honorable discharge of a Communist are just as guilty as the man who belongs to the conspiracy himself."

When John Adams, the Army counsel, interrupted Joe's rambling attack to try to answer a question the senator had raised, McCarthy cut him short. "John, I will not take any double-talk, any evasion on this."

During a recess, Adams released to reporters a letter Army Secretary Stevens had written to Joe on February 16. Stevens had pledged that thereafter no members of the armed forces would receive promotions if they refused to answer questions regarding their loyalty. Nor would they be granted honorable discharges. When asked by the reporters why Peress had been promoted when he was under investigation, Adams acknowledged that he shouldn't have been. But, he added, the Army's inquiry into Peress's past affiliations had failed to uncover the kind of solid evidence that would be needed to justify a court-martial.

Joe flatly rejected the idea that the Army lacked enough evidence to court-martial Peress. "That is a completely incorrect statement," the senator said. He intimated that Secretary Stevens must have been "misinformed," or had

Brigadier General
Ralph W. Zwicker.
The Library of Congress

signed a letter composed by others, "perhaps holdovers from the previous administration."

That afternoon the scheduled witness at a closed hearing was Brigadier General Ralph W. Zwicker, commander of Fort Kilmer, where Irving Peress had been stationed. Zwicker, a graduate of West Point, had served in the infantry during World War II. He had led a special reconnaissance unit during the D-Day landings in France, had commanded an infantry regiment during the deadly Battle of the Bulge in the winter of 1944–45, and had received many military honors for his bravery. After the war, Gen. Eisenhower publicly commended Zwicker, and he rose steadily through the ranks of the Army. He was promoted to brigadier general in March 1953, four months before being assigned to run Camp Kilmer.

Most people saw Ralph Zwicker as a model professional soldier. To McCarthy, however, the general was the man who had first promoted Irving Peress and then given him an honorable discharge. And Joe showed Zwicker no mercy during the hearing.

The general began by trying to explain that he had had nothing to do with the Army's decisions concerning Peress. The dentist's promotion to major resulted from an amendment in the doctors' draft law and applied to more than 7,000 Army doctors and dentists. The order to give the dentist an honorable discharge hadn't been made by Zwicker either. It had originated at First Army Headquarters in New York and had come down to the general to carry out.

Joe would have none of these explanations. "Don't be coy with me, General," he said. "Don't you give me double-talk." McCarthy went on to outline a hypothetical situation that he claimed was identical to the one Zwicker had faced with Major Peress. Would the general have granted an honorable discharge to a soldier if he had learned at the last minute that the man was a thief who had stolen fifty dollars? Would he have given an honorable discharge to a soldier whom he knew to be "a part of the Communist conspiracy," as he had to Major Peress?

Flustered, Zwicker said again that he had "no authority to retain him [Peress] in the service." He added, "I was never officially informed by anyone that he was a part of the Communist conspiracy, Mr. Senator."

Joe ignored this and returned to the hypothetical theft.

MCCARTHY: Would you tell us, General, why fifty dollars is so much more important to you than being part of a conspiracy to destroy a nation which you are sworn to defend?

GEN. ZWICKER: Mr. Chairman, it is not, and you know that as well as I do.

MCCARTHY: Yes, I do know it. That is why I cannot understand you sitting there, General, a general in the Army, and telling me that you could not, would not, hold up his discharge.

Joe kept on grilling Zwicker relentlessly, demanding to know how a hypothetical general—one who had acted the way Zwicker had acted in the Peress case—should be treated. At last Joe reached the ultimate question: "Should he [the general] be removed from the military?"

Zwicker answered without hesitation. "He should by all means be kept if he were acting under competent orders to separate [discharge] that man."

Joe brushed aside the general's answer and persisted in holding him responsible for the decision to discharge Peress. Once again he asked: "Do you think the general who originated the order decreeing the separation—do you think he should be kept in service?"

Zwicker tried to be logical in his reply. First, he said, the question was hypothetical and didn't really apply to the Peress case. And even if it did, it would not be for him to decide. That decision would be up to the Army high command. . . .

McCarthy jumped in before Zwicker had finished, demanding to know the general's personal opinion.

> McCARTHY: You will answer that question, General, unless you take the Fifth Amendment. I do not care how long we stay here, you are going to answer it.
>
> GEN. ZWICKER: Do you mean how I feel about Communists?
>
> McCARTHY: I mean exactly what I asked you, General, nothing else. And anyone with the brains of a five-year-old can understand that question. The reporter [court stenographer] will read it to you as often as you need to hear it so that you can answer it, and then you will answer it.
>
> GEN. ZWICKER: Start it over, please.

The reporter repeated the entire question, ending with: "Do you think he should be removed from the military?"

> GEN. ZWICKER: I do not think he should be removed from the military.
>
> McCARTHY: Then, General, you should be removed from any command. Any man who has been given the honor of being promoted to general and who says, "I will protect another general who protected Communists," is not fit to wear that uniform, General. I think it is a tremendous disgrace to the Army.

Then Joe dismissed Gen. Zwicker, ordering him to reappear the following Tuesday.

The general returned to Camp Kilmer, furious at the way McCarthy had insulted and humiliated him. He wrote out a report on the hearing and sent it to the Pentagon, headquarters of the Department of Defense. General Matthew B. Ridgway, who had returned from Korea and was now chief of staff, read Zwicker's report and was outraged at the way one of his officers had been treated. He brought the report to the immediate attention of Army Secretary Stevens.

Stevens reacted with equal fury to Zwicker's account. He issued an order that no Army officer, including Zwicker, should appear in future before McCarthy's subcommittee. Then he called Joe personally to inform him of the order.

McCarthy did not take Stevens's announcement calmly. According to insiders, the senator started shouting, and the Army secretary responded in kind. At last, Joe asked Stevens if he himself would accept a subpoena to testify. "I'll take the matter under consideration," the Army secretary said, to which Joe replied, "Well, then, consider yourself under subpoena!" And he hung up. That evening, Army officials informed the press that Stevens would appear before Joe's subcommittee the following Tuesday—the day that Zwicker had originally been scheduled to appear.

Stevens was a busy man in the next few days. To win support for his order, he prepared a summary of Zwicker's report and had it distributed to the subcommittee members who had not been present at the hearing. They were stunned by the tone of McCarthy's questioning and promised to do all they could to have a transcript of the hearing released as soon as possible.

Joe was busy, too. During subcommittee hearings in the daytime and speaking engagements at night, he directed a stream of taunts at Secretary Stevens. He referred to him as "a fine, innocent, unknowing secretary of the Army who refuses to clean house." He called Stevens "a good, loyal American who has fallen under the influence of the wrong element," and ended by describing him as "an awful dupe."

The Army secretary took those jibes without answering back. But when McCarthy accused him of being "unfair to loyal officers" by forbidding them to appear before the subcommittee, Stevens had had enough. He issued a statement defending his action: "I cannot permit the loyal officers of our armed services to be subjected to such unwarranted treatment. The prestige and morale of our armed forces are too important to the security of the nation to have them weakened by unfair attacks on our officer corps." Stevens went on to say that he himself would be "glad to appear before the subcommittee" because "since assuming office I have made it clear that I intend to take every necessary action to rid the Army of subversives."

The Army secretary's statement failed to silence McCarthy. Speaking to reporters in Philadelphia, where he had gone to accept a good citizenship award from the Sons of the American Revolution, Joe made his own statement. He charged that the issue Stevens had raised "is whether the Army is supreme over the Congress . . . and can enjoy special dictatorial authority in covering up its own wrongdoings."

On Monday, February 22, the day before Secretary Stevens was set to appear before the subcommittee, Congress responded to demands from both Democrats and Republicans and made public the transcript of Gen. Zwicker's interrogation. The *New York Times* published the entire document, and newspapers across the country reacted with shock and anger. The *Chicago Tribune,* which had always been a strong supporter of McCarthy, recommended in an editorial that the senator should "learn to distinguish the role of investigator from the role of avenging angel." The editorial concluded: "We do not believe Senator McCarthy's behavior toward General Zwicker was justified and we expect it has injured his cause of driving the disloyal from government service."

Reached by reporters at his home, Gen. Zwicker said he agreed "100 percent" with what Joe was trying to do, but not with the way he did it. The general had refused to discuss the Peress case with McCarthy because, he said, "I'm an officer of the Army, and there are certain things I'm not permitted to do. To begin with, I don't know who in the Department of the Army issued the order directing that Peress be given an honorable discharge. I'm not supposed to know."

McCarthy seemed eager to get Secretary Stevens in the witness chair and pressure him to respond to the questions Gen. Zwicker had refused to answer. But the last thing Joe's Republican colleagues wanted was an open confrontation between McCarthy and the Army secretary. Sen. Dirksen requested and was granted a two-day postponement of Stevens's appearance before the subcommittee while he and other Republicans tried to work out some sort of compromise.

Joe went along with the postponement but then changed the subject—as he had often done in the past—in hopes of gaining fresh media attention. He summoned reporters to his office and announced that he had uncovered another "known Communist" who was working for the Army. She was Annie Lee Moss, a civilian employee of the Army Signal Corps. McCarthy said he would hold a public hearing on Mrs. Moss starting the next day, and he invited all the major television networks to cover it. Don Surine, McCarthy's longtime investigator, filled reporters in on additional details. The FBI had alerted Joe to Mrs. Moss's existence, Surine told them, and had helped Joe obtain a photostatic copy of her Communist Party membership card. "It's an open-and-shut damn deal," Surine said.

All the subcommittee members, except for one who was in Europe, attended the first day of hearings on February 23. The witness was Mary Stalcup Markward, who had been an undercover FBI agent from 1943 until 1949. She testified that she knew Mrs. Moss was a Communist from seeing her name on party lists of card-carrying, dues-paying members. However, Mrs. Markward admitted under questioning that she probably could not personally identify Mrs. Moss, since she wasn't sure she had ever met the woman. Mrs. Markward also noted that Mrs. Moss's name had disappeared from Communist Party records sometime in 1945.

Joe assured the members that he, his staff, and the FBI had carefully checked every aspect of the case. Annie Lee Moss, who had been a cafeteria worker at the Pentagon in 1945, was now a clerk in the Army's Signal Corps code room. There she was responsible, Joe said, for "handling the [encoding] and decoding of confidential and top-secret messages." Her name might not appear on the party's recent lists of members, McCarthy acknowledged, but he was confident Mrs. Moss was still a Communist. "There is nothing in the record to show that she ever broke with the Party."

In response, Army Signal Corps officials issued a statement declaring that Mrs. Moss had "no access whatsoever to codes, or to uncoded top-secret, secret, or confidential messages." She was a communications relay machine operator whose only job was to "feed into or receive from automatic machines unintelligible code messages." The officials added that the Army had begun its own investigation into the possibility that Mrs. Moss might be a security risk. They emphasized that their investigation had been well under way "prior to any action by the McCarthy subcommittee."

Reporters got in touch with Mrs. Moss, who was ill at home. She told them "she had no knowledge of Communism whatsoever" and "never was a member of the Communist Party or anything else." She also said she had "never been in a code room in my life."

The next morning, Mrs. Moss answered a summons to appear before the subcommittee even though she was still feeling sick. She entered the hearing room slowly, leaning on the arm of her attorney. When the attorney asked that his client's testimony be postponed until her health improved, Joe was annoyed. In the exchange that followed, McCarthy called Mrs. Moss a Communist several times, and suggested that her attorney was also a Communist.

Annie Lee Moss, with her attorney by her side, is sworn in as a witness before McCarthy's subcommittee. *The National Archives*

Democrat Senator Henry Jackson objected to Joe's labeling the attorney a "Red." Jackson, along with the other Democratic members, had only recently returned to the subcommittee. Joe responded angrily: "If you had been sitting with us over the past months, watching members of the Communist conspiracy violating their oaths as lawyers and misinforming and misadvising clients, then you would not make that objection."

Joe finally acceded to the attorney's request and granted Mrs. Moss a delay. But he couldn't resist adding, "I am not interested in this woman as a person at all." According to McCarthy, the issue concerning Mrs. Moss was the important thing. "Who in the military, knowing that this lady was a Communist, promoted her from a waitress to a code clerk? The information we have is that she has no special ability as a decoding clerk. Yet [we know] she has been handling classified material despite the statement issued by the military."

After Mrs. Moss left the hearing room, two other witnesses appeared that day. The first was supposedly the woman who had recruited Moss into the Communist Party, but she refused to answer any questions, taking the Fifth Amendment over and over. The second witness, Charlotte Oram, also took the Fifth when asked if she had ever been a member of the party. But she did tell the subcommittee she had never heard of Annie Lee Moss until she was summoned the day before. This contradicted the testimony of Mary Markward, who had cited Mrs. Oram as one of those who had had access to the party records in which Moss's name was listed.

The hearing ended early so that Joe and the Republican members of the subcommittee could attend a lunch with Army Secretary Stevens. The gathering had been arranged by Senator Karl Mundt. He and other leading Republicans feared that the party's unity might be shattered if McCarthy and Stevens clashed openly when the Army secretary finally testified before Joe's subcommittee the following day.

Reporters waited outside the room where Joe, Secretary Stevens, and the others were eating fried chicken. Eventually the door opened and Sen. Mundt stepped into the hall to read what he called "a memorandum of understanding" between the Army and the subcommittee. The newsmen caught a glimpse of Secretary Stevens and Joe sitting at opposite ends of a green leather sofa. Stevens's face had a solemn expression, while Joe was smiling broadly.

The reason for McCarthy's smile became clear as Mundt continued reading. The memorandum sounded more and more like a total surrender by Stevens. He agreed to permit Army officers to appear before the subcommittee; to provide the names of all military personnel who had been involved in the promotion and honorable discharge of Irving Peress; and also to make these persons available to the subcommittee if it wanted to question them.

Joe had apparently agreed to only two relatively minor concessions: the temporary postponement of Gen. Zwicker's return appearance before the subcommittee, and the cancellation of Secretary Stevens's appearance scheduled for the following day.

Stevens had come to the luncheon meeting in a hopeful mood. He sincerely believed that he could work out an accommodation with McCarthy that would benefit both the Army and the Republican Party. And in some ways he thought he had. When he returned to his office after the meeting with reporters, he told associates that the senators on the subcommittee had assured him Army officers would be treated with respect when they testified in the future. Only when he studied the final text of the memorandum did he realize that this condition was not spelled out.

Stevens began to wonder if McCarthy had gotten the better of him. Even so, he did not anticipate the harsh press response that greeted him the next day. The *New York Post*'s account of the luncheon began: "Under severe party pressure, the Secretary of the Army surrendered to a senator [Joe] who had humiliated and bullied an Army officer." The *Chicago Sun-Times* was even more scathing: "Secretary Stevens' unconditional surrender to Senator McCarthy is shocking and dismaying."

The most hurtful criticism came from Joe himself. A reporter quoted McCarthy as saying after the luncheon that Stevens "could not have given in more abjectly if he'd gotten down on his knees." Later, Joe denied having made the remark, but by then the harm had been done.

Rumors swirled around Washington that President Eisenhower was about to ask Stevens for his resignation as Army secretary. Nothing could have been further from the truth. Eisenhower's press secretary, Jim Hagerty, wrote in his diary that the president was "very mad and getting fed up—it's his Army and he doesn't like McCarthy's tactics at all." Eisenhower went so far as to inform Hagerty, "My friends tell me it won't be long in this Army stuff before McCarthy starts using my name instead of Stevens's. He's ambitious. He wants to be President. He's the last guy in the world who'll ever get there, if I have anything to say about it."

Eisenhower convened a working group at the White House that included Vice-President Nixon, trusted aide Sherman Adams, and Secretary Stevens. They met in the president's study to draft a statement for Stevens to make in his own defense—a statement designed to counter the impression left by the original memorandum.

The president agreed that Stevens should read the statement from the White House. This would indicate, first to reporters and then to the general public, that the Army secretary had Eisenhower's full support in his confrontation with McCarthy.

22

Exposed on Television

AT SIX-FIFTEEN IN THE EVENING, Press Secretary Hagerty summoned reporters to his White House office and handed out copies of the statement. Then Stevens had a chance to tell the reporters his side of the story.

He began by saying that the memorandum issued after his meeting with McCarthy had been misinterpreted. He stated firmly that, in the meeting, "I never receded . . . from any of the principles upon which I stand." Then he went on to spell out his position in more detail. "I shall never accede to the abuse of Army personnel under any circumstances, including committee hearings. I shall never accede to them being browbeaten or humiliated." Stevens ended on a positive note. "From assurances which I have received from members of the subcommittee, I am confident that they will not permit such conditions to develop in the future."

Before taking questions from reporters, Press Secretary Hagerty made one thing perfectly clear. "On behalf of the president, he has seen the statement. He approves and endorses it one hundred percent."

Even so, the first question concerned Stevens's future. "Will you continue as Army secretary?" a reporter asked.

Caught off-guard, Stevens hesitated before answering, and Hagerty stepped in. "Of course," the press secretary said.

Joe was in his Senate office, surrounded by reporters who had heard that Army Secretary Stevens was about to make a statement and wanted to get the senator's reaction. One of the reporters took down Stevens's words in shorthand over the telephone and read them to McCarthy. This was long before any significant news event was covered instantaneously on twenty-four-hour cable television.

Joe could barely contain his anger. He claimed that Stevens had made "a completely false statement" when he said he had been assured no future Army witnesses would be "browbeaten or humiliated." McCarthy said he had made it clear to Stevens in their meeting that "if witnesses are not frank and truthful—whether military personnel or not—they will be examined vigorously to get the truth about Communist activities." The senator wrapped up his remarks with another swipe at Stevens. "I very carefully explained to the secretary a number of times that he was Secretary of the Army and not running the committee."

After the meeting broke up, McCarthy invited a reporter from *Time* magazine home with him to have a drink and continue the conversation. Joe and Jean had moved into an eight-room house in Washington following their marriage. The house was owned by Jean's mother, Elizabeth Kerr; she rented half of it to the McCarthys and lived in the other half.

Jean was not there when Joe and the *Time* reporter arrived. She had suffered a fractured ankle and was recovering in a hospital. After pouring drinks for his guest and himself, Joe sank wearily into an easy chair and said, "I'm getting old." Later, the reporter wrote, "McCarthy is 44. His digestion is bad, and he has sinus trouble. But he is not slowing down. And he is decidedly not mellowing."

Joe chose to be more agreeable when he went to the Senate the next day. When asked what he thought of the president's backing the Army secretary, Joe smiled and said, "Eisenhower is against browbeating witnesses—I am too." But he added a postscript, saying he would "continue to expose Communists, even if it embarrasses my own party."

Stevens's statement, and Eisenhower's support of it, emboldened some commentators to question McCarthy and his methods more openly. Walter Lippman, one of the nation's most respected political columnists, had criticized Joe before. But he had never gone as far as he did in a column published in late February 1954, calling McCarthy "a candidate for supreme boss—for the dictatorship—of the Republican Party." He went on to spell out the danger he felt McCarthy posed to his party and the entire nation. "This is the totalitarianism of the man: his cold, calculated, sustained and ruthless effort to make himself feared. That is why he has been staging a series of demonstrations, each designed to show that he respects nobody, no office, and no institution in the land, and that everyone

McCarthy brings his wife, Jean, home from the hospital, where she was treated for a fractured ankle. With them is Mrs. McCarthy's mother, Elizabeth Kerr.
The National Archives

at whom he growls will run away." Lippman wrote with such urgency because he believed McCarthy's assault on the Army was part of a determined effort to intimidate President Eisenhower.

The columnist had thousands of readers, ranging from Washington politicians to concerned citizens across the country. Many of them began to look more critically at Sen. McCarthy after Lippman sounded the alarm. Other writers and publications echoed Lippman's charges. *Time* magazine wrote: "No one but the president can get McCarthy out of his dominant position in the headlines—a position from which he gives the false impression of dominating the government."

Insiders in the Republican Party were also troubled by McCarthy's ongoing conflict with the Army. In February, Leonard Hall, chairman of the Republican National Committee (RNC), had called Joe a "great asset" to the party. But on March 2, after a meeting with the president, Hall changed his tune. Referring to the McCarthy-Zwicker exchange, Hall told reporters, "I don't think anyone would say generals in our Army are not fighting Communism." When pressed, Hall said Joe's investigation of Army personnel might hurt Republican chances for victory in the fall midterm elections.

President Eisenhower scheduled a news conference for March 3. A record-breaking 256 reporters attended. Rumors had spread in Washington that the president would openly criticize McCarthy at last, and the reporters wanted to be there to hear him do it, but Eisenhower disappointed them. After an opening statement in which he admitted that the Army had made "serious errors" in its handling of the Peress case, the president went on to say that steps were being taken to make sure such errors did not occur in the future. "I am confident that Secretary Stevens will be successful in this effort," he concluded. And that was it. Eisenhower never mentioned McCarthy's name, and the press conference turned to other issues. Apparently the president was still not ready to confront McCarthy directly.

Joe, too, was caught unawares. He had heard the same rumors as the reporters and had prepared a strong statement in response to Eisenhower's expected attack. After his secretary read her transcription of Eisenhower's actual remarks at the conference, Joe made a few minor changes in his statement. It still seemed over-the-top to the newsmen who had gathered in Joe's office to hear him deliver it.

McCarthy began by asserting yet again that "this silly tempest in a teapot" had only come about because "we [the subcommittee] dared to bring to light the cold, unpleasant facts about a Fifth Amendment Communist officer [Irving Peress] who was promoted, and finally given an honorable discharge with the full knowledge of all concerned that he was a member of the Communist Party." Later, he couldn't resist lobbing another attack at Gen. Zwicker. "If a stupid, arrogant, or witless man in a position of power appears before our committee and is found aiding the Communist Party, he will be exposed. The fact that he might be a general places him in no special class so far as I am concerned."

He concluded by implying that even President Eisenhower was unaware of the seriousness of the problem. "When the shouting and the tumult die, the American public and the president will realize that this unprecedented mudslinging against the committee by extreme left-wing elements of the press and radio was caused because another Fifth Amendment Communist in government was finally dug out of the dark recesses and exposed to public view."

Joe's belligerent remarks may have pleased his ardent supporters, but they did not go over well with moderate Republicans, who thought them extremist.

New York Times columnist James Reston offered his own wry comments on the Eisenhower-McCarthy exchange. "President Eisenhower turned the other cheek today, and Sen. Joseph R. McCarthy, always an obliging fellow, struck him about as hard as the position of the president will allow."

Democrats believed that the president's reluctance to confront McCarthy reflected his determination to avoid doing anything that would hurt Republican candidates in the fall congressional elections. Adlai Stevenson took that tack in a nationally broadcast half-hour speech he gave in Miami on March 6. He claimed that "a group of political plungers has persuaded the president that McCarthyism is the best Republican formula for political success." Stevenson labeled the party "half McCarthy and half Eisenhower" and charged that it had "embarked on a campaign of slander, dissension, and deception in order to win the 1954 elections."

Joe, furious, demanded that the radio networks give him thirty minutes of equal time to reply to Stevenson. When Leonard Hall heard this, he immediately sent telegrams to the networks, asking for equal time in the name of the Republican National Committee instead. Hall made it clear that the RNC would designate its own spokesman. "This is not a matter for personal rebuttal by any individual," he added, in an obvious reference to Joe. Later, a source who asked to remain anonymous leaked the information that President Eisenhower himself had summoned Republican congressional leaders to the Oval Office and told them that McCarthy should no longer be allowed to present himself as a spokesman for the Republican Party.

All the radio networks accepted Leonard Hall's request for equal time, and denied Joe's. If Joe was furious before, he was boiling now. "The networks will grant me time or learn what the law is," he blustered. Meanwhile, Hall announced that Vice-President Nixon had been chosen to reply to Adlai Stevenson. Insider leaks to *Time* revealed that Nixon was the president's personal choice.

It seemed that the tide was finally beginning to turn against McCarthy. On March 9, Ralph Flanders, the seventy-three-year-old Republican senator from Vermont, rose in the Senate to deliver an attack on Joe. Flanders had opposed McCarthy on many earlier occasions, from the argument over sugar rationing in 1947 to the controversy surrounding Senator Millard Tydings's reelection campaign in 1950, but never until now had he denounced the Wisconsin senator in such strong terms.

McCarthy, Flanders charged, was "doing his best to shatter the Republican

Party, by intention or through ignorance." Joe belonged, Flanders said, to "his own one-man party, and its name is 'McCarthyism,' a name which he has proudly accepted."

Surveying the earth's trouble spots, from Eastern Europe to the Far East, Flanders said the world was engaged in a struggle between the forces of freedom and the forces of Communism. And what was Sen. McCarthy doing in this monumental struggle? "He dons his war paint," Flanders said. "He goes into his war dance. He emits his war whoops. He goes forth to battle and proudly returns with the scalp of a pink Army dentist."

McCarthy faced an even greater challenge that evening, when Edward R. Murrow broadcast "A Report on Senator Joseph R. McCarthy" on CBS television. Murrow was one of the most respected figures in radio and television journalism. He had made his reputation with his nightly radio broadcasts from London during the worst of the German bombing raids on the British capital in World War II. By the 1950s, he had become a prominent and popular journalist in the new broadcast medium, television. His weekly television news program, *See It Now,* was watched by millions of Americans.

Edward R. Murrow.
The National Archives

Milo Radulovich.
AP/WIDE WORLD PHOTOS

Murrow had already addressed the harm McCarthy-style investigations could do. Back on October 20, 1953, *See It Now* had covered the case of Lieutenant Milo Radulovich, a young weatherman in the Air Force Reserve who had been discharged abruptly. When Radulovich asked why, he was told it was because his father and his sister were suspected of being Communists or Communist sympathizers. Consequently, he himself was considered a security risk.

Pursuing the matter with the help of a lawyer, Radulovich was granted a hearing by the Air Force, where he learned the reason for the charge against his father. The elder Radulovich, an immigrant from Yugoslavia, kept up with news from his homeland by subscribing to several Serbian-language newspapers. One of the papers was published by an organization that had been labeled Communist by the U.S. government. Suspicion fell on Lt. Radulovich's sister, Margaret, because she had made donations to a number of liberal causes. This was enough to convince the Air Force brass that the lieutenant must have come under the influence of his Communist father and left-wing sister.

At the hearing, a lawyer for the Air Force pulled a sealed manila envelope out of his briefcase and said that it contained the evidence against the Radulovich family. He displayed the envelope to those present but refused to share its contents with Radulovich or his lawyer. The Air Force went ahead with its plan to strip Lt. Radulovich of his commission in the Reserve. But he was told that he might get the commission back if he publicly repudiated his father and sister. Saying "This isn't what Americanism means to me," Radulovich refused, as he put it, "to cut my blood ties."

For some time, Edward R. Murrow and his producer, Fred Friendly, had sought a way to cover the damaging effects of the McCarthy witch-hunts on *See It Now*. However, like many other journalists and politicians, they were hesitant to confront McCarthy's tremendous power. Besides, they had their sponsor, Alcoa (the Aluminum Company of America), to consider. The last thing Alcoa wanted was to alienate a large segment of the program's viewers.

When Murrow and Friendly heard about the Radulovich case, they decided it could provide the perfect focus for the story they wanted to tell. It was a clear-cut example of guilt by association, an unfair tactic that had been employed successfully in so many of Joe McCarthy's anti-Communist investigations. At the same time, McCarthy himself had played no role in the case, so no one could accuse Murrow, Friendly, and their team of attacking McCarthy directly. Even so, as Murrow and the others traveled to Dexter, Michigan, where Radulovich and his family lived, they joked about the likelihood of their being fired.

In Dexter, they filmed emotional and touching interviews with Radulovich and his father, sister, and lawyer. The lawyer, Charles Lockwood, looked straight into the camera and said, "In my thirty-two years of practicing law, I have never witnessed such a farce and travesty upon justice as this thing has developed into."

Viewers across the country were moved by the story of Radulovich and his immigrant father. Many questioned the harsh tactics employed against them by the government and the military, and more than 8,000 sent letters and telegrams to CBS and Alcoa. The messages ran 100 to 1 in support of Radulovich. As a consequence, the Air Force reconsidered its decision and restored the weather forecaster to his former position a month after the broadcast.

McCarthy grasped immediately that the program was an indirect attack on him, and as usual he set out to get revenge. He dispatched his chief investigator, Don Surine, to approach Joseph Wershba, one of Murrow's reporters, and give him a warning to pass along to his boss.

In a memoir, Wershba recounted what happened. Surine came up to him in the Senate and said, "Hey, Joe, what's this Radwich [Radulovich] junk you're putting out?" Wershba tried to escape by saying he had to get to the airport, but Surine cut him short. "What would you say if I told you Murrow was on the Soviet payroll back in 1935?" he asked. "Come on up to the office and I'll show you."

Surine told Wershba to wait outside McCarthy's staff office while he got the evidence. He returned shortly with a photocopy of an article from a 1935 issue of the *Pittsburgh Sun-Telegraph,* a right-wing daily newspaper. The article was an attack on a respected American organization, the Institute of International Education (IIE), for sponsoring a summer seminar at Moscow University for American professors and their Soviet counterparts. Murrow, who worked for the Institute at the time, was listed as a member of the advisory committee that had helped to organize the seminar—a meeting the article claimed was designed to promote the Communist cause.

Wershba understood at once why Surine was showing him the article. McCarthy had dug up "files" on everyone he considered a subversive, and now Murrow, for daring to air the Radulovich story, had been added to Joe's list of targets. But where did Surine's charge that Murrow had been on the Soviet payroll come from?

Surine had a ready explanation. In organizing the seminar, the IIE had to work with VOKS, the Soviet student exchange organization, and VOKS picked up some of the expenses. Hence, the IIE, and Murrow, were for a time on the payroll of a Soviet organization.

Wershba asked if he could show the photocopy of the article to Murrow, and Surine said yes. "Mind you, Joe," McCarthy's investigator felt compelled to add, "I'm not saying Murrow's a Commie himself. But if it looks like a duck, walks like a duck, and quacks like a duck—it's a duck."

As Wershba started to walk away, Surine made what seemed like an offhand remark. "It's a shame," Surine said, "Murrow's brother being a general in the Air Force." Wershba understood the comment for what it really was—a threat that McCarthy could do harm to a member of Murrow's family if the TV host persisted in challenging him.

When Wershba told his boss about the exchange with Surine and showed him the article McCarthy's investigator had given him, Murrow said, "So *that's* what they've got." Obviously, he had been expecting trouble. However, the prospect didn't seem to faze him. The next day, he said to Wershba, "The question now is, when do I go against these guys?" The answer was: as soon as he and his team could put together a convincing case against McCarthy.

Over the next four months, Murrow, Fred Friendly, and Joe Wershba assembled the material that would be included in the broadcast. It consisted mainly of film clips of McCarthy himself, from his conflict with Eisenhower during the election campaign of 1952 through his questioning of Gen. Zwicker in 1954. It was apparent to anyone watching that McCarthy consistently harassed the witnesses who came before his subcommittee. Over and over, he interrupted them when they tried to answer his questions and employed innuendo and half-truths to convince those present—and the often-gullible media—that the witnesses were guilty as charged.

When Murrow and the others watched a near-final cut of the broadcast, some members of the staff revealed their fear of putting it on the air. Murrow looked around and said, "The terror [of how McCarthy would react and what he might do] is right here in this room." Later, after they had talked about the reasons for their fear, Murrow tried to reassure them. "No one man," he said, "can terrorize a whole nation unless we are all his accomplices."

On March 9, 1954, Edward R. Murrow opened the broadcast by saying, "Tonight *See It Now* devotes its entire half hour to a report on Senator Joseph R. McCarthy, told mainly in his own words and pictures. . . . [If] the senator believes we have done violence to his words or pictures and desires to speak, to answer himself, an opportunity will be afforded him on this program."

Twenty-seven minutes later, Murrow concluded the broadcast by summing up its meaning. "No one familiar with the history of this country can deny that congressional committees are useful. It is necessary to investigate before legislating, but the line between investigating and persecuting is a very fine one and the junior senator from Wisconsin has overstepped it repeatedly. . . . We must not confuse dissent with disloyalty," Murrow continued. "We must remember always that accusation is not proof and that conviction depends upon evidence and due process of law."

As soon as the broadcast ended, the New York headquarters of CBS television began to be flooded with phone calls. Forty-eight hours later, weary responders added them up and found that the network had received almost 14,300 calls. The vast majority of callers, 12,294, had praise for the program. Only 1,367 opposed it, and some 600 were a mixture of favorable and unfavorable. A similar proportion of yeas and nays was reflected in the telegrams CBS received: 3,267 senders reacted favorably to the program while only 203 responded negatively.

This positive response from the television audience was not surprising. Sharply critical newspaper columnists like Walter Lippman and senators like Ralph Flanders had helped pave the way for Murrow's scathing report on McCarthy. But the mere fact that the exposé went out to the nation on television automatically ensured that it would reach a far larger audience and have a much greater impact.

That impact was reflected in the comments of TV critics for many of the country's major newspapers. The *New York Times* called the broadcast "crusading journalism of high responsibility and genuine courage." The *New York Herald-Tribune* hailed it as the moment when "television came of age."

McCarthy's right-wing supporters, while outnumbered this time around, were equally fervent in their opposition to the program. Murrow received numerous pieces of hate mail. Some of it was addressed to "Red" Murrow. One correspondent rewrote the poem that is inscribed on the Statue of Liberty to show what he felt about the broadcast: "Send me your Commies, pinkos, and crackpots and I will put them on television."

Joe remained remarkably silent. But he accepted Murrow's invitation to present his side of the story, and his appearance on *See It Now* was set for April 6. At the same time, he sent a telegram to the Aluminum Company of America, the program's sponsor, denouncing its support of Murrow and vaguely threatening to launch an investigation into the firm's activities.

On March 10, the day after the broadcast, Joe went about his business as usual. He was in the middle of another hearing on the situation at Fort Monmouth when an invitation came from Defense Secretary Charles E. Wilson to join him at the Pentagon for lunch. Wilson—along with many other prominent Republicans, including the president—had decided Joe's investigations of the Army had gone far enough.

A Devastating Report

AT THE LUNCH, Defense Secretary Wilson confronted McCarthy with a thirty-four-page report the Army had compiled. It was a carefully documented account of all the attempts—many of them outrageous—that Roy Cohn had made over the previous seven months to win special favors for Private David Schine.

McCarthy was caught completely off-guard. He had no idea the Army had assembled this kind of file on Cohn and Schine, and a quick glance through it showed him how dangerous the report could be if it was released. Joe was weighing how to respond when Wilson dropped another bombshell.

Roy Cohn's threat to "get" Army Secretary Stevens, a key point in the report, had convinced the Defense Secretary that Cohn was behind McCarthy's continuing probes of the Army. If the young investigator was out of the way, Wilson and others close to the president believed, McCarthy's focus would shift elsewhere, sparing both the Army and the Eisenhower administration further embarrassment. And so, before the luncheon came to an end, Secretary Wilson named his price for keeping the report under wraps: Joe must fire Roy Cohn. McCarthy refused even to consider Wilson's demand, strode out of the Pentagon, and returned to his Senate office.

Late that afternoon, Joe had a visit from an old friend, Senator Charles Potter of Michigan, a member of his subcommittee. Secretary Wilson had contacted Potter earlier, explained the situation to him, and sent him a copy of the Army report by messenger. Potter was shocked by what he read, and when Secretary

Wilson asked him to try to persuade McCarthy to change his mind about firing Cohn, Potter agreed to see Joe at once.

McCarthy blew up when Potter repeated Secretary Wilson's demand that he let Cohn go. Although he still hadn't read the entire report, Joe defended Cohn and charged that the Army was trying to blackmail him. He also threatened to tell his right-wing columnist friends what was going on and give them Wilson's and Potter's names.

After his temper cooled, Joe admitted to Potter that he wasn't that concerned about Schine's fate. "Hell, Charlie," he said, "I don't care if they ship him to Siberia. But Roy worries about him." He remained totally loyal to Cohn, his invaluable comrade in the fight against Communism. "If I got rid of Roy," he told Potter, "it would be the greatest victory the Communists have scored up to now."

That evening Potter phoned Secretary Wilson. When he informed him that McCarthy was determined to retain Cohn on his staff, Wilson cut him short. "The man has gone too far," he said. The next day, March 11, Wilson sent copies of the Army report to each member of Joe's subcommittee and several members of the Armed Services Committee. If McCarthy knew of Wilson's action, he didn't let on.

That morning, Annie Lee Moss, recovered from her illness, was scheduled to complete her testimony before the subcommittee. Reporters flocked into the courtroom, and interested spectators filled the remaining seats. After all the subcommittee members except Charles Potter had taken their places, Joe opened the hearing in his usual confident manner.

It was not a good time for Mrs. Moss. Besides her lingering illness, she had learned two weeks earlier that she had been suspended from her $3,300-a-year job as a clerk-typist (a low salary even for 1954). On the day of the hearing, she was unemployed and had no idea where her next paycheck would come from. In a soft voice, she denied any connection with Communists and said again that she had never been a member of the Communist Party.

As the questioning by Joe and Roy Cohn continued, the members of the subcommittee, both Democrats and Republicans, responded more and more sympathetically to Mrs. Moss. She had been born in South Carolina, she said, and had not finished high school. When asked if she had ever heard of Karl Marx, she answered, "Who's that?" She also testified that she had never heard of Mary Markward, the undercover FBI agent who had identified her.

Senator Stuart W. Symington.
The Library of Congress

Mrs. Moss's next words caught the attention of everyone in the hearing room. She remarked that there were three other Annie Lee Mosses living in Washington. At that, the members of the subcommittee exchanged glances. Could McCarthy and Cohn have summoned the wrong Mrs. Moss to testify?

Roy Cohn stepped in at this point to say secret evidence existed that proved the witness was Annie Lee Moss, the former Communist. Unfortunately, he could not show the proof to the subcommittee because it was classified.

Two Democratic members of the subcommittee, Senator John L. McClellan and Senator Stuart W. Symington, did not accept Cohn's explanation. Sen. McClellan denounced what he called Cohn's "usual practice of convicting people by rumor and hearsay and innuendo." The audience applauded McClellan, a rare happening in a Senate hearing. Later, they cheered again when Sen. Symington looked at Mrs. Moss and said, "I may be sticking my neck out, but I believe you're telling the truth."

Joe McCarthy had left the hearing by then to tend to other business. Senator Karl Mundt, who was filling in for him, did nothing to stop the crowd's unusual response or interrupt the criticisms of Cohn. Mundt was one of those who had received a copy of the Army report on Cohn and Schine. Perhaps its content made him hesitate to stand up for Cohn.

Sen. Symington had the last word at the hearing. He assured Mrs. Moss that if the Army did not rehire her, he would personally see to it that she got a job somewhere else. As the subcommittee members, reporters, and spectators filed out of the hearing room, it was clear to everyone that Joe's case against Annie Lee Moss—the case that Don Surine had called "an open-and-shut damn deal"—had collapsed completely.

Many newsmen and political commentators echoed that opinion in the days that followed. Walter Lippman thought the utter failure of the Moss hearing played a major role in "the breaking of a spell" that Joe had cast over public opinion. Edward R. Murrow played excerpts from the hearing on *See It Now,* and audience response ran nine to one against McCarthy and Roy Cohn. One letter writer wrote that she was "sickened" by the way Mrs. Moss had been treated.

If the media response to the Annie Lee Moss hearing seemed unusually harsh, it was nothing compared to the outcry that greeted the leaking to the press of the Army report on Cohn and Schine. The United Press news agency called the report "a dynamite-laden document . . . landing like a bombshell." The *New York Times* ran a banner front-page headline in bold type: "Army Charges McCarthy and Cohn Threatened It in Trying to Obtain Preferred Treatment for Schine." Inside, the paper printed the entire text of the document.

The publication of the report threatened to have a more devastating effect on McCarthy's reputation and popularity than any previous attack had had. Not even the Murrow TV exposé could match its impact. The American public held the Army in the highest esteem. It had achieved tremendous victories in World War II and now served as the nation's front line of defense in the cold war. After reading the report, average Americans found themselves asking how Senator McCarthy—whom most of them still admired as an anti-Communist fighter—could have tolerated Roy Cohn's bullying of top Army officials and his brazen attempt to blackmail them.

Beyond that, many wondered in private what was behind Cohn's obvious obsession with David Schine. Why was he so determined to have Schine with him in New York every evening and weekend? What sort of relationship did they have, exactly? However, no journalist or politician raised these questions in public. In the 1950s, certain subjects, including homosexuality, were simply not discussed openly.

Joe appeared to be blind to the implications of Cohn's obsession. But he was acutely aware of the dangers the Army report posed to him personally. And from the moment he rejected Defense Secretary Wilson's demand that he fire Roy Cohn, he knew the report would inevitably be leaked to the press. The question then became: How could he defend himself and protect Cohn?

That evening, Joe held a hastily arranged meeting with Cohn and other aides to hammer out a response. The plan they came up with was as daring—and risky—as the way Joe kept changing the number of Communists he claimed were at work in the State Department back in 1950. Under Joe's direction, the team would draft eleven interoffice memos, back-dated to the previous fall and winter, that had supposedly been exchanged among McCarthy, Cohn, and Francis Carr, an ex-FBI man who served as executive director of the subcommittee.

The memos would be designed to answer and disprove each of the key charges against Cohn contained in the Army report. For example, the Army document related that, in December 1953, Roy Cohn increased the pressure on Secretary Stevens and Army counsel John Adams to get special favors for Private David Schine. However, one of the back-dated memos would show that it was John Adams, not Cohn, who was putting on the pressure.

In this hastily contrived memo to Joe, Francis Carr purportedly wrote, "I couldn't get you on the telephone. What I want to tell you is that I am getting fed up with the way the Army is trying to use Schine as a hostage to pressure us to stop our hearings on the Army. John Adams constantly refers to Schine as 'our hostage' whenever his name comes up."

The memos went so far as to suggest that Adams was trying to blackmail Roy Cohn for his own ends. January 14, 1954, was the day, according to the Army report, when Cohn threatened to "wreck the Army" if they didn't give him what he wanted with regard to Schine. But another memo from Carr to Joe conveyed a very different account of that day's events. Carr supposedly told Joe that John Adams had phoned Cohn on that date to say "this was the last chance" for Cohn to arrange for Adams to be offered a partnership in a New York law firm at a salary of $25,000 a year (a very large amount in 1954).

McCarthy, Cohn, and Carr finished writing the memos at a late hour, and Joe arranged for them to be typed and copied overnight. The next morning, March

12, when the Army report dominated the front pages of all the nation's newspapers, Joe called a press conference at noon to tell his side of the story. With Roy Cohn sitting beside him, McCarthy praised his chief assistant and said he would do everything he could to make sure Cohn remained in his job.

As Joe did when cornered, he responded to the attack with a bold counter-attack. After denying to the press that he or anyone on his staff had sought special favors for David Schine, he claimed the Army had mounted a campaign against him and Cohn to get them to call off their investigations. Then he handed out copies of the eleven back-dated memos.

While most reporters from right-wing publications accepted at face value the memos and McCarthy's denials that anyone from the subcommittee had pressured the Army, many other journalists reserved judgment. The memos seemed almost too neat in the way they addressed the content of the Army report, and many were awkwardly written. The Army's strong response later that day cast further doubt. Army counselor John Adams stated forcefully that the memos' "blackmail charge was fantastic and false." Army Secretary Stevens asserted that everything in the memos was "utterly untrue."

Among those most upset by McCarthy's press conference were the Republican members of the subcommittee. Joe had told them nothing in advance about the conference, nor had he given them copies of the eleven memos he planned to hand out. Earlier, Senator Karl Mundt had been stunned by the Army report's account of Roy Cohn's extreme behavior. Now the senator was even more concerned about Joe's eleven memos, with their countercharges against the Army.

Mundt announced that he would make a motion to form an impartial Senate committee to investigate both the Army report and the McCarthy memos. He told reporters he thought it would be a bad idea for the subcommittee to initiate the inquiry. "I don't want to have it conducted by a committee on which the staff is involved and the chairman [McCarthy] is involved."

While the media were still hashing over the Army-McCarthy conflict, Vice-President Nixon went on network television and radio to present the Eisenhower administration's belated response to Edward R. Murrow's TV report on Joe. Nixon made the point that the "responsible leadership" of the Republican Party believed firmly that procedures for dealing with Communism "must be fair and they must be proper."

Then, in a clear reference to McCarthy (whom he didn't mention by name),

Nixon said that some anti-Communist fighters believed that "Reds should be shot like rats." He agreed, he said, that "they're a bunch of rats. But just remember this: When you go out to shoot rats, you have to shoot straight, because when you shoot wildly it not only means that the rats may get away more easily, but you might hit someone else who's trying to shoot rats, too." He went on to make the point even more explicitly: "Men who have in the past done effective work exposing Communists in this country have, by reckless talk and questionable methods, made themselves the issue, rather than the cause they believe in so deeply."

After the Nixon speech, there could be no doubt in anyone's mind that the Eisenhower administration sided with the Army in its standoff with Joe. The meaning of the vice-president's remarks was certainly not lost on McCarthy. When he was asked to comment on Nixon's talk, Joe confined himself to saying

Vice-President Richard M. Nixon discusses the McCarthy situation with President Eisenhower. *The National Archives*

he thought "the American people were sick and tired of the constant yack-yack-ing" about his being too harsh in his investigations. His anger emerged in private, though, when, according to his friend Urban Van Susteren, he called the vice-president "that prick Nixon."

Joe's subcommittee held a closed executive session on March 16 to decide what steps to take next. The meeting lasted more than two hours, and when Joe emerged, he was smiling broadly. Other participants said the discussion had been heated. Karl Mundt had tried to convince his colleagues to join him in proposing that a separate committee be set up to handle the investigation of McCarthy's clash with the Army. The other members felt it should be done by the subcommittee itself.

Since McCarthy obviously could not chair a probe that involved his own activities, Mundt was persuaded to accept the post of temporary chairman. The hearings would be public (a suggestion of Joe's), and the subcommittee would not undertake any other investigations until they were completed. A new counsel would replace Francis Carr, who was credited with writing many of the eleven controversial memos, and new staff members would be appointed also.

Joe joked with reporters as he discussed the plans for the hearings. He made a point of saying he was pleased by the appointment of Sen. Mundt as temporary chairman. When asked about his own role, McCarthy said he expected to testify under oath and participate in the hearings as a member of the subcommittee. But he wasn't sure he would vote on the subcommittee's final determinations.

If Joe was angry that hearings were being held at all, he didn't show it. He was a skilled-enough politician to realize that, given the heated feelings on both sides, hearings of one sort or another were probably inevitable. Perhaps he was confident that, once they began, he would be able to dominate the proceedings as he had done so often since he had become a power in the Senate.

As if to show how confident he was, Joe flew with Don Surine to Chicago on March 17 for the first of four speaking engagements. That evening he addressed a crowd of more than 1,200 that had gathered in the grand ballroom of the Palmer House Hotel for a St. Patrick's Day dinner. Before he even began to speak, shouts of support erupted from the audience: "Give 'em hell, Joe!" and "Pour it on—you're in your own ball park tonight!"

In return, he gladly gave the crowd what it wanted to hear. His confrontation with the Army, he said, had been stirred up by "Pentagon politicians appointed by the Truman-Acheson regime" who wanted to derail his search for Communists in government. He also charged that the subcommittee's vote to halt all other inquiries during the Army-McCarthy hearings was "a rather major, if temporary, victory for those who fear exposure of Communists."

Joe went on to affirm his determination to continue the struggle against subversion at whatever cost. He "did not give a tinker's damn," he said, about attacks on his anti-Communist methods, "no matter how high or how low my critics are, or from which political party they come." To emphasize the point, he repeated the phrase "no matter how high or how low," making it clear to his listeners that he defied everyone up to and including the president. He concluded the speech by stating that he had not initiated this clash with the administration, "but I might have to finish it." As he turned to step down from the podium, the ballroom resounded with applause.

In the days that followed, Joe repeated his performance at a gathering of 450 Chicago automobile dealers, and before large crowds in Milwaukee and Oklahoma City. Despite fatigue, an attack of laryngitis, and a nagging fever, he rose to each occasion and belted out his familiar themes. Portraying himself as a lone fighter against subversion, he implied that anyone who opposed him was either a Communist, a pro-Communist, or a Communist dupe—some naive individual who served the purposes of the Communists without knowing it.

Many Americans still bought McCarthy's arguments, but a growing number did not. While Joe was basking in the admiration of his Midwestern supporters, a chorus of voices spoke out against him. Among them was a respected and influential Episcopal bishop, the Very Rev. Francis B. Sayre, Jr., who delivered a highly critical sermon from the pulpit of the National Cathedral in Washington. "For the sake of ten guilty ones he [McCarthy] will damn an army. For the sake of twenty, he is willing to wreck a whole administration. For the sake of thirty or forty or fifty, he will divide a nation right down to its democratic roots."

Even more telling was the sudden drop in Joe's approval ratings in both local and national polls. The *San Francisco News* asked its readers in early March if they admired McCarthy. Influenced perhaps by the Murrow television exposé and the broad coverage the media were giving his conflict with the Army, 641 of the respondents said "No," they did not, and only 161 replied "Yes."

On the national level, a Gallup poll published on March 2 showed that Joe's approval rating had fallen four points since January. Three weeks later, on March 23, a new Gallup poll revealed that McCarthy's rating had fallen another eight points. Now only 38 percent of those surveyed gave him a favorable rating, while 46 percent, according to Gallup, had an unfavorable impression.

Back in Washington, Joe called a meeting of the subcommittee for March 24. He said the members would discuss new plans to investigate Communist infiltration of defense plants. Sen. Symington and the other members objected, reminding Joe of the agreement they'd reached not to launch any new investigations while the Army-McCarthy hearings were under way. Joe persisted, claiming he could work on other projects because the hearings weren't really about him. "This isn't my case," he argued. "This is a case involving my chief counsel and the Army legal counsel."

Sen. McClellan, a Democratic subcommittee member, refused to accept that reasoning. He emphasized to reporters that "McCarthy is indeed a party to the quarrel being investigated."

Now the focus shifted to another unresolved question: whether Joe would be allowed to participate as a member of the subcommittee during the hearings. In a meeting with the press, he said he had "given no thought whatsoever" to leaving the subcommittee for the duration. He went on to insist that he expected, as a member, to have the right to cross-examine any witness who testified against him.

President Eisenhower had other ideas. When asked at his weekly press conference if he thought McCarthy should take part in the hearings, the president adopted an objective tone, but his meaning was unmistakable. "I am perfectly ready to put myself on record flatly, as I have before, that in America if a man is a party to a dispute, directly or indirectly, he does not sit in judgment on his own case."

At that point, Sen. Mundt stepped in and suggested that Joe temporarily give up his membership. If he refused, Mundt said, the issue would have to be brought before the full Senate for a final decision. A three-hour, closed-door session of the subcommittee followed, at the end of which Joe agreed to step down. McCarthy won a major concession, though. He, Roy Cohn, and their new counsel, as well as Army Secretary Stevens, his associates, and their counsel, would have the same right to cross-examine witnesses that the members of the subcommittee had.

McCarthy in a clip from the film he prepared to be shown on Edward R. Murrow's TV program *See It Now* on April 6, 1954. The film was a reply to Murrow's criticism of the senator in an earlier broadcast.
AP/WIDE WORLD PHOTOS

On April 6, Joe finally replied on *See It Now* to the charges Edward R. Murrow had directed toward him during the earlier broadcast. Joe did not appear in person. Instead, he was filmed seated at a desk, staring into the camera, as he repeated Don Surine's claims that Murrow had played a suspicious role in arranging an exchange of Russian and American professors back in the 1930s. Speaking of Murrow in the present, Joe called his TV host "the cleverest of the jackal pack which is always found at the throat of anyone who dares to expose Communists and traitors."

If Joe thought his appearance on the show would swing public opinion in his favor, he was mistaken. The next day, CBS officials reported that the initial response of viewers ran overwhelmingly in favor of Murrow and against McCarthy. Meanwhile, both the subcommittee and the Army were hard at work searching for new counsels. They didn't have much time; the hearings were scheduled to start on April 22.

After rejecting several candidates because they were either too pro- or too anti-McCarthy, the subcommittee announced that Ray H. Jenkins, a wealthy criminal lawyer from Knoxville, Tennessee, would be their special counsel. At a press conference, Jenkins said, "I have no record, publicly or otherwise, with regard to Senator McCarthy or what has come to be called McCarthyism. I have no prejudice, and no bias."

Earlier, the Army had named Joseph N. Welch, a native of Iowa who was now a lawyer with a prominent Boston law firm, to be its counsel. When asked his position regarding McCarthy, Welch refrained from naming the senator in his response. "I am a registered Republican and a trial lawyer," he said. "I'm just for facts." Welch said he would be aided at the hearings by two junior law associates from his firm, James D. St. Clair and Frederick G. Fisher, Jr. He added that all three of them would serve without pay.

Shortly before the hearings began, Welch disclosed that Frederick Fisher would not be taking part in them after all. The young lawyer had once been a member of the National Lawyers Guild, an organization that the House Un-American Activities Committee had labeled subversive. Joseph Welch knew what McCarthy might try to make of that association, so he had asked Fisher to withdraw from the case. In explaining Fisher's sudden departure, Welch told reporters, "I didn't want a diversionary affair."

24

McCarthy on the Receiving End

HUNDREDS OF MEMBERS of the public lined up in the corridor outside the Senate caucus meeting room on the morning of April 22, 1954. Each hoped to get one of the 400 seats allotted to spectators on the opening day of the Army-McCarthy hearings. Inside the room, more than a hundred reporters from all over America milled about while television technicians from the three major networks set up the cameras that would cover the hearings from start to finish. Preliminary estimates suggested that as many as 20 million people might watch the telecasts.

Joseph Welch, the recently appointed counsel for the Army, recorded his initial impressions of the hearing room: "It was utter confusion. Photographers leaped up and down to get pictures. Messengers crawled beneath chairs. The cameras turned to follow the action. People sat, stood, and moved in every inch of space, and the whole crowded room was bathed in the bright lights of television." Places had been set aside at one end of a long wooden conference table for the members of the subcommittee, three representatives of the Army, and McCarthy, Cohn, and Francis Carr.

Joe did not look happy when he entered the caucus room and took his seat at the table. In the weeks before the start of the hearings, he had been drinking heavily, and he wore a gloomy, unsmiling expression. Perhaps his dark mood was due to a realization that he faced an uphill battle. The most recent Gallup poll showed that eight out of ten of those questioned had read or heard of the Army-McCarthy conflict, and 46 percent of them sided with Army Secretary

Joseph N. Welch, chief lawyer for the Army in the Army-McCarthy hearings.
The Library of Congress

Stevens, while only 23 percent backed McCarthy. The rest said they weren't sure whom to believe.

Before the hearings began, each side in the dispute had agreed to make available to the other, and to the media, the charges they intended to pursue and the evidence they'd gathered to support them. The Army's charges were an expanded version of its earlier report on all the various ways that Roy Cohn, with McCarthy's backing, had tried to win special favors for David Schine.

Joe's charges drew heavily on the eleven interoffice memos supposedly written by Francis Carr and others—memos implying that on the contrary, it was the Army that had been harassing Joe and Cohn. In addition, the subcommittee's document claimed that Cohn and Army counsel John Adams had once been "close personal and social friends," and that their friendship had continued even after Cohn was said to have made "serious threats against the Army."

Chairman Mundt opened the day's proceedings with a brief statement. It emphasized the subcommittee's commitment to "a maximum degree of dignity, fairness, and thoroughness" as the hearings progressed. Sen. McClellan, the senior Democrat on the subcommittee, was less optimistic. He stated candidly that the charges in the case were "so diametrically in conflict" that he saw no way in which they could be reconciled. The best the subcommittee could do, he said, was to uncover the facts, weigh the accusations made by both sides, and issue some sort of final report. "It will be an arduous and a difficult task," he concluded, "but it is one that must be done."

From the outset, Joe seemed determined to make the subcommittee's task as difficult as possible. The Army was slated to present its case first, and the subcommittee would follow. The hearing had been under way for less than seventeen minutes when Joe interrupted it to raise a point of order—a question as to whether the rules for such hearings were being properly followed. McCarthy was objecting to Counsel Adams and Secretary Stevens saying their charges had been "filed by the Department of the Army." The senator's face flushed a deep red as he declaimed, "I maintain it is a disgrace and reflection upon every one of the million outstanding men in the Army to let a few civilians, who are trying to hold up an investigation of Communists, label themselves as the Department of the Army."

This was the first of hundreds of points of order McCarthy would introduce during the course of the hearings. He may have thought this was an effective way to interrupt the proceedings and inject his thoughts and opinions. The members of the subcommittee soon came to resent the interruptions. As for the television viewers at home, most were shocked at first, and then annoyed, by Joe's rude behavior. It wasn't long before radio and TV comedians began to imitate the senator's flat, droning voice saying "point of order" over and over. If Joe was aware that he was being laughed at, he didn't let on.

Secretary Stevens took the stand on April 24 for the first of what would be thirteen days of testimony. Under subcommittee counselor Ray Jenkins's relentless cross-examination, Stevens came across as sincere but often confused and awkward in his answers. He replied to one of Jenkins's questions about a phone call from Roy Cohn by saying, "I don't think I did, probably." The Army's counsel, Joseph Welch, knew he had to turn the situation around somehow before Stevens became a laughingstock on the witness stand.

At last, on April 27, Welch saw an opening. That morning, Ray Jenkins introduced as evidence a photo taken in late November 1953, shortly after David Schine had begun basic training at Fort Dix. McCarthy, Roy Cohn, and Frank Carr had met Secretary Stevens in New York to discuss the ongoing Fort Monmouth investigation. Afterward, Cohn had said he'd like to visit David Schine at nearby Fort Dix, and Stevens quickly arranged the trip. When they arrived, a photograph was taken of the group with Colonel David Bradley, a key officer at the base. In the picture, Schine stood between Stevens and Bradley.

Roy Cohn remembered the photo when he was gathering evidence for the hearing. He thought it would indicate that Stevens and Schine had been on good terms, since both men were smiling. Ray Jenkins agreed and asked a subcommittee staff member to obtain a copy of the "picture of Stevens with Schine." The man promptly did so, but then he had the picture altered so that it showed only Stevens and Schine. He said later he thought that was what Jenkins wanted.

During the hearing on April 27, Ray Jenkins displayed the picture to everyone present, unaware that it had been changed. Jenkins went on to allege that Secretary Stevens had specifically asked to have his picture taken alone with Schine. This, Jenkins said, proved there were no ill feelings between Stevens and Schine at the very time the Army claimed Roy Cohn had begun harassing the Army secretary.

It so happened that Joseph Welch, in preparing for the hearings, had seen the original photograph and remembered it. Now he charged that Ray Jenkins had presented as evidence "a doctored or altered photograph . . . as if it were hon-est." He went on to contend that, in the original, "Stevens was photographed in a group" and that he was smiling at Col. Bradley, not at Schine.

Welch's revelation created a tremendous stir in the hearing room and in the media. The subcommittee spent long hours trying to find out who had done the doctoring and for what purpose—or purposes. Reporters and columnists remembered how Joe had used an altered photograph to help defeat Senator Millard Tydings, and they speculated that he was behind this attempt to sway public opinion in favor of David Schine.

As for Welch, he had achieved his goal of swinging the spotlight away from Secretary Stevens's inept testimony. He also had beaten McCarthy at his own game. Joe long ago had learned that unproved charges (and doctored photos) had a far greater effect on public opinion than lengthy recitals of the facts later on. Now, before the facts were in, Welch had used the altered photo of Stevens and Schine to cast doubt on the subcommittee's case.

McCarthy protested that he had had nothing to do with the doctoring. In this instance he was probably telling the truth, but the American people had already formed their opinion, and most of them did not believe him. Joe wasn't about to give in, however. His frustration and anger rose to the surface when Welch had James Juliana, an aide to Roy Cohn, on the witness stand. Welch was question-ing Juliana about the photo, which, before it was altered, had hung on the wall of David Schine's New York office. "You did know what hung on Schine's wall when that was handed to you, sir."

"I did not know what hung on Schine's wall," Juliana said.

Welch held up the picture, which had been introduced as evidence. "Did you think this came from a pixie? Where did you think this picture that I hold in my hand came from?"

Joe interrupted the proceedings to say, "Will counsel for my benefit define—I think he might be an expert on that—what a pixie is?"

McCarthy probably thought his question would fluster Welch and shift the gathering's focus away from the photo, but it had the opposite effect. Welch quickly replied, "Yes. I should say, Mr. Senator, that a pixie is close relative to a fairy."

Laughter broke out in the hearing room. Everyone present knew that James Juliana worked for Roy Cohn. They also knew that "fairy" was a slang word for homosexual. They inferred that the Army's counsel was calling Cohn a fairy—and they laughed.

"Shall I proceed, sir?" Welch asked Joe. "Have I enlightened you?"

There was no way McCarthy could top Welch, so he merely repeated himself. "As I said, I think you may be an authority on what a pixie is." The senator sat back in his chair, and Welch continued his questioning of Juliana.

This sort of exchange was repeated over and over in the days and weeks that followed. Joe would continually interrupt the presentation of the Army's case with a point of order or some other objection. His goal was obvious: to wear down the opposition—in this case, the Army and its counsel, Joseph Welch—until they were so tired of the fight that they would, in effect, surrender and let

Joseph Welch (left) raises a point with Sen. McCarthy (right) during the Army-McCarthy hearings. *The Library of Congress*

him have his way. That was why he kept calling the Army's case against Cohn and Schine a mere "distraction." He wanted to put it behind him, he said, so he could get on with the "serious business" of rooting out Communists in defense plants.

But the Army and Welch were just as determined not to let McCarthy emerge victorious this time. They had a strong case against him and Cohn, and they intended to pursue it to a successful conclusion, no matter how long it took. Backing them up, silently but strongly, was President Eisenhower, who still hesitated to intervene personally but made his position clear to Vice-President Nixon and others he met with behind the scenes.

Not every Republican agreed with the president. Conservative senators like Karl Mundt and Everett Dirksen feared that the hearings were damaging the party's image among voters. Many Republican senators and congressmen would be up for reelection in the fall of 1954. Dirksen and Mundt worried that the longer the hearings went on, with their charges and countercharges, the more the Republican candidates' chances for victory would suffer.

The senators had good reason for their concerns. TV viewership of the hearings increased as the hearings continued instead of declining, as some had predicted. The Army-McCarthy telecasts proved to be a new kind of phenomenon, and a preview of TV news spectaculars to come. Viewers might not grasp all the details of what was discussed, but they became involved with the central figures in the hearings as if they were characters in a soap opera. Secretary Stevens was the sincere and kindly uncle who meant well even when he couldn't express himself clearly. Roy Cohn was the fast-talking, shifty-looking wise guy whom you'd have doubts about if he tried to sell you a house or a car. By contrast, lawyer Welch was the good neighbor with a crinkly smile and a sharp wit who always made you laugh.

And Joe—well, Joe just wasn't appealing on television, especially when you saw him every day. You began to notice his wrinkled suit, and the combover that only made him look balder, and the dense five-o'clock shadow that gave him the appearance of a man who hadn't shaved in a couple of days. Then there was the glowering expression he wore most of the time, and the low, threatening monotone of his voice. It was no wonder his poll ratings kept going down while Welch's went up.

During the hearing on May 4, McCarthy made a rash move that got him into

Cartoonist Herblock's comment on the manufactured "evidence" that McCarthy introduced at a key point in the Army-McCarthy hearings.
The Library of Congress

more trouble. He and Cohn had been trying to establish that Secretary Stevens had attempted to block their Fort Monmouth investigation. Now Joseph Welch introduced as evidence a letter from Army files proving that Stevens had done everything he could to facilitate the investigation.

Not to be outdone, Joe fell back on a ploy he had often used when he wanted to change the subject. He reached into his briefcase and pulled out what he said was a copy of a letter J. Edgar Hoover had sent to an Army general on January 26, 1951. According to Joe, the letter was one of several the FBI had sent to top Army officials, warning them of security lapses at the Fort Monmouth Signal Corps laboratories. Waving the piece of paper in front of him (as he had once waved documents he said listed the names of Communists at work in the State Department), Joe charged that whoever had received the letter "was derelict when these repeated warnings from the FBI were ignored."

Such dramatic gestures had worked for Joe in the past, but not this time. Welch denied any knowledge of the letter, calling it "this purported copy." When asked, Joe maintained that he had not gotten it from anyone at the FBI but had been told that the original could be found in the Army's files. Responding quickly, Army staffers spent hours that evening searching for the letter, but found no trace of it. Meanwhile, Robert Collier, a subcommittee staff member, took McCarthy's copy to the FBI to show to J. Edgar Hoover himself.

The next morning, Collier reported that the FBI had no such letter in its files, either. But it did have a copy of a top-secret, fifteen-page memorandum that was sent by Hoover on the same date and to the same general as Joe's one-and-a-half-page "letter." Collier said the FBI had told him the letter contained a number of paragraphs with the exact same wording as paragraphs in the memorandum. But it was in no way a copy of the much longer document.

Joe responded by bluffing. He claimed that the letter *was* a copy of the

Sen. McCarthy displays a range of emotions while he listens to testimony in the Army-McCarthy hearings. *The National Archives*

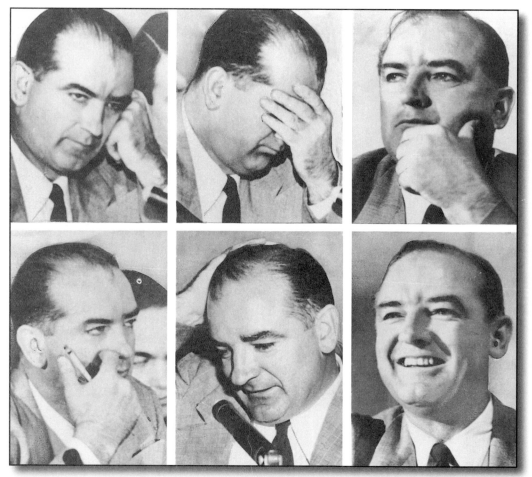

memorandum, with classified security information omitted. Collier immediately contradicted McCarthy. He had raised that possibility in his meeting with J. Edgar Hoover, he said, and the FBI director had ruled it out.

While Joe was trying to think of a reply, Welch chuckled and said, "Mr. Collier, as I understand your testimony, this document that I hold in my hand is a copy of precisely nothing, is that right?" Collier was forced to agree.

The next day, Ray Jenkins, the subcommittee's counsel, called Joe to testify as to how he had obtained the so-called letter. Joe stated that it had been given to him in the spring of 1953 by a young Army Intelligence officer. The officer was disturbed, he said, because nothing was being done about clear indications of Communist infiltration in the top-secret radar laboratories at Fort Monmouth.

Ray Jenkins accepted Joe's explanation, but Joseph Welch had serious reservations about it. In his cross-examination, he tried to get McCarthy to reveal the name of his informant, but Joe refused. Then Welch took another tack, asking Joe to whom he had shown the document after receiving it. McCarthy evaded the counsel's questions by saying "I don't remember," or "I don't recall," or "I wouldn't know." But Welch was relentless; as soon as McCarthy ducked one question, the Army's counsel lobbed another at him. Their exchange was eerily similar to the many occasions when Joe had badgered a witness unmercifully during one of his investigations. Only this time he was on the receiving end.

As the hearings continued, Joe maintained a seemingly impossible schedule. Almost every morning at seven-thirty or eight, he and Jean met with Cohn and Carr over breakfast at their home to plot their strategy for the day. The quartet left the McCarthy house promptly at nine to walk the few blocks to the Senate Office Building, where the hearings were held. Both Joe and Roy Cohn had received anonymous threats, so they were surrounded by bodyguards supplied by the Washington police department.

When the hearing broke for lunch, the group usually went to the dining room at a nearby hotel. Joe's suit jacket would be soaked with perspiration by then, so he'd hang it over his chair back to dry while he gulped down his lunch and a few drinks.

The hearing generally ended for the day around four-thirty. Joe, his aides, and Jean would then retire to his Senate office, where they went over the day's proceedings and made plans until seven or seven-thirty. Dinner followed, sometimes at Joe's home but more often in a favorite restaurant. During the meal, Joe would down one straight shot of vodka after another. After dinner, they all went back to Joe's office to work some more. Jean, Roy Cohn, and Carr usually left for home before eleven. But Joe would stay on, hunting for documents he intended to refer to, or reading the transcripts of earlier hearings. And all the while he was drinking.

Occasionally Mark Catlin, an old friend from Wisconsin who was now a Washington lobbyist, would stay with Joe during one of his all-night working binges. Later, Catlin recalled how Joe would often talk about whom he was going to "get" during the next day's hearing. Or he would ramble on in a deadly serious tone about all the Communists who still were at work in the government, eating away at the nation's strength and security.

Catlin had known Joe four years earlier, when he had just embarked on his anti-Communist crusade. At that time, Catlin thought the pursuit of Communists was a sort of game for Joe—a game he enjoyed playing because it brought him publicity and fame. But now Catlin sensed that Joe had come to believe completely in his struggle against Communism. He seemed like a man with a mission, a man obsessed.

Every so often as the night wore on, Joe would doze off at his desk for a few minutes. But then he would wake up abruptly, reach for his glass, and go back to work. When Catlin finally left the senator's office around six A.M., Joe would still be there, napping and waking up and then napping again. As far as Catlin could tell, that was the only sleep Joe got before going home for breakfast and the next day's strategy session.

By May 7, the hearings had been going on for twelve days, with no end in sight. Republican Party leaders were anxious to halt the proceedings before they did any more harm to the party's image. They sought the help of Wisconsin party leader Tom Coleman, who had aided Joe in the early stages of his political career. Coleman agreed to approach a friend of Roy Cohn's with a proposal: If Cohn would resign from his position with the subcommittee, John Adams would at the same time resign from his position with the Army. They'd each say they were making a personal sacrifice in order to bring the hearings to a close, save the taxpayers further expense, and serve the best interests of the nation.

Joe reluctantly agreed to the proposal. He hated the thought of losing Cohn but realized it was probably the only way to get the Army off his back so he could resume his anti-Communist investigations. With Joe's assent, Cohn began

G. David Schine (left) and Roy Cohn (right) listen intently while Sen. McCarthy (center) asks a question in the Army-McCarthy hearings. *Wisconsin Historical Society*

writing his letter of resignation. But the Army refused to go along with the plan. Secretary Stevens and other top Army brass did not want the hearings to be cut short before all the evidence they had gathered against Joe and Roy Cohn had been presented in a public forum.

Angry and frustrated, Senator Everett Dirksen appealed to the administration to put pressure on the Pentagon to get the Army to change its mind. But the White House refused to intervene. This made it unmistakably clear to Dirksen—and to McCarthy—that the president remained firmly behind the Army in the dispute. And so the hearings continued as originally planned, with one minor change. Each day's proceedings were extended by an hour and a half in the hope that the hearings would move along at a faster pace.

25

"Have You No Sense of Decency, Sir?"

ARMY LEGAL ADVISOR John Adams took the stand on May 12. His testimony, unlike Secretary Stevens's, was concise and to the point. In two days of examination and cross-examination, he offered a vivid account of Roy Cohn's repeated attempts to get special treatment for David Schine. Joe indicated his contempt for Adams by reading newspapers during much of the testimony.

The rest of the audience paid close attention to Adams when he described situations like a luncheon at which Cohn had behaved strangely: "Mr. Cohn became extremely agitated, became extremely abusive. He cursed me and then Senator McCarthy. The abuse went in waves. He would be very abusive and then it would kind of abate and things would be friendly for a few moments. Everybody would eat a little more, and then it would start again. It just kept on."

Adams added that, besides being abusive, Cohn's language was frequently obscene. "The thing that Cohn was angry about, the thing that he was so violent about, was the fact that, one, the Army was not agreeing to an assignment for Schine and, two, that Senator McCarthy was not supporting his staff in an effort to get Schine assigned [to duty] in New York."

The media made the most of Adams's lively testimony, and it was obvious to many observers that Adams's remarks were doing serious damage to McCarthy's case. To counteract the negative impact, Sen. Dirksen and Sen. Mundt went on the attack when it came their turn to cross-examine Adams. Dirksen testified that Adams had come to see him in January and had requested that the subcommittee stop issuing subpoenas to Army personnel. Adams had also brought up the problems the Army was having with Roy Cohn. Later, Sen. Mundt told much the same story. Neither senator claimed that Adams had been trying to blackmail them, but that clearly was the implication.

Legal advisor Adams inadvertently lent credence to the senators' statements. When questioned about events that led to the Army's compiling a chronology of Cohn's attempts to win favors for Schine, Adams told of attending a January 21 meeting with presidential aide Sherman Adams, Attorney General Brownell, and U.N. Ambassador Henry Cabot Lodge. He went on to say that it was Sherman Adams who had suggested at the meeting that the Army begin to keep such a chronology.

Democratic members of the subcommittee were as startled as the Republican members by Adams's disclosure. But when Democratic Senator Stuart Symington tried to question Adams further about the high-level meeting, Adams told Symington he had received instructions not to discuss it. Hearing this, McCarthy was heard to mutter what everyone in the hearing room was thinking: "I can't believe the White House is intervening in the case of a private [David Schine]."

The next day, the administration released a letter from President Eisenhower to Secretary of Defense Charles E. Wilson. The letter prohibited any testimony concerning the January 21 meeting on the grounds of the separation of powers between the executive [the presidency] and the legislative [Congress].

Joe was furious when he learned of the prohibition. He railed to reporters that someone had placed "an iron curtain" between the subcommittee and the truth about the charges against him, Roy Cohn, and their aides. "I frankly thought all along that Mr. Adams [John Adams] was the one who had instigated this. Now there is no way of knowing who did." He said he did not blame the president. "I don't think his judgment is that bad."

Was Joe so naive that he believed President Eisenhower had no knowledge of the Army's chronology? Or that the president had not approved the letter to the Secretary of Defense? Perhaps for once Joe held back from expressing what he really thought, judging that with so much else at stake, it wasn't the moment to risk an open confrontation with Eisenhower.

With feelings at a fever pitch on both sides, Sen. Dirksen decided it was time to take a break. He moved that the subcommittee recess for a week, and his motion was approved on a party-line vote. Democratic members feared this was just another Republican attempt to cut the hearings short. Chairman Mundt reassured them by saying, "I think we all want these hearings to continue, and we want to get out all the facts."

During the recess, a new Gallup poll brought fresh evidence that the television broadcasts of the hearings weren't doing McCarthy any good. His popularity rating had continued to slide and now stood at 49 percent unfavorable. Some Republican leaders were backing away from him, too. Senator Homer Ferguson of Michigan, who chaired the Republican Policy Committee, told reporters that Joe would not be a welcome speaker in the party's fall campaigns.

The hearings resumed on May 24 with Secretary Stevens and legal advisor Adams again on the stand. Both did their best to minimize the importance of the secret meeting on January 21 by affirming that the chronology of Roy Cohn's attempts to pressure the Army had been compiled at the urging of the Pentagon, and the Pentagon alone. Joe made it clear he didn't believe them.

At the next session, Joseph Welch called to the stand General Cornelius Ryan, the commanding officer at Fort Dix, to help document the special treatment Private David Schine had been accorded during his eight weeks of basic training. Schine, Ryan said, had received sixteen passes to leave the base, whereas most privates received only three or four. He had been permitted to make more than 250 long-distance telephone calls; other recruits got to make between five and ten. Once he had gone AWOL (absent without leave) on a holiday without being penalized.

Ryan went on to say that in permitting this, he was only following orders that came from Secretary Stevens—at a time when McCarthy and Cohn claimed that Stevens had been holding Schine "hostage." Ryan could not testify as to how much pressure Cohn had put on Stevens. He could state that he himself had received twenty-nine pressuring phone calls and visits from Cohn and his aides.

McCarthy and Cohn objected strongly to the introduction of this evidence. McCarthy interrupted Ryan's testimony with yet another point of order. Calling Welch a "clever little lawyer," McCarthy said, "He is now recounting events in the private life of David Schine. I am not going to sit here and listen to it. May I say, Mr. Chairman [Mundt], we have much more important work to do. We should be investigating Communists!" With that, McCarthy rose from his seat and strode out of the hearing room.

Perhaps he intended his walkout to impress the crowd and steer the session in a different direction. It probably had the opposite effect. The public had already formed a largely negative impression of Schine's behavior at Fort Dix, and General Ryan's testimony merely reinforced it. In any case, Joe returned to the hearing room before the session ended.

The Army rested its case on May 26, the twenty-first day of the hearings. The next day, McCarthy and Cohn planned to begin the presentation of their case with testimony from Cohn about the eleven interoffice memoranda he and his aides had written. But first, Sen. Symington raised the unresolved issue of the Hoover "letter" that Joe had introduced earlier. Symington made it clear he wasn't accusing anyone. "I have never said that anybody committed anything wrong in receiving it [the 'letter']. But I do say that, regardless of his personal opinion, no man who takes an oath of office not to divulge secrets has the right to decide to do it."

Joe was well aware that Symington was referring to him, and it ignited his temper. He tore into Symington and his fellow Democrats, challenging their patriotism. He also attacked the presidential directive that had cut off discussion of the secret meeting on January 21. On the other hand, he had nothing but praise for those in government who had supplied him with confidential information over the years "in defiance of any presidential directive."

Chairman Mundt tried to turn the discussion back to Cohn's testimony, but Joe wasn't through yet. "As far as I am concerned," he said, "I would like to notify all two hundred million federal employees that I feel it is their duty to give us any information which they have about graft, corruption, Communism, treason—and that there is no loyalty to a superior officer which can tower above and beyond their loyalty to their country." (Joe's math was more than a little off; the entire U.S. population in 1950 was just 151 million.)

President Eisenhower was stunned when told of McCarthy's diatribe. According to Jim Hagerty, he paced back and forth in the Oval Office as he tried to put his thoughts and feelings into words. "This amounts to nothing but a wholesale subversion of public services," the president said. "McCarthy is making exactly the same plea of loyalty that Hitler made to the German people. Both tried to set up personal loyalty within the government while both were using the pretense of fighting Communism.

"McCarthy is trying deliberately to subvert the people we have in government, people who are sworn to obey the law, the Constitution, and their superior officers. I think this is the most disloyal act we have ever had by anyone in the government of the United States."

Publicly, the White House issued a statement by Attorney General Brownell that was personally approved by the president. It declared that the executive branch's responsibility "cannot be usurped by any individual who may seek to set himself above the laws of our land." A short while later, Brownell linked the statement directly to McCarthy in a speech that the president had also approved. Brownell called Joe's appeal for information from government employees an "open invitation to violate the law."

Back at the hearings, Roy Cohn spent nine days on the stand describing the main points of his and McCarthy's case. He proved to be a tough, sharp-witted advocate, but the subcommittee members and the audience found it hard to believe some of what he said. Despite all the evidence the Army had presented, he stated with a straight face, "There was never any request by us for any kind of preferential treatment for Schine." And he adopted a deferential tone when asked about the eleven memoranda. "As far as I know, sir, they are memoranda from Senator McCarthy's file concerning various of these matters in our relations with Mr. Adams and Mr. Stevens."

Ray Jenkins, the subcommittee's legal counsel, began his cross-examination of Cohn with the question that was on everyone's mind. What had made Cohn seek Schine's company so often while his colleague was undergoing basic training? By raising the issue so early in the proceedings, Jenkins hoped to defuse it.

Cohn was ready with a quick response. Schine, he said, was absolutely indispensable. He learned quickly and knew more about the subcommittee's business than anyone else. But when Jenkins asked Cohn to produce examples of projects Schine had worked on during his frequent leaves from his military duties, Cohn stalled. At last he came up with a single six-page document.

Jenkins left the matter at that. When it was Joseph Welch's turn to cross-examine the witness, he pointed to the six-page document and asked Cohn, "Who wrote that?"

"I believe David Schine did," Cohn replied.

"At what time?"

Cohn paused. "I don't know, sir."

"Prior to his induction?" Welch asked.

"I don't know. It might very well have been."

Welch was persistent. "You wouldn't say it was afterward?"

"No, I can't say that, sir."

"So," Welch said, "the first document I pick up is one that he might very well have done before his induction."

Cohn was clearly flustered. "Yes, sir," he muttered.

Then Welch embarrassed Cohn further by producing receipts from several New York nightclubs and expensive restaurants. When questioned about the receipts, Cohn was forced to admit that he and Schine had gone to the establishments while Schine was on weekend passes from Fort Dix. Although Welch didn't hammer it home, he had made his point. Obviously the "indispensable" Schine hadn't spent all of his leave time working on subcommittee business.

Next Welch zeroed in on the eleven interoffice memoranda that McCarthy and Cohn were relying on to disprove the Army's case. He made no attempt to hide his opinion of the documents: "I do not wish to conceal from anyone in this room that I have grave suspicions about the authenticity of these memoranda."

Roy Cohn did his best to deflect Welch's incessant questioning, but Welch kept finding new angles to pursue. On June 9, he got Cohn into a corner by asking why Cohn had climbed three flights of stairs to dictate one of the memoranda to McCarthy's secretary, Mary Driscoll, when there were two secretaries on the floor where Cohn was working who could have done the job. In response, Cohn could only splutter unconvincingly that that was what he had done.

Mrs. Driscoll was no help when she took the stand. Through his questioning, Welch demolished her nervous attempts to back up Cohn's claim that she had typed the memoranda as Cohn dictated them to her over the course of several months. At one point, she blurted out that she had "no independent recollection" of any of the documents. When Welch asked her to produce the notebooks in which she had taken down Cohn's dictation, she fumbled for an answer and finally said she had destroyed them. The audience in the hearing room greeted several of her least convincing answers with outbursts of laughter.

Joe sat through most of Welch's June 9 interrogations without interrupting, but observers said later that his grim expression revealed how hard it was for him to restrain himself. After the lunch break, Welch brought Cohn back to the stand and started to question him further about his and Schine's work habits when the Army private was on leave. Joe finally lost control. He waited until there was a brief break in the questioning and called out, "Mr. Chairman, point of order—point of order!"

Sen. Mundt recognized him, and Joe launched, slowly and deliberately, into a typical attack, this one aimed directly at Welch. "I think we should tell him [Welch] that he has in his law firm a young man named Fisher whom he recommended, incidentally, to do work on this committee, who has been for a number of years a member of an organization which was named . . . as the legal bulwark of the Communist Party, an organization which always swings to the defense of anyone who dares to expose Communists."

McCarthy was referring to Frederick Fisher, the young lawyer from Welch's Boston law firm whom Welch had initially invited to be a member of his staff in the Army-McCarthy hearings. When Welch had learned of Fisher's past affiliation with the leftist National Lawyers Guild, he had asked the young lawyer to leave the staff before the hearings began.

McCarthy must have known the facts of the Fisher story. But the facts of a case had never mattered to him when he launched one of his attacks, and they obviously didn't matter to him now. In his zeal, he failed to notice the worried looks Roy Cohn, seated near him, was aiming in his direction, or that his colleague was silently mouthing the words, "No! No!"

Cohn and Welch had reached an agreement two days earlier, by which Cohn promised not to bring Frederick Fisher's name into the hearing if Welch would not mention the embarrassing fact that Cohn had twice found ways to avoid the draft. Cohn had told Joe of the agreement, and Joe had okayed it. Why was he ignoring it now?

Cohn dashed off a note and passed it to McCarthy. "This is the subject which I have committed to Welch we would not go into," the note said. "Please respect our agreement as an agreement because this is not going to do any good." Joe skimmed the note, then turned and smiled at Cohn. "I know Mr. Cohn would rather not have me go into this," he said, "but I feel I must."

Switching his attention back to Welch, he continued. "I am not asking you at this time to explain why you tried to foist him [Fisher] on this committee. Whether you knew he was a member of that Communist organization or not, I don't know. I assume you did not, Mr. Welch, because I get the impression that,

Roy Cohn reminds McCarthy of the deal he, Cohn, has made with Joseph Welch, but the senator ignores him. *The Library of Congress*

while you are quite an actor, you play for a laugh. I don't think you have any conception of the danger of the Communist Party."

Chairman Mundt interrupted to point out that Welch had never promoted Fisher as an assistant counsel, but McCarthy barged on, repeating much of what he'd said earlier about Fisher, before finally coming to a halt.

Then Welch launched his counterattack. "Until this moment, Senator," he said, "I think I never really gauged your cruelty or your recklessness." Some observers thought they detected tears in his eyes; certainly there was deep emotion in his voice.

"Fred Fisher is a young man who went to the Harvard Law School and came into my firm and is starting what looks to be a brilliant career with us," Welch continued. He went on to say that he had invited another lawyer in the firm, James St. Clair, to be his chief assistant in his work for the subcommittee, and had asked St. Clair to pick someone else in the firm to work with him. St. Clair had chosen Frederick Fisher.

After arriving in Washington, the three of them had had dinner together.

Welch now reported that he had said, "'Boys, I don't know anything about you except I have always liked you, but if there is anything funny in the life of either one of you that would hurt anybody in this case, you speak up quick.'

"Fred Fisher said, 'Mr. Welch, when I was in law school and for a period of months after, I belonged to the Lawyers Guild,' as you have suggested, Senator." Welch fixed his gaze on McCarthy. "I said, 'Fred, I just don't think I am going to ask you to work on the case. If I do, one of these days that will come out and go over national television and it will just hurt like the dickens.'"

He paused briefly. "So, Senator, I asked him to go back to Boston. Little did I dream you could be so reckless and so cruel as to do an injury to that lad. It is true he is still with Hale & Dorr [Welch's Boston law firm]. It is true that he will continue to be with Hale & Dorr. It is, I regret to say, equally true that I fear he shall always bear a scar needlessly inflicted by you.

"If it were in my power to forgive you for your reckless cruelty, I would do so. I like to think I am a gentleman, but your forgiveness will have to come from someone other than me."

A hush had fallen over the hearing room, but Joe appeared to be unaware of it. He tried to pick up where he had left off in his attack on Fisher, but Welch cut him short. "Senator, may we not drop this? We know he [Fisher] belonged to the Lawyers Guild, and Mr. Cohn nods his head at me. I did you, I think, no personal injury, Mr. Cohn."

"No, sir," Cohn said quickly.

Still looking at Cohn, Welch said, "I meant you no personal injury, and if I did, I beg your pardon." He focused again on McCarthy. "Let us not assassinate this lad further, Senator. You have done enough. Have you no sense of decency, sir, at long last? Have you left no sense of decency?"

Joe, stubborn as ever, started in again on Fisher's membership in a "Communist organization." Welch refused to hear it. "Mr. McCarthy, I will not discuss this with you further. . . . If there is a God in heaven, it will do neither you nor your cause any good. I will not discuss it further. I will not ask Mr. Cohn any more questions. You, Mr. Chairman, may, if you will, call the next witness."

The hearing room resounded with loud, sustained applause. Chairman Mundt made no move to stop it. Joe, his face red, sat silently in his seat. For once in his life, he had nothing to say.

26

Censured

THE MEDIA MADE THE MOST of the clash between Welch and McCarthy. Newspapers across the country ran photographs of Joseph Welch in tears as he spoke of Fred Fisher, and then smiling afterward amid stacks of congratulatory messages. By contrast, most photos of Joe showed him either smirking or glowering. Even some of McCarthy's strongest supporters among the press, like the *Wisconsin State Journal,* called his performance "reprehensible."

Joe's closest friends realized how deeply he had been humiliated. Urban Van Susteren, who watched the hearings on television, said, "It made me sick," while Roy Cohn commented later, "The blow was terribly damaging to Senator McCarthy."

And how did Joe react? On the surface, he seemed as cocky and confident as ever. But when he himself took the stand on June 9 as a witness before the subcommittee, he wasn't as quick on his feet as he'd been when the hearings began. Perhaps he'd been more affected by Welch's condemning words than he'd let on. Or perhaps too much alcohol and too little rest were finally taking their toll.

Whatever the explanation, Joe often had to be prompted by Roy Cohn during his four days on the stand. He had nothing new to offer, merely a rambling repeat of his familiar speech about the serious threat of Communist subversion in the U.S. government. None of the senators or counsel present challenged him on that score, however; they were still afraid of being labeled as "soft on Communism" by their political opponents. Even Joseph Welch called Irving Peress a "no-good Communist" at one point, and told Joe, "I admire the work you do, when it succeeds."

The subcommittee was less accepting when Joe tried to defend Cohn and Schine against the Army's charges of favoritism. Even the Republican members found it hard to believe McCarthy when he said of Schine, "I think he is the most modest young man I have seen," and later, referring to Cohn, "I believe he is just a normal young man. He is very brilliant. I don't think that he has a hotter temper than anyone else."

During this phase of the hearings, the Republican members of the subcommittee held an after-hours executive session. They made a motion to call a halt to the hearings after Joe and his aide Francis Carr testified. The Democrats protested—they wanted a chance to interrogate David Schine—but the motion passed on a party-line vote.

And so, after McCarthy concluded his testimony and Francis Carr had weakly defended his role in preparing the eleven questionable memoranda, the Army-McCarthy hearings came to an end on June 17. They had lasted 36 days and taken up 187 hours of network television time. Millions of fascinated viewers had watched the proceedings, and 15,000 had attended one or more of the hearings in person.

The jury—in this case, the members of the subcommittee—would not announce their verdict until September, when they issued their final report. In the meantime, nationwide polls and other samplings of public opinion revealed that the American people had found the Army's case against McCarthy, Cohn, and Schine far more credible than the defense the three of them had presented.

Joe's own approval ratings were equally revealing. In the Gallup poll published immediately after the hearings, his popularity rating had fallen to 34 percent, its lowest yet. More telling, 41 percent of the business and professional people who were polled expressed "extreme disapproval" of McCarthy, while only 14 percent expressed "high approval."

At first, Joe dismissed such polls as inaccurate, claiming he still enjoyed the support of the majority of "real Americans." His claim was reinforced by the fan mail he continued to receive and the backing he got from groups like the Republican convention in his home state of Wisconsin. The convention passed a resolution in the summer of 1954 commending McCarthy for his "crusade against subversives."

Joe relaxed with Jean on a vacation in Mexico that summer. When he returned to Washington in mid-July, expecting to resume his usual schedule, he called a meeting of the subcommittee. He told reporters he would soon launch a one-man hearing in Boston to investigate alleged Communist subversion in the city's defense plants.

But things had changed in Washington. Senator William Knowland of California had been named Senate majority leader after Sen. Taft died of cancer the previous summer. Now Knowland had to tell Joe he couldn't start a one-man hearing outside Washington during the final weeks of the Congressional session because it would be sure to anger the other subcommittee members, even some of the Republican members. What Knowland didn't say was that Joe's power to intimidate his fellow senators had been seriously weakened.

This truth had been brought home to Joe even more clearly on June 11. His longtime foe Senator Ralph Flanders rose on the floor of the Senate that afternoon and introduced a resolution to censure McCarthy—that is, to condemn his actions as wrong and express disapproval publicly. Flanders said that the Republican Party had reached a fork in the road and must decide which direction to take. "On the one hand we move in the path and under the influence of

Senator Ralph Flanders, on June 11, 1954, hands McCarthy a note alerting him that Flanders plans to introduce a resolution against him that afternoon in the Senate. *Marquette University Archives*

the great Lincoln," he said. "If we turn the other way, we choose the leadership of the junior senator from Wisconsin. In the words of Joshua, who led the children of Israel into the Promised Land, 'Choose you this day whom you will serve.'"

Flanders then introduced the resolution itself: "Resolved, that the conduct of the senator from Wisconsin, Mr. McCarthy, is unbecoming a member of the United States Senate, is contrary to senatorial traditions and tends to bring the Senate into disrepute, and such conduct is hereby condemned." There were no specific charges in the resolution; those would be thrashed out in a Senate debate.

Given the altered political climate in Washington since the Army-McCarthy hearings, Flanders was hopeful that the censure resolution would be favorably received. He knew from preliminary surveys conducted by his political allies that twenty-four senators could be counted on to vote in favor of censuring McCarthy, and eighteen others were likely to join them. He also knew that at least twenty senators were strongly opposed to the measure, and the rest were undecided.

Joe may not yet have grasped which way the political winds were blowing, but Roy Cohn did. Realizing he had lost the support of the subcommittee, Cohn resigned from his post as counsel on July 20. McCarthy tried to get Cohn to reconsider his decision, but he refused. Joe made no effort to conceal his disappointment. He called Cohn's departure "a victory for the Communists and their fellow travelers," and claimed that Cohn was appreciated by the millions who had seen him at work during the hearings. "I know that they will resent as deeply as do I the treatment to which he has been subjected," McCarthy said.

Senate debate on the Flanders resolution to censure Joe began on July 30. In an opening statement, Sen. Flanders laid out three specific charges against McCarthy: his contemptuous treatment of the Gillette-Hennings committee, which had been set up to investigate the underhanded tactics used by Joe and others to defeat Senator Millard Tydings in 1951; sending Roy Cohn and David Schine to Europe on a tour that "compromised the honor of the nation and the Senate"; and McCarthy's "habitual contempt" for people whom he had called as witnesses, such as the New York lawyer Dorothy Kenyon and Gen. Zwicker.

Flanders conceded that "the senator's work has resulted in some desirable dismissals." But, he added, "So far as I am aware he [McCarthy] has never claimed credit for a single successful prosecution."

Before the debate began, both political parties had agreed that the Flanders

Senator Ralph Flanders of Vermont, McCarthy's longtime opponent.
The Library of Congress

resolution should be discussed in an open-minded, nonpartisan way. However, the remarks of Republican senators in the aftermath of Flanders's opening statement made it clear that they were determined to defeat the resolution. Among other things, the Republicans charged that it was too general.

Senator J. William Fulbright, Democrat of Arkansas, responded to this criticism by adding several more examples of alleged misconduct to the resolution. Among them were Joe's appeal to government employees to give him classified information in violation of the law, and his insulting comments about witnesses like Annie Lee Moss and esteemed Americans like General George Marshall. Fulbright concluded his Senate speech by saying, "His [Joe's] abuses have recalled to the minds of millions the most abhorrent tyrannies which our whole system of ordered liberty and balanced power was intended to abolish."

Fulbright's speech did nothing to lessen Republican opposition to the proposed censure. Newspapers reporting on the Republicans' position predicted that if the resolution was put to a vote, it would go down to defeat. Determined to prevent that, Sen. McClellan suggested that a special committee be formed to study the charges against Joe and report its findings before the Senate adjourned.

The notion of a committee appealed to many senators who were reluctant to take a position on McCarthy during an election year. After heated debate, the Senate voted 75–12 to form a committee composed of three Republicans and three Democrats, appointed by Vice-President Nixon on the recommendation of the Senate majority and minority party leaders.

In public, Joe adopted a defiant attitude toward these developments. He said he welcomed the opportunity to cross-examine his critics on the Senate floor. "I assure the American people that the senators who have made the charges will either indict themselves for perjury, or they will prove what consummate liars they are."

To close friends, though, it was clear that McCarthy was deeply hurt. He couldn't understand why former friends and allies like J. Edgar Hoover and Richard Nixon had turned away from him. Nor could he grasp why his approval ratings in the polls kept on dropping, or why staunch supporters like the Hearst chain of newspapers had begun to criticize him. Weren't the public and the press aware that Communists and Communism were just as much of a threat to the American way of life as they'd always been?

The Senate majority leader, William F. Knowland of California, and the minority leader, Lyndon B. Johnson of Texas, had the difficult task of selecting the committee members who would weigh the charges against Joe. Johnson, known as the "Master of the Senate," was more forceful than Knowland. He was all in favor of censuring Joe; he also knew that, if the resolution was to have any hope of passage, the committee members would need to be moderate conservatives. Otherwise, they would be open to the charge of being prejudiced against Joe.

Johnson compiled a roster of six candidates whom he described as "men who are symbols for patriotism, integrity, and judicial temperament." All came from the South or West, where McCarthy was not as popular as in other regions, and none was known to be either strongly for or against the Wisconsin senator. When Johnson discussed his choices with Knowland, the Californian approved them all. "I would be perfectly willing to go before them on trial of my life," he said. Vice-President Nixon agreed, saying, "This is an outstanding committee."

Joe appeared to be content also. He told an audience at an American Legion convention in Illinois that he was "completely satisfied." But when asked about the resolution, he replied scornfully that some "nice little boys in the Senate" had attacked "someone for doing the skunk-hunting job they didn't have the guts to do themselves." The "someone" of course was McCarthy.

The committee, under the chairmanship of Senator Arthur V. Watkins, Republican of Utah, announced that it would conduct public hearings, but they would not be broadcast or televised. It also announced that it would investigate just five charges against Joe out of the many that had been suggested. These were McCarthy's scornful treatment of the Gillette-Hennings committee; his invitation to government employees to give him classified information; his possession and manipulation of the so-called "letter" to J. Edgar Hoover; his abuse of various fellow senators in the course of his investigations; and his attack on Gen. Zwicker. Excluded were hearsay evidence and any evidence that was not directly related to one of the five charges, in order to prevent McCarthy from going off on any tangents during the hearings.

Joe and Jean took another brief vacation, this time to California. On their return, Joe told reporters he considered the hearings "a great waste of time."

Senate Majority Leader William Knowland of California (left) and Senator Walter George of Georgia (center) discuss with Senate Minority Leader Lyndon B. Johnson (right) the censure proceedings against Sen. McCarthy. *The National Archives*

Senator Arthur Watkins.
The Library of Congress

He said he planned to accept several of the charges. "For instance, the fact I said Senator Flanders is senile is unquestioned. It will be freely admitted. He [Flanders] can prove he's not if he can and wants to."

The hearings opened on August 31, 1954, in the Senate Caucus Room, where the Army-McCarthy hearings had concluded two months earlier. Once again every seat in the room was filled, and once again McCarthy tried to divert the proceedings by interrupting the chairman's opening statement. But Chairman Watkins refused to acknowledge him: "We are not going to be interrupted by these diversions. We are going straight down the line." When McCarthy persisted, Watkins pounded his gavel on the table over and over again until Joe finally sat down. After that, McCarthy often stayed away from the hearings, and when he was there, he was unusually quiet. *New York Times* columnist James Reston wrote of Joe, "He is fenced in for the first time and he is being hurt, for regardless of what the Senate does about his case, each day's hearing is a form of censure of its own."

Reston was referring to McCarthy's profanities and insulting remarks that were read into the public record during the hearings. Committee members were visibly distressed to hear Sen. Fulbright described as "Senator Half-bright,"

Senator Robert C. Hendrickson ridiculed as "the only human being who ever lived so long without brains or guts," and the continuous slurs directed at Gen. Zwicker, whose confrontation with McCarthy was read in full.

McCarthy's lawyer, Edward Bennett Williams, tried to mount a strong defense of his client. McCarthy undercut Williams's efforts at every turn. He expressed no regret for asking government employees to provide him with classified information: "My comments expressed my feelings then," he testified, "and they express my feelings now." He was not about to retract his criticism of Gen. Zwicker, either. "I think any man who says that it is right to give honorable discharges to known Communists is not fit to wear the uniform of a general. I said it then. I will say it now. I will say it again."

Joe's stubborn refusal to admit any wrongdoing on his part did not sit well with the committee members. Their displeasure was evident in the stern tone of their final report, which was issued on September 27. The six members recommended unanimously that McCarthy be censured on two counts: his "vulgar and insulting" treatment of Sen. Hendrickson and the Gillette-Hennings committee; and his slurs on the character and abilities of Gen. Zwicker, which they called "inexcusable" and "reprehensible."

As was to be expected, Joe's ultraconservative Republican friends, such as Sen. Dirksen and Sen. McCarran, vowed to fight the recommendations. But a majority of newspapers across the country praised the work of Sen. Watkins and his committee. A commentator for the *Louisville Courier-Journal* wrote: "These six inoffensive and austere men [the committee members] have by their unanimity and moderation both destroyed the McCarthy myth and elevated the prestige of a Senate which has suffered severe blows. . . . The nation owes them thanks."

Joe had little to say publicly, but close associates said he was depressed by the committee's decision. He was also surprised and saddened when many Republican leaders made it clear that, in the wake of the Army-McCarthy hearings and the Watkins committee report, he would not be welcome as a campaigner in their local elections that fall. Perhaps as a result of these disappointments, Joe suffered one of his periodic sinus attacks and checked himself into Bethesda Naval Hospital for treatment.

Many Republicans continued to employ his scare tactics when they spoke on behalf of their party's candidates. Vice-President Nixon made a practice of calling all Democratic candidates "left-wingers." He went on to warn that, if elected, the Democrats would again tolerate the employment of "Reds and Communist sympathizers" in government as they had in the Truman years.

Such tactics had proved effective in 1950 and 1952, but did not succeed in 1954. Perhaps the Republicans had cried wolf once too often. Or perhaps it was because there had been signs of change in the Soviet Union in the year and a half since Stalin's death. Ambassador Charles Bohlen reported from Moscow that the new Soviet leaders, Nikita Khrushchev and Nikolai Bulganin, had begun to relax some of the rigid policies of the Stalin regime. Thousands of political prisoners were coming home from Stalin's notorious labor camps. More consumer goods were appearing in the stores. Books, plays, and movies were starting to deal with personal themes instead of political propaganda. The title of a new novel, *The Thaw*, by the respected Soviet writer Ilya Ehrenburg came to define this period of transition. Ehrenburg used the phrase to represent not just the usual spring thaw but also the easing of restrictions within the Soviet Union.

McCarthy smilingly accepts a plaque awarded him by the Amityville, New York, American Legion Post for "distinguished service to our nation in the field of anti-subversion." *The National Archives*

Whatever the reasons, American voters in November 1954 turned away from the Republican message of fear and returned the Democrats to control of both the House and the Senate. Now that both sides in the cold war had arsenals of nuclear weapons at their command, a majority of voters seemed to be more interested in finding ways to avoid a future conflict than in raking over old charges of subversion and espionage.

But not Joe. He blamed the Republican losses on the failure of their candidates to speak out loudly and clearly about the dangers of Communist subversion in government. "Republicans have got to learn before the next election that they can't duck the real issues and can't talk about sweet nothings." He apparently meant the possibility of peaceful coexistence with the Soviet Union, a notion that some political leaders in the U.S. and other Western countries had begun to take seriously.

The debate on the Watkins committee's recommendations for McCarthy's censure, which had been postponed until after the election, was set to begin on November 8. Everyone concerned realized how serious a matter censure was. Only two senators in American history had been censured for their behavior, one in 1902, the other in 1929.

A Gallup poll released on the 8th was anything but encouraging for Joe. It showed that of the 55 percent of Americans who had followed the doings of the Watkins committee, 56 percent felt he deserved to be censured for his attacks on the Gillette-Hennings committee, and 47 percent thought he should be censured for the disrespectful way he had treated Gen. Zwicker.

Thousands upon thousands of other Americans continued to support McCarthy, believing he was the victim of an attack by pro-Communist forces in the government. Every day, Sen. Watkins, Sen. Flanders, and Sen. Fulbright received thousands of phone calls, letters, and telegrams denouncing them as "traitors," "cowards," and "dirty Reds." The Catholic War Veterans of Brooklyn and Queens, New York, launched a nationwide campaign to collect signatures for a "Save McCarthy" petition, and by early November they claimed to have rounded up more than 250,000 names. Even more ambitious was the goal of another national organization called Ten Million Americans Mobilized for Justice. They aimed to gather 10 million signatures from people opposed to the censure.

Just before the debate began, McCarthy received a patriotic service medal from the American Coalition, a right-wing organization. In a message accompanying the award, the group's president wrote, "If you are destroyed then it

Two representatives of the Catholic War Veterans of New York present McCarthy with the signatures of 250,000 citizens protesting the censure debate, November 8, 1954. *Marquette University Archives*

follows, as night follows day, that your distinguished anti-Communist colleagues in the Congress and in the government will be savagely assaulted, and they too eliminated."

In accepting the award, Joe adopted a somber tone. He pledged to continue the struggle "even if the Senate censures me—and I think they will—for fighting the dirtiest fighters in the world, Communists. I will go on until either the Communists lose or we die."

During the first days of debate, one after another of McCarthy's Republican supporters took the floor of the Senate to defend their hero. Senator Herman Welker praised him as "one of the greatest living champions of human liberty, and one of the greatest living foes of Communist slavery." Senator Barry Goldwater of Arizona said censuring Joe would be a "global victory for Communism." Senator William E. Jenner suggested that the entire censure resolution be set aside, claiming it "was initiated by the Communist conspiracy."

Democratic senators were eager to respond, but Minority Leader Lyndon Johnson convinced them to hold their fire. Johnson feared that if the debate became too partisan, moderate Republicans, who were now leaning toward censure, would change their votes. However, Johnson moved quickly to block Majority Leader William Knowland when he tried to introduce amendments intended to weaken the resolution.

In the midst of the debate, Joe distributed the text of a speech that he said he

Two of McCarthy's female fans demonstrate against his censure.
The National Archives

Republican Senator William E. Jenner defends his friend McCarthy on the floor of the Senate.
The Library of Congress

intended to deliver the next day. Reporters and fellow senators were startled by the personal nature of his remarks. "From the moment I entered the fight against subversion back in 1950 at Wheeling, West Virginia, the Communists have said that the destruction of me and what I stand for is their number-one objective in this country," McCarthy wrote.

He went on to imply that Sen. Watkins and the other members of the censure committee were dupes of the Communists. "I would have the American people recognize, and contemplate in dread, the fact that the Communist Party—a relatively small group of deadly conspirators—has now extended its tentacles to that most respected of American bodies, the United States Senate; that it has made a committee of the Senate its unwitting handmaiden."

Joe said he realized it was likely he would be censured. He followed that up with a loaded question. "As you vote 'aye' on this resolution I urge you to weigh carefully the question: who has really won by this vote of censure?" He concluded his remarks with a promise "to continue to serve the cause to which I have devoted my life, no matter what happens."

Joe did not deliver the speech in person, claiming he didn't have enough time. But he entered it into the *Congressional Record,* and it was published in full in the *New York Times.*

The following weekend, Joe and Jean, accompanied by Barry Goldwater, flew to Milwaukee to attend a testimonial dinner in Joe's honor. More than 1,500 guests interrupted his remarks with frequent applause, and at the end they serenaded him with a song specially composed for the occasion. It began, "Nobody's for McCarthy but the people, and we all love our Joe."

Afterward, reporters asked him how the censure resolution, if passed, would affect his political future. "Not at all," McCarthy replied. "I think I would not even be up for censure except for the fact that I am exposing Communists."

Back in Washington, Joe's speech accusing Sen. Watkins and his committee of being "unwitting handmaidens" of the Communists had aroused Watkins's ire. The senator made no attempt to conceal his feelings in a speech he delivered on November 16 as part of the ongoing debate. Watkins sharply criticized McCarthy for his false and insulting charges, and urged his fellow senators to add a section to the censure resolution denouncing them. Wallace Bennett, Utah's other senator and Watkins's longtime colleague, volunteered to introduce such an amendment immediately.

The next day, Joe checked himself into Bethesda Naval Hospital again. He told reporters he was suffering from a painful attack of bursitis in his right elbow. It had been caused, he said, when he bumped the elbow on the sharp edge of a table while shaking hands after the Milwaukee dinner. The Senate agreed to adjourn the debate until November 29, when Joe said he would be able to return. But the official Capitol physician checked with McCarthy's doctors to make sure his injury wasn't just a delaying tactic.

Congressional friends of Joe's, including Sen. Dirksen and Sen. Goldwater, visited him in the hospital. They pleaded with him to apologize to Sen. Watkins and several other senators who felt they had been insulted. If he'd just make that gesture—and extend an apology to those, like Gen. Zwicker, who were named in the charges—Joe's friends were confident the censure resolution could still be defeated. Sen. Dirksen had gone so far as to draft a letter of apology for Joe to consider sending.

Joe refused. He'd never yielded a point to anyone in what he saw as his personal crusade against Communism, and he wasn't about to start now. If he had to suffer for his beliefs, so be it. He'd rather stand by his guns than apologize to those he believed were helping the Reds. When Dirksen tried to give him the letter, Joe shoved it aside. "I will never let them think I would ever crawl," he said. And when Goldwater urged him not to be hasty, Joe threw a pen at him, let loose a stream of curses, and pounded on the bedside table with his good hand.

As promised, McCarthy returned to the Senate on November 29. His right arm was bandaged from wrist to elbow and supported by a sling. He surprised his senatorial friends and foes by requesting that debate on the resolution be cut short and a vote taken within two days. He said he was eager to get back to hunting subversives.

That evening, 13,000 people crowded into New York's Madison Square Garden for a rally in support of Joe. It was sponsored by Ten Million Americans Mobilized for Justice, the organization that was gathering the signatures of millions of Joe's supporters. McCarthy remained in Washington because of the hearings, but both Jean and her mother spoke on his behalf. So did many others, including Roy Cohn. "If the Senate votes to censure," Cohn warned, "it will be committing the blackest act in our whole history."

On the evening of December 2, 1954, after three more days of debate, the Senate voted 67–22 to condemn Senator Joseph R. McCarthy for "contempt and abuse" of both the Gillette-Hennings committee and the Watkins committee. The latter charge was the one Sen. Bennett of Utah had introduced just two weeks earlier at the urging of Sen. Watkins. All forty-four Democrats voted in favor of condemnation, while the Republicans were evenly divided. McCarthy himself simply voted "present."

Two things about the vote puzzled those who'd followed the debate closely. First, they questioned why the wording of the resolution was changed from "censure" to "condemn." Sen. Fulbright explained that the word "condemn" had been used in the last such resolution that had been adopted, back in 1929. "Actually," he said, "'condemn,' as I read it, is a more severe term than 'censure.'"

Second, they asked why the charge regarding Joe's abuse of Gen. Zwicker had been dropped from the resolution without a vote being taken. Insiders offered various explanations, but the one that made the most sense to observers at the

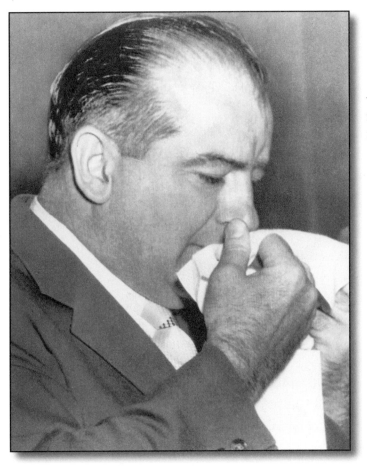

Overcome by emotion, McCarthy wipes away tears while addressing a rally in his honor in Washington in 1954. *The Library of Congress*

time concerned the general's connection to Irving Peress, the Army dentist accused of being a Communist. From the start of the censure process, the senators involved had excluded any examples of mistreatment arising from McCarthy's anti-Communist investigations. They were well aware that many innocent people had been abused during those inquiries. If the senators drew attention to these misdeeds, however, they feared they'd be labeled "Communist sympathizers," or worse. So in the end they limited themselves to cases in which Joe had belittled and demeaned his fellow senators.

When Joe left the Senate chamber after the vote, reporters crowded around to ask what he thought of the decision. "Well, it wasn't exactly a vote of confidence," he quipped.

27

"His Time to Die"

JOE MIGHT HAVE WEATHERED the censure easily. No formal punishment—no prison sentence or period of probation—was connected to it. Nor did it contain any criticism of his work as an anti-Communist investigator. There was no reason he couldn't have resumed his inquiry into suspected Communist subversion in defense plants where he had left off.

But he didn't, and his supporters wondered why. Always before, he had rebounded with renewed energy after a setback, but not this time. One evident reason for this was his loss of political power. When the Democrats took back control of Congress in January 1955, McCarthy had to hand over the chairmanship of his Government Operations Committee to the senior Democratic member of the committee, Senator John McClellan. No longer would Joe have the final say as to who or what was investigated.

That was by no means the only reason for McCarthy's retreat. He was terribly upset when President Eisenhower, who had made no comments during the censure hearings, invited Sen. Watkins to the White House for a friendly chat after the hearings had ended. Later, it was reported that the president had commended Watkins for his "very splendid job" as chairman. Although the press report didn't say so, it was also evident that Eisenhower was pleased with the Senate's verdict.

Joe had long suspected that Eisenhower was against him; now he was certain. He responded with some of his old fire, issuing a statement that probably did more harm to his own battered reputation than it did to the president. Joe apologized to his followers for having endorsed and campaigned for Eisenhower in 1952. He went on to charge the president with a "shrinking show of weakness" toward the whole issue of Communist subversion.

Eisenhower's press secretary, Jim Hagerty, responded by reminding the press and the public of a recent message from the president, enumerating all the Communists his administration had prosecuted. Hagerty added that the attorney general was at present bringing the figures up to date.

McCarthy probably expected to be rejected by the White House. But it's doubtful he anticipated the highly negative response his statement received in other quarters. The chairman of the Republican National Committee, Leonard Hall, said Joe had made "a great mistake." In his home state of Wisconsin, the Republican State Committee, after sharply criticizing Joe, praised Eisenhower for "working carefully, diligently, and aggressively to remove subversives from the government."

Some press outlets expressed doubts about Joe's mental health. The *Chicago Sun-Times* wondered if McCarthy had "taken temporary leave of his senses" when he attacked the president. The *Rocky Mountain News* of Denver was even blunter: "He has simply blown his stack."

In the days that followed, the president gave a dinner for departing committee chairmen and failed to invite Joe, making clear to McCarthy that he would no longer be welcome at the White House. Later, Joe was one of three Republican senators who, the president publicly announced, could not be counted on to support the party's legislative program.

McCarthy told friends that he wasn't hurt by these slights, only amused. But his behavior revealed him to be in a deep depression. He rose late in the morning, and he failed to show up for many Senate proceedings. When aides sought him out, they'd find him at home, usually with a drink in hand, watching soap operas on television. On the days he did go to his Senate office, he often refused to take phone calls, even from close associates.

Most senators concern themselves with more than one issue, as Joe had done when he'd first arrived in Washington. But since the Wheeling speech, McCarthy had gradually devoted almost all his energy and drive to fighting Communism. Now the Senate, by censuring him and then depriving him of his power base on the Government Operations Committee, had in effect told him he was no longer needed. And he didn't know what to do.

Jean tried to cheer up her husband. She assembled his Marine medals and anti-Communist awards and displayed them in a corner of the living room, where he couldn't help but see them. She read aloud articles in the press that praised him and assured him that his reputation was bound to be restored. Joe had begun to talk vaguely of retiring, but Jean, claiming that the country needed him, urged Joe to announce that he planned to run for reelection to the Senate in 1958.

Buoyed by Jean, McCarthy did make a last attempt to assert himself on the anti-Communist issue. In the spring of 1955, President Eisenhower agreed to join the leaders of Britain and France in discussions with the new leaders of the Soviet Union, Khrushchev and Bulganin. This summit conference, as it was called, would take place in June in Geneva, Switzerland. Not much in the way of formal agreement was expected from the meeting. The leaders simply wanted to exchange views and take the measure of one another two years after the death of Stalin.

Joe and some other ultraconservative Republicans bitterly opposed the president's attendance at the conference. They argued that he shouldn't even talk with the Soviet leaders until the Soviet Union had changed its aggressive ways. In an attempt to prevent Eisenhower from going, Joe introduced a resolution in the Senate. It declared that the president would not take part unless the conference agenda included a full discussion of the so-called captive nations of Eastern Europe—Poland, Hungary, Czechoslovakia, and the rest—which the Soviet Union had dominated since World War II. Joe and his cohorts knew that the Soviet Union would never agree to such a discussion. As a result, the conference would inevitably be called off, and President Eisenhower would be embarrassed for ever having agreed to attend it.

McCarthy and his colleagues misread the temper of the times, however. A majority of Americans had gradually changed their view of the cold war. The very real possibility of a nuclear conflict loomed as a far greater threat than subversion, and the need to find ways to prevent such a catastrophe through diplomacy became more urgent. Consequently, most Americans favored exploratory meetings like the Geneva summit.

So did their representatives in government. Even as staunch an anti-Communist as Richard Nixon advised President Eisenhower not to take Joe's resolution seriously. He didn't—and neither did the Senate. When the resolution came up for a vote in that body, it went down to crushing defeat by a vote of 77–4. Afterward, Eisenhower made a remark to associates that was widely quoted in Washington and beyond. "It's no longer McCarthyism," the president said. "It's McCarthywasm."

Joe's self-confidence suffered another severe blow when the media stopped paying attention to him. From his days as a young judge in Wisconsin, he had thrived on publicity. Along the way, he had mastered the art of self-promotion, inflating his wartime record in the South Pacific, manipulating the press at every step in his political rise, and getting front-page coverage for his anti-Communist investigations. Now, suddenly, no one was interested in what he had to say.

Joe began to take part in even fewer Senate sessions. And he began to drink more heavily. By the summer of 1956, his drinking had become so severe that he was forced to enter the Bethesda Naval Hospital for detoxification. Jean covered up for him by telling reporters he was being treated for an old knee injury he had suffered on Guadalcanal.

McCarthy played almost no part in local or national campaigns during the presidential election of 1956. When he sent letters offering his help to all the Republican candidates in Wisconsin who were running that fall, only one candidate responded positively. Joe spoke on his behalf at a tavern-restaurant in the Milwaukee suburb of West Allis before a disappointingly small audience. It was a far cry from the Wisconsin audiences of thousands who had come to applaud Joe during his reelection campaign just two years earlier.

Joe and Jean stopped off in Appleton while they were in Wisconsin. One evening, after a day of steady drinking, McCarthy suffered an attack of delirium tremens, a kind of seizure, at the home of Urban Van Susteren. In front of Jean and his friends, he crouched down on the living-room floor, screaming that he was being surrounded by snakes. Later, after Joe had calmed down, Jean tearfully confided to Van Susteren that her husband was suffering from severe liver damage. She said his doctors had warned him the condition could be fatal if he didn't stop drinking.

Jean had long wanted to have a child, and the McCarthys had been trying to adopt one for several years. Finally, with the help of their friend Francis Cardinal Spellman of New York, they obtained a five-week-old girl from the New York Foundling Hospital in January 1957. They named her Tierney Elizabeth after her two grandmothers: Tierney was Joe's mother's maiden name, and Elizabeth was the name of Jean's mother.

Francis Cardinal Spellman.
The National Archives

Joe was entranced by his baby daughter, and Jean told friends she hoped and prayed his upbeat mood would last. It didn't. By early April, on a visit by himself to Wisconsin, Joe was again drinking heavily. His friend Steve Swedish visited him at his Milwaukee hotel. He looked ill, Swedish said later, and seemed to stagger as he moved about the room. Leaning toward Swedish, he said in a low voice that he was being persecuted by Communists who called him constantly on the phone. "They're murdering me!" Joe said urgently.

Back in Washington, McCarthy was readmitted to Bethesda Naval Hospital on April 28. At first, Jean told reporters his knee had been acting up again. A day later, she said he'd gotten a virus while in Wisconsin, and it had turned into a bad cold. In fact, his liver had begun to fail, but Jean was still trying to cover for him.

On the afternoon of May 2, 1957, McCarthy received the last rites of the Catholic Church from a priest, and that evening at 5:02, with Jean at his side, he died. He was forty-eight years old.

The death certificate gave the cause of death as "hepatitis, acute, cause unknown." *Time* magazine, however, reported that Joe had died of cirrhosis of the liver, a disease known to be brought on by excessive drinking. Jean, intent as always on defending him, insisted that her husband had died of hepatitis, not alcoholism, and ardent McCarthyites followed her lead.

In their obituaries, liberal newspapers like the *New York Times* and the *Washington Post* described Joe as a demagogue—a person who tries to stir up people by appealing to their emotions and prejudices in order to become a leader and achieve his or her own selfish ends. The two papers said that McCarthy had undermined the nation's civil liberties, done irreparable harm to many innocent government employees, and tarnished America's image abroad. Conservative newspapers such as the *Chicago Tribune* assumed a very different stance. In an editorial, the *Tribune* wrote, "The senator was no Communist; hence he was no hero to the 'liberals.'" An ultraconservative newspaper in New Hampshire, the *Manchester Union Leader,* charged that "McCarthy was murdered by the Communists because he was exposing them. . . . The Communist Party realized that if it was to survive and succeed in its conspiracy to seize control of the United States, it had to destroy McCarthy before he destroyed the Party."

In January 1957, McCarthy feeds his adopted daughter, Tierney Elizabeth, while his wife, Jean, looks on. *Marquette University Archives*

After Sen. McCarthy's funeral on May 6, 1957, United States Marines carry
his body from St. Matthew's Roman Catholic Cathedral in Washington, D.C.,
to a waiting hearse. Watching the departure from the bottom of the cathedral
steps is McCarthy's widow, Jean, who holds on to the arm of her late husband's
brother William. *AP/WIDE WORLD PHOTOS*

Reactions of Joe's fellow senators divided along political lines. His longtime friend Karl Mundt said, "His passing takes out of the American political arena a courageous fighter against Communism and a stalwart advocate of our traditional American concepts." His frequent opponent Stuart Symington said only, "I am deeply distressed," and would never discuss McCarthy again.

President and Mrs. Eisenhower offered their "profound sympathy" to Jean. Former Secretary of State Dean Acheson, who had been the subject of many of Joe's fiercest attacks, told the press, "I have no comment at all." Then he used a Latin phrase, *De mortuis nil nisi bonum,* which means "Say nothing about the dead unless it is good."

On May 6, a formal funeral service was held at St. Matthew's Cathedral in Washington, where Joe and Jean had been married four years earlier. In attendance were Vice-President and Mrs. Nixon, Roy Cohn, Senator William Knowland, a White House assistant representing President Eisenhower, and 2,000 other mourners. Another service followed, at Jean's request, in the Senate chamber where McCarthy had delivered so many of his anti-Communist speeches. Jean wept quietly in her seat as one after another of Joe's Senate allies extolled him.

Barry Goldwater inserted his comments into the *Congressional Record.* "Do not mourn Joe McCarthy," Goldwater began. "Be thankful that he lived, at the right time, and according to the talents vested in him by his Maker. Be grateful, too, that when it came his time to die, he passed on with the full assurance that, because he lived, America is a brighter, safer, more vigilant land today."

After the Senate service, McCarthy's remains were flown to Wisconsin, accompanied by Jean. The next day, more than 30,000 people paraded respectfully through St. Mary's Church in Appleton to view the open casket. In late afternoon, the coffin was taken to St. Mary's Cemetery, where Joe was buried beside his parents in a grassy plot overlooking the Fox River. His grave was only seven miles from the farm where he grew up.

EPILOGUE

Another McCarthy?

Today, more than fifty years after his death, Joe McCarthy remains as controversial a figure as he was in life. Ardent believers still think of him as a true American hero who alerted the country to the threat of Communist subversion until he was silenced by evil forces on the left. A greater number recall him as a demagogue who played cynically on the nation's fears of the Soviet Union and nuclear war to keep his name on the front pages of the nation's newspapers.

His most enduring legacy, though, may be the word "McCarthyism," which has found a permanent place in our language. It refers to tactics McCarthy himself used so successfully: guilt by association and unfounded accusations.

The tactics themselves are standard procedure for many politicians, even today. Just as accusations of Communism or association with Communism did in the McCarthy era, accusations of terrorism or terrorist leanings stirred up fear and resentment in the aftermath of 9/11. Claims that a candidate speaks for "real Americans," suggesting that rival candidates do not, or that an opposition candidate has "socialist"—read "Communist"—ideas, have typically been part of recent political campaigns. Anyone familiar with McCarthy's methods can recognize this kind of reckless speechmaking for what it is.

Can another McCarthy appear on the political stage and wreak havoc? It's entirely possible. In any kind of major crisis, people tend to look for someone or something to blame—a simple answer to a complex problem. A would-be leader who claimed to have the answer would probably attract followers, perhaps millions of followers, as McCarthy did.

Thoughtful Americans, however, would probably question and challenge the new leader's simplistic solutions, especially if they conflicted with the Constitution and its Bill of Rights. Eventually, the challengers would expose the new leader's failings and take steps to correct any damage that had been done. It took more than four years to bring Joe to heel—but his opponents ultimately succeeded. And if the new leader's opponents were lucky, the leader's weaknesses, like McCarthy's tendency to act alone rather than build a strong supporting organization, would help their cause.

There's no way to be sure that a dangerous leader will or will not rise up in the future. One thing is certain: Our democratic form of government, with its checks and balances, has survived serious assaults in the past. With luck, and the attentiveness and dedication of its citizens, the nation and the principles on which it relies will continue to prevail.

After McCarthy's Death . . .

JEAN KERR MCCARTHY obtained permission from the Catholic Church to complete the adoption process for her daughter, Tierney Elizabeth, and raise the little girl on her own. In 1961, Jean remarried. Her second husband was G. Joseph Minetti, a conservative Democrat from Brooklyn, New York, who served on the Civil Aeronautics Board in Washington. He, in turn, adopted little Tierney. Also in 1961, Jean donated all of Joe McCarthy's personal papers to the archives of Marquette University, his alma mater. But she placed a severe restriction on them: The papers will "remain closed to all use until 2050." This was probably a last attempt by Jean to protect her first husband's image. Jean McCarthy Minetti died of cancer in 1979.

ROY M. COHN returned to New York City after resigning as counsel to McCarthy's committee, and he built a successful career as an attorney for the rich and powerful. Among his clients were Donald Trump, several Mafia chieftains, and the Catholic Archdiocese of New York. He never worked again with David Schine.

Cohn lived with his widowed mother, Dora, until her death in 1969, when Roy was forty-two. Although he dated several women, including the television journalist Barbara Walters, those close to him knew he was really attracted to men. Cohn never admitted to being homosexual, though, not even after he was diagnosed with the AIDS virus in 1984. Instead, he insisted that he was being treated for liver cancer. Roy Cohn died in 1986 of complications from AIDS; he was fifty-nine.

In 1993, Cohn reappeared as a major character in Tony Kushner's Pulitzer Prize–winning play *Angels in America.* Kushner portrays Joe McCarthy's former associate as an amoral hypocrite who vigorously denies his sexuality to the end of his life. *Angels in America* was made into a television miniseries in 2003. It starred Al Pacino as Roy Cohn and won both a Golden Globe Award and an Emmy.

G. DAVID SCHINE went back to his father's hotel and movie businesses after completing his military service. Then and later, he refused to comment on the Army-McCarthy hearings or his friendship with Roy Cohn.

In 1957, Schine married a former Miss Sweden, Hillevi Rombin, and they eventually had six children. Meanwhile, Schine achieved considerable success in the music and film industries. He was the executive producer of *The French Connection,* the 1971 crime thriller that was nominated for eight Academy Awards, including Best Picture, and won them all.

Schine's life came to a tragic end in 1996 when he, his wife, and their eldest son, Berndt, were killed in the crash of their private plane moments after takeoff from the Burbank, California, airport. David Schine was sixty-eight years old.

JOSEPH N. WELCH, the legal counsel who took on Sen. McCarthy in the Army-McCarthy hearings, became an actor after retiring as a lawyer. In 1959, he was cast as a judge in the film version of the best-selling mystery novel *Anatomy of a Murder.* Welch said he took the part "because it looked like that was the only way I'd get to be a judge." The movie was a huge hit and Welch received a 1959 Golden Globe nomination as best supporting actor for his performance. He died a year later, in 1960, at the age of sixty-nine.

LYNDON B. JOHNSON, who shepherded the censure of McCarthy through the Senate, was John F. Kennedy's choice for vice-president in his winning campaign for the presidency in 1960. Johnson succeeded Kennedy as president following the latter's assassination in November 1963. He ran for reelection in 1964 and won in a landslide over his Republican opponent, Senator Barry Goldwater.

During his presidency, Johnson used his knowledge of the legislative process to push a number of important bills through Congress. Among them were Medicare, Medicaid, and, in the area of civil rights, the Voting Rights Bill of

1965. He lost public support, however, because of his failure to bring the unpopular war in Vietnam to an end.

After deciding not to run for a second full term in 1968, Lyndon Johnson retired to his Texas ranch, where he died in 1973 at the age of sixty-four.

RICHARD M. NIXON, one of Joe McCarthy's earliest supporters, succeeded Lyndon Johnson as president in January 1969. This was a remarkable comeback for Nixon, who had been defeated in his earlier bid for the presidency against the Kennedy-Johnson ticket in 1960.

Ironically, it was Richard Nixon, the arch anti-Communist, who opened the way for renewed diplomatic relations with Communist China when he made a state visit there in the spring of 1972. The success of his China trip played a key role in Nixon's landslide reelection to a second term that fall. He negotiated a cease-fire agreement with Vietnam early in 1973, thereby pointing the way toward the conclusion of the longest war in American history.

Nixon's popularity was at an all-time high in May 1973 when it was threatened by revelations of his involvement in a criminal break-in at Democratic Party offices in the Watergate Hotel during the previous year's election campaign. An investigation of what became known as the Watergate scandal exposed other instances in which Nixon and his staff had engaged in illegal activities, and this led to the president's resignation under pressure in August 1974.

Unlike Joe McCarthy, who sank into depression after his censure, Nixon fought hard to restore his reputation after he left the White House. He largely achieved his goal through the publication of his memoirs and a number of other books, mainly about foreign policy issues. In April 1994, Richard Nixon suffered a stroke, and he died four days later at the age of eighty-one.

Bibliography
and Source Notes

BIBLIOGRAPHY

I HAVE LONG WANTED TO WRITE about Joe McCarthy and the witch-hunts he conducted in the early 1950s, because they coincided with an important period in my own life. I was a junior in high school when McCarthy launched what became his first major anti-Communist campaign with a speech in Wheeling, West Virginia, in February 1950. And I was a senior in college when the Army-McCarthy hearings that effectively ended his career were telecast in their entirety in the spring of 1954.

McCarthy's activities never affected my family or me directly, but they had a significant effect on my college education. I describe that effect in Chapter 18, where I am the college junior whose philosophy professor declines to discuss Marxism, the philosophical basis of Communism, in class for fear of losing his job.

In preparing to write the book, I was confronted by a mountain of research material. Among the books I found most useful was *The Life and Times of Joe McCarthy: A Biography* by Thomas C. Reeves (New York: Stein and Day Publishers, 1982). Published twenty-five years after McCarthy's death, it presents a more balanced view of the man than some of the biographies that were published immediately after his passing. In an attempt to offer a comprehensive portrait of McCarthy, it devotes more space to his formative years in Wisconsin and includes extracts from interviews Reeves conducted with members of McCarthy's family, Wisconsin friends and colleagues, and some of his early political opponents, all of whom were still very much alive when Reeves did his research. I drew extensively on extracts from these interviews for the early chapters of my book.

At the other end of the time spectrum, *Shooting Star: The Brief Arc of Joe McCarthy*, by veteran *New York Times* reporter and columnist Tom Wicker (Orlando, Fla.: Harcourt, 2006), has the advantage of a long perspective. Wicker, as a young reporter in early 1957, had a brief encounter with McCarthy shortly before the latter's death, but his book is written from the viewpoint of an astute observer familiar with the ways of Washington, whose purpose is to evaluate McCarthy and his actions from a distance of almost fifty years. I found his cool, judicial tone a welcome relief from some of the more heated tomes published in the late 1950s. These include *Senator Joe McCarthy* by Richard H. Rovere, a longtime political commentator for *The New Yorker* (New York: Harcourt Brace Jovanovich, 1959). Writing in a fast-paced, journalistic style, Rovere strives to make a strong case against McCarthy, and he does so, but at the expense of a full-scale biographical study. For example, he devotes almost no space to McCarthy's youthful years, his military service during World War II, or his early political career in small-town Wisconsin.

Other books helped me to see McCarthy in a broader context. Ted Morgan in *Reds: McCarthyism in Twentieth-Century America* (New York: Random House, 2003) begins his narrative with the Russian Revolution of 1917 as seen through the sometimes panicked eyes of American observers, and ends the chronicle with the buildup to the Iraq War in 2002–3. In the middle of the book, Morgan presents a condensed but accurate account of the key role Joe McCarthy played in America's response to what was sometimes called the "Red Menace."

For an intriguing left-wing view of McCarthy and his times, the British journalist Cedric Belfrage's *The American Inquisition, 1945–1960: A Profile of the McCarthy Era* (Indianapolis: Bobbs-Merrill, 1973) is worth examining. You may not agree with Belfrage's conclusions, but chances are you'll be stimulated by his lively writing style.

Another book worth reading for its different take on one of Joe McCarthy's most famous, or infamous, hearings is *Ordeal by Slander* by the subject of that hearing, Owen Lattimore (New York: Carroll & Graf Publishers, 2004). This is a paperback reprint of the hardcover edition, published in 1950, written in the immediate aftermath of the hearing and rushed into print two months later. Lattimore's book not only presents a spirited self-defense but also offers advice to other Americans who might find themselves facing similar charges of being disloyal to their country.

Yet another illuminating book about the period is *The Age of McCarthyism: A Brief History with Documents* by Ellen Schrecker (2nd ed., New York: Palgrave, 2002). Especially valuable is the compilation of key documents that composes more than half of the book. Among them is a large section of Joe McCarthy's 1950 Wheeling, West Virginia, talk that launched what would become his anti-Communist crusade.

Along with books about McCarthy and his investigations, I read a number of books about the other Senate and House investigative committees that competed for attention with Joe's. *Washington Gone Crazy: Senator Pat McCarran and the Great American Communist Hunt,* by Michael J. Ybarra (Hanover, N.H.: Steerforth Press, 2004), portrays the workings of the Senate Internal Security Subcommittee chaired by Senator Pat McCarran, archconservative Democrat from Nevada. The subcommittee's 1952 investigation of alleged Communist influence in the United Nations led to the dismissal of many capable and experienced staff members.

I also read several books and articles about the House Un-American Activities Committee and its numerous hearings into the supposed Communist infiltration of the entertainment industry. One book, *Red Star over Hollywood: The Film Colony's Long Romance with the Left,* by Ronald and Allis Radosh (San Francisco: Encounter Books, 2005), admits that many innocent actors, directors, and writers had their careers destroyed by the HUAC-fostered blacklists that deprived them of their livelihoods. But the Radoshes insist that HUAC still provided a useful service by exposing the hard-core Communists who attempted to inject Communist propaganda into the movies they acted in, wrote, and directed in the 1930s, 1940s, and early 1950s.

Taking the opposite view, Victor S. Navasky, in his National Book Award–winning book *Naming Names* (New York: The Viking Press, 1980), sees little if anything of value emerging from the HUAC hearings. He questions the motives of the committee members and believes the employment blacklists they inspired did great harm not only to those who were named as Communists by their former friends and colleagues, but also to the often conflicted witnesses who did the naming.

In 2006, I was fortunate to attend a debate between Ronald Radosh and Victor Navasky before a New York audience that obviously included many aging veterans of the HUAC hearings. It was equally apparent that few of those present had forgiven the men and women who, they believed, had given their names to the committee more than fifty years earlier. One elderly gentleman in a wheelchair shouted, "How can I ever forgive the bastard who told lies about me to save his own wretched skin?"

Finally, a play and a documentary film offer their own distinct insights into the anti-Communist investigations of the late 1940s and early 1950s.

The play is *Are You Now or Have You Ever Been?*, Eric Bentley's skillful compilation of some of the most significant HUAC hearings into the purported Communist activities of such Hollywood and Broadway celebrities as playwright Lillian Hellman, dancer-choreographer Jerome Robbins, movie and stage director Elia Kazan, and African American singer-actor Paul Robeson. (It is one of three plays by Bentley contained in the book *Rallying Cries,* Washington: New Republic Book Company, 1977.) The script can be performed as a staged reading, which makes it a good choice for a student cast.

Last but far from least, there is Emile de Antonio's critically acclaimed documentary record of the Army-McCarthy hearings, *Point of Order* (issued as a DVD in 2005 by New Yorker Video). Tightly edited from kinescopes (the predecessors of videos) of the hearings, this ninety-seven-minute 1964 movie climaxes with the dramatic exchange between Joe McCarthy and Joseph Welch after McCarthy exposed Welch's young legal associate, Fred Fisher, as a onetime leftist. Watching McCarthy's performance today, it's easy to see why the original television audience turned so decisively against him.

Source Notes

(A note about the notes: In my research, you'll see that I made extensive use of the Internet, especially Wikipedia. But I accompanied it with parallel research in the *Columbia Encyclopedia* because I still put more faith in a traditionally edited and cross-checked encyclopedia than in what may be a more loosely assembled Internet source.)

Chapter 1. Background information on Joe McCarthy's boyhood and young adult years: Reeves, *The Life and Times of Joe McCarthy*. Quotations of Leo D. Hershberger, Joe's sisters and brothers, and others: from interviews conducted by Reeves.

Chapter 2. Information about McCarthy's college years at Marquette University: Reeves. Quotations of Charles Hanratty: his interviews with Reeves. Background information on the Great Depression in the United States and the rise of the Soviet Union in the 1920s and early 1930s: Wikipedia, the *Columbia Encyclopedia,* and the author's extensive reading on both topics.

Chapter 3. Information on Joe's experiences as a young lawyer: Reeves. Joe's discussions with Mike G. Eberlein and quotations of Eberlein and his secretary May Voy: Reeves's interview with Mrs. Allen Voy, October 25, 1976. Joe's unsuccessful campaign for district attorney of Shawano County: Reeves. Background information on the Spanish Civil War: Wikipedia, the *Columbia Encyclopedia,* and *The Spanish Civil War* by Hugh Thomas (New York: Harper & Row Publishers, 1961). Information on the situation in China in the 1930s, with the Nationalists battling the Communists and both of them struggling against the invading Japanese: Wikipedia, the *Columbia Encyclopedia,* and *Red Star over China* by Edgar Snow (New York: Random House, 1938).

Chapter 4. Quotes of Urban Van Susteren and Louis Cattau about Joe's use of the age factor in his campaign for district judge against Edgar V. Werner: From interviews

Van Susteren and Cattau had with Reeves in 1975 and 1976. Excerpts from Joe's 1939 speech urging Americans to stay out of the impending European war: news story in the *Appleton Post-Crescent*, as reported by Reeves. Buildup to World War II, the signing of a nonaggression pact between the Soviet Union and Hitler's Germany, and Germany's invasion of Poland in September 1939: Wikipedia, the *Columbia Encyclopedia,* and *World War II* by C. L. Sulzberger (New York: American Heritage Press,1985). McCarthy's speedy working style as a judge and his decision to enlist in the Marines after Pearl Harbor: from interviews conducted by Reeves with Urban Van Susteren, Charles Hanratty, and others. Main events in World War II in the summer of 1942: Sulzberger, *World War II.*

Chapter 5. McCarthy's Marine Corps experiences, including his initiation at sea during which he suffered his only wartime injury; the supposed citation for devotion to duty signed by Admiral Chester Nimitz; and Joe's brief service as a tail gunner on combat missions: Reeves, bolstered by quotes from Marines who served with Joe, subsequently interviewed by Reeves. Joe's unsuccessful primary campaign for the U.S. Senate while still in uniform and his subsequent (and successful) reelection campaign for his judgeship: Reeves.

Chapter 6. Events in the European war in the first half of 1945; the Yalta Conference; the death of President Roosevelt; the suicide of Adolf Hitler and the end of fighting in Europe; the Potsdam Conference; the situation in the ongoing war against Japan; America's development of the atomic bomb; the dropping of the bomb on Hiroshima and Nagasaki; the Soviet Union's entry into the Pacific war; and Japan's surrender: Wikipedia entries, the *Columbia Encyclopedia,* and Sulzberger, *World War II.* Joe's plans for his 1946 senatorial campaign: Reeves. Background on the La Follette family, and Joe's main opponent for the Republican nomination, Senator Robert M. La Follette, Jr.: Reeves, Wikipedia, and the *Columbia Encyclopedia.*

Chapter 7. How McCarthy got rid of two Republican rivals for the nomination and won the endorsement of political boss Tom Coleman: Reeves, abetted by interviews with Loyal Eddy and Urban Van Susteren. McCarthy's nonstop primary campaign across Wisconsin by car and plane: Reeves, enhanced by interviews with Ray Kiermas, a new friend of Joe's. La Follette, leading in the polls, refuses to debate McCarthy: Reeves, citing news stories in the *Milwaukee Journal.* McCarthy's upset victory over La Follette in the Republican primary: Reeves, including quotes from interviews with Loyal Eddy and Tom Coleman.

Chapter 8. Debate exchange between McCarthy and his Democratic opponent, Howard McMurray, in which Joe accuses McMurray of being disloyal: *Milwaukee Journal,* October 17, 1946, as reported by Reeves. McCarthy's living arrangements in Washington with Ray Kiermas and his family: Reeves's interviews with Kiermas and article "The Private Life of Senator McCarthy" by Eleanor Harris in the *American Weekly,* August 16, 1953. McCarthy's opposition to David Lilienthal's nomination to be chairman of the Atomic Energy Commission: Reeves. Additional information on Lilienthal: Wikipedia, the *Columbia Encyclopedia.*

Chapter 9. Information on the investigation by the House Un-American Activities Committee of suspected Communists at work in Hollywood: Wikipedia entries; the *Columbia Encyclopedia;* Navasky, *Naming Names;* and Radosh, *Red Star over Hollywood.* The postwar housing problem in the U.S.: Reeves. Joe's sponsorship of and participation in a committee to survey the entire housing situation, and his ensuing clash with "Mr. Republican," Senator Robert Taft of Ohio: Reeves. McCarthy's first meeting with Jean Kerr, who would soon become his chief research assistant: Reeves. Article credited to Joe that appeared in a paperback book on the housing crisis, *How to Own Your Own Home,* published by the Lustron Corporation: Reeves. McCarthy's involvement in the Malmédy case, in which German prisoners of war claimed they had been tortured by their American captors: Reeves; also Wicker, *Shooting Star.* How the Malmédy investigation was overshadowed first by the Soviet Union's test of its own atomic bomb, in August 1949, and then by the final victory of the Chinese Communists over their Nationalist adversaries in October 1949: Reeves, Wikipedia articles, and entries in the *Columbia Encyclopedia.*

Chapter 10. McCarthy's charge that the city editor of the *Madison Capital Times,* Cedric Parker, is a Communist: Reeves. Background information on Alger Hiss and the Hiss case: Wikipedia, the *Columbia Encyclopedia,* and Reeves. President Truman's plans to develop a hydrogen bomb, and the arrest of German atomic scientist Klaus Fuchs as a Soviet spy: Wikipedia, the *Columbia Encyclopedia,* and Reeves. Joe's Wheeling, West Virginia, speech, in which he claimed there were 205 Communists at work in the State Department: Reeves, Wicker. Joe's contradictory comments on the number of Communist employees in subsequent talks given in Reno and Las Vegas, Nevada, and Huron, South Dakota: Reeves, Wicker.

Chapter 11. Account of Joe's speech to Congress, in which he tries to explain the shifting numbers of Communists he claimed were at work in the State Department: Reeves,

Wicker. Democrats demand a full investigation of McCarthy's charges, and Republicans rally around Joe, not wanting him to be exposed: Reeves, Wicker. Charges against, and testimony of, New York lawyer Dorothy Kenyon: Reeves, Wicker. Maneuvering between McCarthy and the Democratic chairman of the investigating subcommittee, Millard Tydings: Reeves, Wicker, Wikipedia, and *Columbia Encyclopedia* entries on Senator Tydings.

Chapter 12. Joe's claim that China expert Owen Lattimore is the "top Soviet agent" in the U.S.: Reeves, Wicker, Wikipedia article on Lattimore. Controversy over whether President Truman should order the release of FBI loyalty files regarding Lattimore and others charged by McCarthy: Reeves. McCarthy's lengthy Senate speech denouncing Lattimore: Reeves, the *Congressional Record*. Lattimore's quote that McCarthy couldn't look him "straight in the eye": Lattimore, *Ordeal by Slander*. Lattimore's strong denial of the espionage charge: Reeves, *Ordeal by Slander*. McCarthy's witnesses against Lattimore fail to prove that he was, or is, a Communist agent: Reeves, *Ordeal by Slander*. Despite the lack of evidence, a majority of Americans tell pollsters they believe McCarthy's charges: Reeves. To aid Democrats, President Truman agrees to partial release of the FBI and State Department files on Lattimore: Reeves, *Ordeal by Slander,* Wicker.

Chapter 13. Senate subcommittee members examine files on Lattimore, find nothing to support McCarthy's charges; McCarthy claims the files have been altered—"raped," as he puts it: Reeves. Tydings committee shifts its focus to John Stewart Service, another State Department China expert whom McCarthy accuses of being disloyal: Reeves, Wikipedia article on Service, the *Columbia Encyclopedia*. Service impresses senators when he testifies before subcommittee, but not Joe: Reeves. Excerpt from McCarthy's Wisconsin speech in which he continues to attack Service: the *Ashland* [Wisconsin] *Daily Press,* August 1, 1950. Senator Margaret Chase Smith, Republican of Maine, gives a Senate speech, "A Declaration of Conscience," in which she indirectly criticizes McCarthy for making unwarranted charges against people without supporting evidence: Reeves, Wikipedia biography of Smith, Smith's website. McCarthy's sneering response: the *New York Times,* June 3, 1950, as reported by Reeves. North Korea invades South Korea on June 25, 1950, marking the start of what became the Korean War: Reeves, Wikipedia article, the *Columbia Encyclopedia*. Background to the conflict: Reeves, Wicker, Wikipedia, the *Columbia Encyclopedia*. President Truman's response to the outbreak of war: Reeves, Wicker. Joe's attack on the president and Secretary of State Dean Acheson for not being prepared for the war: Reeves, Wicker.

Chapter 14. Tydings committee's final report absolving Kenyon, Lattimore, Service, and others of McCarthy's charges against them is issued on July 17, 1950; McCarthy predictably denounces its findings as a "whitewash": Reeves, Wicker. Anecdote about Jean Kerr and an FBI agent's attractive young wife who caught McCarthy's eye: Wicker. McCarthy's efforts to get revenge on Millard Tydings by undermining the latter's reelection campaign, and Tydings's bitter reaction when he is defeated: Reeves, Wicker. Back-and-forth developments in the Korean War in the fall and winter of 1950-51: Reeves, Wicker, Wikipedia articles. McCarthy and other conservatives criticize Truman for what they see as his weak leadership: Reeves. General Douglas MacArthur seeks authorization to carry the fight on into Communist China, and to use tactical nuclear weapons if necessary, but Truman rejects the general's proposals: Reeves. MacArthur lets it be known he strongly disagrees with the president's policies, leaving Truman no option except to fire him for disobedience: Reeves, Wicker. McCarthy joins other right-wingers in protesting the general's firing, calling him "the greatest American I know," but Truman stands by his guns: Reeves, Wicker, Wikipedia articles on the progress of the Korean War.

Chapter 15. Background material on General George Marshall's life and military career: Wikipedia articles, the *Columbia Encyclopedia*. Excerpts from McCarthy's Senate speech denouncing Marshall: the *Congressional Record*, June 14, 1951. Congress attempts to rein in McCarthy via a subcommittee investigation of unfair tactics he allegedly employed during Senator Tydings's 1950 reelection campaign, but final report contains no specific charges against McCarthy: Reeves, Wicker. Focus shifts to the upcoming 1952 elections, in which McCarthy is up for reelection and a new president will be chosen. McCarthy starts out backing General MacArthur for president, but switches his allegiance to General Dwight Eisenhower when Republican delegates turn in Ike's direction: Reeves, Wicker. McCarthy's health isn't good, and he begins to drink more heavily: Reeves. Joe sounds enthusiastic about Eisenhower's eventual nomination, but there are deep differences between the two men: Reeves, Wicker.

Chapter 16. Joe's surgeries: Reeves. Backing for Joe from right-wing commentators and John Wayne: Reeves. Joe's successful attempt to get Eisenhower to delete support for General Marshall from his Milwaukee speech: Reeves, Wicker, *The Ordeal of Power: A Political Memoir of the Eisenhower Years,* by Emmet John Hughes (New York: Atheneum, 1963).

Chapter 17. Joe's refusal to campaign for Henry Cabot Lodge and against John F. Kennedy in Massachusetts: Reeves, Wicker. In wake of Eisenhower's decisive victory, and his own, Joe chooses to head the Senate Committee on Government Operations and its Permanent Subcommittee on Investigations, saying these positions will give him the most power: Reeves, Wicker. McCarthy plans new investigations of the Federal Communications Commission and Communist professors in the nation's colleges: Reeves, Wicker. Joe hires Roy Cohn to be his chief counsel: Reeves, Wicker, and Wikipedia and *Columbia Encyclopedia* biographies of Cohn. The trial of Julius and Ethel Rosenberg for espionage and Roy Cohn's role in it: Reeves, Wicker, and Wikipedia and *Columbia Encyclopedia* articles about the Rosenbergs. Hiring of G. David Schine as a "consultant" to the committee: Reeves, Wicker, and Wikipedia and *Columbia Encyclopedia* articles on Schine.

Chapter 18. Controversy over Charles Bohlen's nomination to be ambassador to the Soviet Union: Reeves, Wicker, and Wikipedia and *Columbia Encyclopedia* entries on Bohlen and the cold war. Case of philosophy professor at Western Reserve University who was reluctant to discuss Marx and Marxism in class: the author's experience in 1953. Roy Cohn and David Schine's trip to Europe in search of books by Communist writers in American-sponsored libraries: Reeves, Wicker.

Chapter 19. Speculation about Joe's political ambitions: Reeves, Wicker. Opposition by the president to Joe's announcement that he plans to investigate the CIA: Reeves, Wicker. Reactions to the distressing news that the Soviet Union has tested a hydrogen bomb, which the U.S. had successfully tested just nine months earlier: Reeves, Wicker, and Wikipedia and *Columbia Encyclopedia* accounts of nuclear weapons developments in the early 1950s. Testimony of General Richard C. Partridge: the *Congressional Record*. Joe's marriage to Jean Kerr: Reeves, Wicker.

Chapter 20. McCarthy's investigation into allegedly subversive activities of civilian employees at the Army's radar laboratories at Fort Monmouth, New Jersey: Reeves, Wicker. McCarthy expands investigation to General Electric plant in Schenectady, New York: Reeves. Roy Cohn's attempts to win special privileges for David Schine after Schine is drafted into the Army: Reeves, Wicker. Accusations against Army dentist Irving Peress: Reeves, Wicker.

Chapter 21. Exchanges between McCarthy and General Ralph Zwicker: *Communist Infiltration in the Army,* record of February 1954 hearings, as excerpted by Reeves. Background of Annie Lee Moss: Reeves, Wicker, Wikipedia, the *Columbia Encyclopedia*. Quotes of President Eisenhower regarding McCarthy's Army investigations and the Senator's long-term ambitions: unpublished diaries of Press Secretary Jim Hagerty, as excerpted by Reeves.

Chapter 22. Quotes of Army Secretary Stevens and Press Secretary Hagerty at news conference: Hagerty's unpublished diaries, as excerpted by Reeves. Senator Ralph Flanders's speech attacking McCarthy: the *Congressional Record,* March 9, 1954. Background of Edward R. Murrow: Reeves, Wicker, Wikipedia, the *Columbia Encyclopedia.* Murrow's TV report on McCarthy: Reeves, Wicker. Murrow's earlier report on McCarthy's role in the case of Milo Radulovich: Reeves, Wicker, memoir of Murrow's TV associate Joe Wershba.

Chapter 23. Confronted by Army report of Cohn's attempts to get special treatment for Schine, McCarthy refuses to fire Cohn: Roy Cohn, *McCarthy* (New York: New American Library, 1968). Annie Lee Moss returns as a witness before McCarthy's subcommittee and wins sympathy of Democratic members: Reeves, Wikipedia, the *Columbia Encyclopedia.* McCarthy's subcommittee decides to hold full inquiry into Army-McCarthy dispute: the *New York Times,* March 17, 1954. Decline in McCarthy's favorability ratings: Gallup Poll, March 21, 1954. Army appoints Boston lawyer Joseph N. Welch to be its special legal counsel in the Army-McCarthy hearings: the *New York Times,* April 3, 1954.

Chapter 24. Joseph Welch's impression of the Senate caucus room: the *New York Times,* April 23, 1954. Joe's first "point of order": Cohn, *McCarthy.* Secretary of the Army Stevens's testimony on April 24 and the days that followed: U.S. Senate, *Special Senate Investigation on Charges and Countercharges Involving Secretary of the Army Robert T. Stevens, [et al.], and Senator Joe McCarthy, Roy Cohn, and Francis P. Carr.* 83rd Cong., 2nd sess., 1954 (hereafter referred to as *Army-McCarthy Hearings*). Disputed photograph of Schine and Secretary Stevens: Reeves, *Army-McCarthy Hearings.* Conservative Republicans eager for hearings to end: Reeves, *Army-McCarthy Hearings.* McCarthy introduces as evidence a spurious 1951 letter from J. Edgar Hoover to an Army general, warning of security problems at top-secret Signal Corps laboratories at Fort Monmouth, New Jersey: Reeves, *Army-McCarthy Hearings.* Joe's schedule during the hearings: *Time* magazine, May 3, 1954. Mark Catlin's impressions of McCarthy: Reeves interview with Catlin.

Chapter 25. Testimony of Army Counsel John G. Adams: Reeves. Wicker, *Army-McCarthy Hearings.* Army rests its case on May 26, 1954: Reeves, Wicker, *Army-McCarthy Hearings.* Testimony of Roy Cohn, and Joseph Welch's cross-examination: Reeves, *Army-McCarthy Hearings.* Joe attempts to gain an advantage in the hearings by raising the issue of Welch's legal colleague, Fred Fisher, who was briefly a member of a left-wing lawyers' organization: Reeves, Wicker, *Army-McCarthy Hearings.* Welch defends Fisher and ends by asking Joe, "Have you no sense of decency, sir?" Reeves, Wicker, *Army-McCarthy Hearings.*

Chapter 26. Negative reaction to Joe's confrontation with Welch: *Madison Capital Times,* June 11, 1954, *Washington Star,* June 10, 1954, as cited by Reeves. Joe's faltering performance on the witness stand: *Army-McCarthy Hearings,* as excerpted by Reeves. Hearings come to an end on June 17; meanwhile, Senator Ralph Flanders on June 11 introduces resolution in the Senate to censure McCarthy: the *Congressional Record,* 83rd Cong., 2nd sess., June 15, 1954, Reeves, Wicker. Roy Cohn resigns as Joe's legal counsel: the *New York Times,* July 21, 1954, Reeves, Wicker. Committee formed to decide on censure charges against Joe: Reeves, Wicker. Censure proceedings begin on August 31, 1954, under the chairmanship of Senator Arthur Watkins: *Watkins Committee Hearings,* as excerpted by Reeves and Wicker. Debate resumes on November 8 after a break for the midterm elections: Reeves, Wicker. On November 9, McCarthy releases text of speech in which he charges Communists are behind censure attempt: the *New York Times,* November 10, 1954, Reeves, Wicker. Supporters organize rallies in defense of Joe and present him with awards: the *New York Times,* November 12, 1954, Reeves. Senate votes to "condemn" Joe on two counts: the *New York Times,* December 3 and 4, 1954, Reeves, Wicker.

Chapter 27. Joe's despairing mood after the censure: Cohn, *McCarthy,* as excerpted by Reeves. President Eisenhower congratulates Senator Watkins for doing "a very splendid job" of chairing the censure committee, Joe responds by breaking openly with the president: the *New York Times,* September 5, 1954, as recounted by Reeves. Joe no longer welcome at the White House: *Madison Capital Times,* January 20, 1955, as excerpted by Reeves, Wicker. Joe's resolution in the Senate to block President Eisenhower's participation in a July 1955 meeting with new Soviet leaders in Switzerland is soundly defeated: the *New York Times,* June 17–23, 1955, as recounted by Reeves and Wicker. Press starts to ignore McCarthy: Cohn, *McCarthy,* as excerpted by Reeves. By the late summer of 1956, Joe's alcoholism requires frequent hospital detoxification: *Milwaukee Sentinel,* September 5, 1956, as recounted by Reeves. Joe suffers attack of delirium tremens during a gathering at home of Urban Van Susteren: Reeves's 1977 interviews with Van Susteren. The McCarthys adopt a baby girl in January 1957: Cohn, *McCarthy,* Reeves, Wicker. Joe dies in Bethesda Naval Hospital, May 2, 1957: *Milwaukee Journal,* May 3, 1957, as excerpted by Reeves. Formal funeral service held in Washington's St. Matthew's Cathedral on May 6, followed by a second service in the Senate chamber and burial in Appleton, Wisconsin: *Appleton Post-Crescent,* May 6, 7, and 8, 1967, as recounted by Reeves, Wicker.

After McCarthy's Death

Jean Kerr McCarthy: Her second marriage, to G. Joseph Minetti: *Time* magazine, September 15, 1961. Mrs. Minetti's restrictions on the use of Senator McCarthy's personal papers: fact sheet from the Marquette University Archives.

Roy Cohn. Cohn's later life and death from AIDS: Nicholas von Hoffman, "The Snarling Death of Roy M. Cohn," article in *Vanity Fair* magazine, March 1988; Wikipedia biographical entry. Information on Tony Kushner's Pulitzer Prize–winning play *Angels in America: A Gay Fantasia on National Themes:* Wikipedia. The play itself: New York: Theatre Communications Group, 1993–94.

G. David Schine. Life after the Army-McCarthy hearings and death with wife and eldest son in the crash of the family's private plane: Wikipedia.

Joseph N. Welch. Biographical entry and quote about his decision to play a role in the film *Anatomy of a Murder:* Wikipedia.

Lyndon B. Johnson. Life, career, and death: Wikipedia and the *Columbia Encyclopedia.*

Richard M. Nixon. Life, career, and death: Wikipedia and the *Columbia Encyclopedia.*

Index

Page numbers in *italics* refer to photos and illustrations.

Abraham Lincoln Brigade, *17,* 18, 92

Acheson, Dean, *82;* and Bohlen, 160; and Korea, 111–12, 113; McCarthy's claims against, 96, 113, 123; on McCarthy's death, 265; refusal to release State Dept. files, 83–84, 89; Stimson's support for, 96

Adams, John G.: Army-McCarthy hearings, 222, 230, 232–33, 234; and Cohn influence on Schine military service, 185, 212, 213; Peress investigation, 187

Adams, Sherman, 144, 145, 176, 185, 196, 233

Aluminum Company of America (Alcoa), 204, 207

American Civil Liberties Union, 94

American Coalition, 251–52

American Legion Post, *250*

Americans for Democratic Action, 94

anti-Semitism, 172, 180

Appleton, Wisc., 24, 25, 37, 38, 144, 261, 265

Aschenbrenner, Ed, 16

atomic bombs, 41–42, 73, 78, 154. *See also* hydrogen bombs; nuclear weapons

Atomic Energy Commission, 62, 63, 173

Austria, 22

Baarslag, Karl H., 167

Baldwin, Sen. Raymond E., 72, 73

Beall, J. Glenn, 147

Belgium, 71

Bennett, Sen. Wallace, 255, 256

Benton, Sen. William F., 130–31, 140, 148, 149

Bessie, Alvah, 64

bibliography, 271–74

blacklists, 66, 163

Blau, Fred, 56

Bohlen, Charles E., *159,* 159–63, 250

book burning, 165

Bradley, Col. David, 223–24

Bridges, Sen. Styles, 90

Browder, Earl, 117

Brownell, Herbert, 181, 233, 236

Buckley, William F., Jr., 148

Budenz, Louis F., 103–4

Bulganin, Nikolai, Prem., 250, 260

Bundy, William P., 170

Bush, Dr. Vannevar, 78

Butler, John Marshall, 116–19

Byrnes, James F., 81, 83

Camp Lejeune, N.C., 29

career. *See* political career of McCarthy; political fall of McCarthy

Carr, Francis, 212, 215, 222, 223, 229, 230, 242

cartoons, political, *viii,* ix, *59,* 99, *140, 171, 227*

Catholic War Veterans, 251, *252*

Catlin, Mark, 230

Cattau, Louis, 16

censorship and library policy, 165, 167–68

censure, 244–57, 258

Central Intelligence Agency (CIA), 122, 170–72, *171*

Chamberlain, P. M. Neville, 22

Chambers, Whittaker, 77

Chennault, Anna, 75

Chennault, Lt. Gen. Claire, 75

Chiang Kai-shek, Pres., 18, 27, 73–75, 77, 103, 106–7

China: civil war, 74–75; communism, 18, 106 (*see also* People's Republic of China); Gen. Marshall and U.S. foreign relations, 127, 128–29; invasion and control by Japan, 18, 27, 39–40; invasion by the Soviet Union, 41; Lattimore and U.S. foreign relations, 100, 101; Nixon diplomatic visits, 270; Service and U.S. foreign relations, 106–7

China Lobby, 75, 102

Churchill, P. M. Winston, 39, 40, 41, 46, 56, 126

Clay, Gen. Lucius D., 71

Cohn, Albert, 153

Cohn, Roy Marcus: after McCarthy's death, 268–69; and the Army-McCarthy hearings, 214–17, 220–42, *231, 239;* background, 153; as character in *Angels in America,* 269; GE investigation, 180; Govt. Operations Comm., *155,* 155–57, *156,* 165–68, 176, 177, *178,* 179; and the McCarthy censure hearings, 256; at McCarthy's

funeral, 265; military draft issues, 181, 238; and the Moss investigation, 210, 211; resignation, 230, 244; Rosenberg trial, 154–55; and Schine's military service, 181–82, 185, 186, 208–9, 211–13; Voice of America investigation, 165–68, *166, 172*

Coleman, Thomas E., 42–43, 44–45, 47–48, 50, 230

Collier, Robert, 228, 229

communism: China, 18 (*see also* People's Republic of China); Communist Party U.S.A., 12, 60, 83; *Daily Worker,* 56, 92, 103; decline in the U.S. during WWII, 12; Eisenhower rhetoric against, 145; "Fifth Amendment Communists," 179, 180, 185, 200; "if it looks like a duck," 205; McCarthy rhetoric against, 57, 76, 77, 216, 251; perceived as a threat, 60, 63, 76–78; Republican Party rhetoric against, 147–48; rise in the U.S. during the Depression, 12; as a Senate election issue, 56–57; Soviet Union and the cold war, 60, 71, 211, 250, 251, 260; VOKS student exchange, 205; Wisconsin Communist Party, 44, 56; Young Communist League, 153

Congressional Record, 255, 265

Connally, Sen. Thomas T., 89, 100, 102

constitutional rights. *See* U.S. Constitution

Corry, Patricia, 58

Czechoslovakia, 22, 39

"Declaration of Conscience," 109–11

demilitarized zone (DMZ), 150, 181

Democratic Party, 56, 170, 182–83, 258

Dewey, Gov. Thomas E., 68

Dirksen, Sen. Everett: and the Army investigation, 192; Army-McCarthy hearings, 226, 231, 232, 233; McCarthy censure hearing, 249, 255–56;

opposition to "taking the Fifth," 179
Dmytryk, Edward, 64
Douglas, Helen Gahagan, 119
Driscoll, Mary, 237
Dulles, Allen, 171, 176
Dulles, John Foster, 151, 161

Eberlein, Michael G., 15, 16, 19, 20
Eddy, Loyal, 42, 44, 46, 47, 53
Einstein, Dr. Albert, 78
Eisenhower, Pres. Dwight D. "Ike": and
    the Army-McCarthy hearings, 231,
    233, 235–36; background, 132; and the
    CIA investigation, 170; employment
    and the Fifth Amendment, 179; and
    Gen. Zwicker testimony, 188, 200; as
    general during WWII, 39, 126, 132,
    133; on McCarthy's death, 265; more
    stringent hiring policy, 168; opposition
    to McCarthy, 135–36, 142, 143, 196,
    198, 214, 217, 226, 260–61; political
    cartoon, viii, ix; power struggle with
    McCarthy, viii, ix, 135–36, 142–45,
    168, 185, 200–201, 213–15, 214,
    258–59; pres. campaign 1952, 132–33,
    134, 135–36, 136, 142–45, 148–49;
    presidency, 150, 160; summit conf.
    with Soviet Union, 260; support for
    Bohlen, 161, 162–63; support for
    Marshall, 135, 142–43, 145; support for
    Watkins, 258; trip to Korea, 150; and
    the Voice of America investigation, 168
Ellender, Sen. Allan J., 158–59
Ellis, Lt. Col. Burton F., 72
England, 18, 22, 23, 202
espionage: Fuchs investigation, 78–79;
    and govt. employees, 60, 235–36, 245,
    247, 249; Hiss investigation, 77–78;
    McCarthy's accusations, 96–104, 107–
    8, 114–15, 177–80, 181; Rosenberg
    trial, 153–55, 154, 173, 177

Evjue, William T., 139

Fairchild, Sen. Thomas, 140, 141, 147, 149
fall from favor. See political fall of
    McCarthy
Federal Bureau of Investigation (FBI):
    Bohlen file, 161, 162; leaking
    information to McCarthy, 91; letter
    presented during Army-McCarthy
    hearing, 227, 227–28, 235; Lilienthal
    file, 63; list of disloyal organizations,
    61; Moss file, 192, 193; role in
    background investigations, 60, 83
Federal Communications Commission
    (FCC), 151
Ferguson, Sen. Homer, 234
film industry: Anatomy of a Murder, 269;
    The French Connection, 269; HUAC
    investigation, 64–66, 65; support for
    McCarthy 1952, 139
Fisher, Frederick G., Jr., 219, 238–40, 241
Flanagan, Francis, 153
Flanders, Sen. Ralph E., 60, 162, 201–2,
    207, 243, 243–45, 245, 251
Fort Monmouth Radar Laboratory, 176,
    177–80, 178, 207, 227–29
Foster, William Z., 60
France, 18, 22, 23, 39, 126
Franco, Gen. Francisco, 17, 23
Freedom House, 169–70
Friendly, Fred, 204, 206
Fuchs, Dr. Klaus, 78–79
Fulbright, Sen. J. William, 245, 248, 251,
    256

General Electric Company (GE), 180–81
Genghis Kahn, 125
George, Sen. Walter, 247
Germany: Marshall Plan, 128; occupation
    of France, 39, 126; occupation of
    Poland, 22, 23; occupation of the Soviet

Germany *(cont.)*
    Union, 27; Potsdam Declaration, 40;
    and the Spanish Civil War, 17; WWII,
    17, 22–23, 26, 27, 39, 40, 70–73, 126,
    202
Giblin, James Cross, 271
Gillette, Sen. Guy M., 131, 134, 141, 244,
    247
Goldwater, Sen. Barry, 252, 255–56, 265,
    269
Grand Chute, Wisc., *x*, 1, 25
Great Depression, 7, *11*, 11–12, 14, 17, 18
Green, Sen. Theodore F., 99, 120
Greenglass, David, 153, 154
Gromyko, Andrei A., *159*
Guadalcanal Island, 29, 31
guilt: by association, 61, 77, 204, 266; by
    "taking the Fifth," 65, 179, 180, 183, 185

Hagerty, Jim, 196, 197, 235, 259
Hall, Leonard, 201, 259
Hanratty, Charles, 10, 12
Hayden, Sen. Carl, 141, 150
health problems of McCarthy: broken
    foot, 30–31; bursitis, 255; drinking
    heavily, 134, 220, 230, 259, 261, 262;
    fatigue and laryngitis, 216; herniated
    diaphragm, 137; sinusitis, 2, 8, 100,
    134, 249
Hearst, William Randolph, 92, 135, 139,
    246
Hendrickson, Sen. Robert C., 249
Hennings, Sen. Thomas, 141, 150, 244, 247
Herblock (Herbert Block), *59*, 99, *227*
Hershberger, Leo D., 4, 7
Hickenlooper, Sen. Bourke, 77, 94, 98,
    103, 106, 114
Hirohito, Emperor of Japan, 42
Hiss, Alger, 77–78, *78*, 96, 138, 139
Hitler, Adolf, 17, 22, 27, 40, 170, 235
"Hollywood Ten," 64–66

homosexuality, 168, 176, 212, 225, 268–69
Hoover, J. Edgar, *90*; anti-communist
    warnings, 76; and the Army-McCarthy
    hearings, 228, 229, 235; and Bohlen,
    162; and Kerr's jealousy, 115; and
    Lattimore, 98; and Lilienthal, 63; and
    McCarthy censure, 246; and Service,
    108; support for McCarthy, 90–91, 153;
    See also Federal Bureau of Investigation
House Un-American Activities
    Committee (HUAC), *66*; blacklists,
    66, 163; coordination with Govt.
    Operations Comm., 158; Hiss
    investigation, 77–78, *78*; Hollywood
    film industry investigations, 64–66,
    163; McCarthy had no direct
    connection, 64; misuse of personnel
    files, 83; overview, 64; public school
    teachers investigation, 163; resources,
    273; subversive organizations list, 92,
    219; unfriendly witnesses, 65
housing shortage and housing bills, 66–68,
    69–70
How to Own Your Own Home by Lustron
    Corp., 70
Hughes, Emmett John, 142, 163
Hungary, 39
Hunt, H. L., 117
Hurley, Patrick, 107
hydrogen bombs, 173. *See also* atomic
    bombs; nuclear weapons

image and public perception, McCarthy's
    use of: claims against State Dept.,
    77, 81–82, 84, 88, 212; and military
    service, 27, 31, 34, 37, 42; as a new
    attorney, 13, 20; as a new senator, 58;
    revenge on Tyding, 117–19, 201, 224
India, 150
Institute of International Education (IIE),
    205

Institute of Pacific Relations, 103
International Information Administration
  (IIA), 165–68
investigations, general principles:
  bipartisan board for govt. employees
  (*see* loyalty review); "disloyalty"
  in context of, 60–61, 206; and due
  process of law, 61, 144, 206; guilt by
  association, 61, 77, 204, 266; guilt by
  "taking the Fifth," 65, 179, 180, 183,
  185; order by Pres. Truman, 60–61; *See
  also* House Un-American Activities
  Committee; U.S. Senate, Internal
  Security Subcomm.
investigations by McCarthy: torture of
  German prisoners, 72–73; Parker,
  76–77; State Dept. employees, 77–85,
  80, 86–95, *87,* 96–104, 212; Voice of
  America, 163, 165–68, *166;* CIA, 170–
  72, *171;* Army, 174–80, 183–96, 207;
  GE, 180–81; Peress, 183–86, 187–92,
  195–96, 200; Moss, 192–95, 209–11;
  Radulovich, 202–7; Murrow, 205, 218;
  defense plants, 217, 226, 243, 258
investigations of McCarthy: for
  misstatement of facts, 27, 34, 73, 83;
  for tax evasion, 76–77, 141, 150; by the
  Senate to expel, 130–31, 134, 140–41,
  148, 150, 244; Army-McCarthy
  hearings, 208–9, 214–17, 219–42, *225,
  228, 231,* 243, 274
"Iron Curtain," 46, 56
isolationist policy, 23, 44
Italy, 17
Ives, Sen. Irving M., 111

Jackson, Sen. Henry, 194
Jaffe, Philip, 107–8
Japan, 18, 26, 27–28, 29, 31, 39–42
Jenkins, Ray H., 219, 223–24, 229, 236
Jenner, Sen. William, 115, 148, 252, *254*

job security. *See* unemployment
Johnson, Louis A., 120, 128
Johnson, Sen. Lyndon B., 151, *152,* 246,
  247, 253, 269–70
Juliana, James, 224, 225

Kaufman, Judge Irving, 154
Kennedy, John F., 146, 147, 151, 176, 269
Kennedy, Joseph P., 146, 147, 153
Kennedy, Patricia, 147
Kennedy, Robert "Bobby," 153, 183
Kenyon, Dorothy, 92, *93,* 94, 114, 244
Kerr, Elizabeth (mother-in-law), 198, *199,*
  256
Kerr, Jean, *116;* "From the Record,"
  117–19; housing book, 70; Lincoln
  Day speeches tour, 185–86; marriage
  to McCarthy, *175,* 175–76 (*see also*
  McCarthy, Jean Kerr); *McCarthyism:
  The Fight for America,* 138; meeting
  McCarthy, 68; relationship with
  McCarthy, 115–16; working with
  McCarthy, 70, 77, 115, 116–18, 129–30
Khrushchev, Nikita, Prem., 250, 260
Kiermas, Dolores, 57
Kiermas, Ray, 48, 54, 57, 115, 176
Kim Il Sung, Pres., 112
Knowland, Sen. William F., 90, 243, 246,
  247, 253, 265
Kohler, Gov. Walter, 143, 144, 145
Korean War, 111–13, 119–25, *121,* 131–32,
  148–49, 150, 181

La Follette, Belle Case, 43
La Follette, Gov. Philip, 43, 44
La Follette, Sen. Robert M., Jr., 26, 38, *43,*
  43–45, 47, 50–53
La Follette, Sen. Robert M., Sr., 43
Landon, Alf, 16
Lardner, Ring, Jr., 65
Lattimore, Owen, 75, 96–104, *97,* 114, 147

Lawton, Maj. Gen. Kirke B., 177
League of Women Voters, 94
Lee, Rep. Robert, 82, 83, 86, 89, 106
Lehman, Sen. Herbert H., 100
Lewis, Fulton, Jr., 139
library policy, 165, 167–68
life events of McCarthy: birth, ix;
    childhood and adolescence, 1–4, *2, 3;*
    university years, 8–13, *9;* as an attorney,
    12–13, 14–17, 19, 22; as a judge, 22, *24,*
    24–26, 37–38, 42, 54; in the military,
    26–28, 29–38, *30, 32, 33, 35, 36;* move
    to Wash. D.C., 57–63, *58;* relationship
    with Kerr, 115–16, *116;* marriage
    to Kerr, *175,* 175–76; adoption of
    daughter, 261–62, *263;* death, funeral,
    and burial, 262–63, *264,* 265
Lilienthal, David E., *62,* 62–63, *77*
Lincoln Day speeches, 79–85, *80,* 185–86
Lippman, Walter, 198–99, 207, 211
Little Wolf High School, 4–7, *5, 6*
lobbies, 70, 75, 102
Lodge, Sen. Henry Cabot, 57, 106, 114,
    146, 147, 151, 233
loyalty review: Eisenhower admin., 168,
    187; personnel file access issues, 89,
    96, 105–6, 114, 151; Truman admin.,
    61–62
Lucas, Sen. Scott, 86–87, 88
Luce, Henry, 75
Lustron Corporation, 70, 150

MacArthur, Gen. Douglas, *112,* 113, 120–
    25, 132, 133, 134
magazines. *See* media
Malmédy. *See* torture, investigation
Mao Zedong (Tse-tung), Chrmn., 18,
    73–74, *74,* 106, 128
Markward, Mary Stalcup, 193, 195, 209
Marquette University, 7, 8–13, *9,* 268
Marshall, Gen. George, *127;* background,
74, 126–28; McCarthy's claims against,
    126, 128–29, 130, 135, 137, 142, 163,
    245; Sec. Defense during Korean War,
    120, 123, 125, 128
Martin, Joseph, 124
Marx, Karl, 164–65, 209
Maybank, Sen. Burnet R., 69
McCarran, Sen. Pat, 161, 162, 249
McCarthy (grandfather), 1
McCarthy, Anna Mae (sister), 1
McCarthy, Bridget (mother), 1, 7
McCarthy, Howard (brother), *2*
McCarthy, Jean Kerr (wife): and adopted
    daughter, 261, *263,* 268; and the Army-
    McCarthy hearings, 229, 230; fractured
    ankle, 198, *199;* at husband's funeral,
    264; new home, 198; prior to marriage
    (*see* Kerr, Jean); second marriage to
    Minetti, 268; support for husband,
    255, 256, 260, 261, 262, 268; trips with
    husband, 242, 247
McCarthy, Sen. Joseph Raymond "Joe," *ii,*
    69, 182, 199; archives, 268; biographies
    on, 271–72; conflict of interest and
    Lustron, 70, 150; early jobs, 4, 7, 8;
    education, 1–13, *3, 5, 6, 9;* farm, *x,*
    1; finances, 35, 42, 54, 115; health
    (*see* health problems of McCarthy);
    investigations of (*see* investigations of
    McCarthy); and the Kennedy family,
    146–47; on the Korean War, 113, 120,
    124, 173; legacy, 255, 266; life events
    (*see* life events of McCarthy); love of
    boxing, 2, 5, 10; love of gambling, 10,
    14, 15, 25–26, 29–30, 42, 90; no direct
    connection to HUAC, 64; personality,
    10–11, 15, 25, 76, 116–19; physical
    appearance, 1–2, 226; political career
    (*see* political career of McCarthy;
    political fall of McCarthy); political
    strategies (*see* political strategies of

McCarthy); poultry business, 2–4, 58; relationship with family, 25; religion, 1, 25; support during censure hearings, *250*, 251–52, *252*, *253*, *254*, 255, 256, *257*; voice quality, 8, 223, 226

McCarthy, Tierney Elizabeth (daughter), 261–62, *263*, 268

McCarthy, Tim (father), 1, 7

McCarthy, William (brother), *2*, 176, *264*

"McCarthyism": culture of fear which made possible, 60, 71, 104, 111, 163–65, 173, 206, 241, 251, 257; first use of term, 99; Flanders' opposition to, 202; as McCarthy's legacy, 266; political cartoons, *140, 141*; possibility today, 266–67; resources, 272–73; rise of influence, 140

McCarthyism: The Fight for America by Kerr, 138

"McCarthywasm," 261

McClellan, Sen. John L., 210, 217, 222, 245, 258

McFarland, Sen. Ernest W., 131

McLeod, Scott, 151, 160, 162

McMahon, Sen. Brien, 88

McMurray, Howard J., 54, 56–57

media: coverage of Army-McCarthy hearings, 220, 223, 226, 234, 241; coverage of McCarthy censure hearings, 249, 257; drama to increase sales, 92; end of McCarthy coverage, 261; lack of interest in accuracy, 77; McCarthy's use of the, 95, *95*, 96, 99, 177, 180, 192, 261; obituaries for McCarthy, 263; rise in opposition to, 192, 198–99, 201, 207, 211, 216–17; television (*see* television)

Miller, Ruth McCormick, 116–17

Milwaukee, Wisc. *See* Marquette University

Minetti, G. Joseph, 268

Minetti, Jean Kerr McCarthy (widow), 268

Monroney, Sen. Mike, 172

Morse, Sen. Wayne, 111

Moss, Annie Lee, 192–95, *194*, 209–11, 245

Mundt, Karl E.: during Army investigation, 195; during Army-McCarthy hearings, 213, 215, 217, 222, 226, 232–33, 234, 235, 238–39, 240; and Cohn influence on Schine military service, 210–11; on McCarthy's death, 265; Permanent Subcomm. on Investigations, 151

Murchison, Clint, 117, 185

Murrow, Edward R., *202*, 202–7, 211, 214, 218–19

Mussolini, Benito, P. M., 17

National Council for Prevention of War, 71

National Lawyers Guild, 238, 240

National Security Council (NSC), 170

Nazis. *See* Germany, WWII

Nellor, Ed, 115

New Deal, 44, 45, 56, 62

newspapers. *See* media

New York, N.Y., *11*

Nimitz, Adm. Chester, 33, 34, 37

9/11 terrorist attacks, 266

Nixon, Pat, 175, 265

Nixon, Sen. Richard M.: after McCarthy's death, 270; and the CIA investigation, 170–71; death, 270; and Eisenhower-McCarthy power struggle, 196, 201, 213–15, *214*; on Hiss, 78; HUAC, 64, 66, 78, 90; and McCarthy censure, 246; at McCarthy's funeral, 265; as pres., 270; relationship with McCarthy, 172–73, 175, 215; Senate election 1950, 119; support for Eisenhower's summit conf., 260; support for Gen. MacArthur,

Nixon, Sen. Richard M. *(cont.)*
124; support for McCarthy, 90, 249–
50; "Tricky Dick," 119; as vice pres.
running mate 1952, 135, *136,* 148;
Watergate, 270
North Atlantic Treaty Organization
(NATO), 132
North Korea (People's Democratic
Republic of Korea), 40, 112, 113, *122,*
150, 181. *See also* Korean War
nuclear weapons, 123, 251, 260. *See also*
atomic bombs; hydrogen bombs

Oram, Charlotte, 195

Parker, Cedric, 76–77, 116
Partridge, Gen. Richard, 174–75
Pearl Harbor, Hawaii, 26, 29
Pearson, Drew, 99
Pegler, Westbrook, 139
People's Republic of China, 74, *74,* 75, 88,
103, 121–23, 128. *See also* China
Peress, Irving, 183–86, *184,* 187–92, 195–
96, 200
Persons, Maj. Gen. Wilton B., 144
petitions, to save McCarthy, 251, *252,* 256
Philippine Islands, 27
Poland, 22, 23, 39
political career of McCarthy: as a
Democrat, 12, 15; campaign for district
attorney, 15–16; campaign for judge,
19, 20–22; plans to run for Senate, 26,
31, 32, 34, 42; as a Republican, 34, 77;
Senate campaign 1944, 35–38; Senate
primary campaign 1946, 45, 46–53, *49,*
52; Senate campaign 1946, 54–57, *55;*
first public anti-Communist views, 63;
housing bills, 66–68, 69–70; torture
investigation, 72–73; Senate hearings
1950, 76–85, *80,* 86–95, *87,* 96–104,
105, 114–15; Lincoln Day speeches,

79–85, *80,* 185–86; Senate investigation
to expel, 130–31, 134, 140–41, 148,
150; Senate campaign 1952, 132,
133–34, 149; help with pres. campaign
1952, 134, 139–45, 146; chrmn. Govt.
Operations Comm., 151, 153, *155,*
155–57, 258; opposition to Bohlen
nomination, 160–63; investigation of
Voice of America, 163, 165–68, *166;*
investigation of the CIA, 170–72, *171;*
investigation of the Army, 174–80,
183–96; investigation of GE, 180–81;
investigation of Peress, 183–86,
187–92, 195–96, 200; investigation of
Moss, 192–95, 209–11; investigation
of Radulovich, 202–7; and Cohn
influence on Schine military service,
211–13; *See also* political fall of
McCarthy
political fall of McCarthy: rise in
opposition to, 172, 191, 192, 196,
198–202, 207, 211, 216–17, 242, 251;
Murrow's television report, *202,* 202–7,
213; end of Moss investigation, 209–11;
McCarthy's rebuttal to Murrow, *218,*
218–19; Army-McCarthy hearings,
214–16, 220–42, *225, 228, 231, 239,*
243, 274; censure, 244–57, 258;
opposition to Eisenhower's summit
conf., 260–61; lack of Republican
support, 261
political strategies of McCarthy: anti-
Communist rhetoric, 57, 76, 77, 216,
251; bluffing with no evidence, 82,
83, 85, 87–88, 103–4, 106, 213, 229;
bullying, 72, 188–92, 196, 198, 206,
223, 224–26, 235, 248–49, 257;
manipulation of facts, 88, 89, 91–92,
106, 108, 114, 117–19, 131, 139, 170,
172, 194; manipulation of image
(*see* image and public perception);

manipulation of the media, 81, 84, 95, *95*, 96, 99, 177, 180, 192, 261 (*see also* media); manufactured evidence, 212–13, 224, *227*, 235, 237, 242, 247; meet and greet, 4, 15, 21, 48, 51, *130*; negative campaigning, 16, 21–22, 47, 50, 76, 117–19, 129–30; pamphlets, 50, 51; "personal" postcards, *36*, 37, 48, 54, 117, 119; power, *viii*, ix, 47, 115, 142, 169, 186, 195, 204, 258; revenge, 116–19, 125, 205–7, 230; timely revelation of new threat, 80–81, 192, 205, 227, 238, 254; used by politicians today, 266

Pope Pius XII, 176

Potter, Sen. Charles, 208–9

presidential elections, U.S.: 1948, 68; 1952, 104, 125, 132–36, 137–45, 148–49, 173; 1956, 169, 261; 1960, 269, 270; 1964, 269; 1968, 270; 1972, 270

Progressive Party, 16, 43, 44, 45

Prohibition, 10, 146

Quantico, Va., 28, 29

radio. *See* media

Radulovich, Milo, *203*, 203–5

Reese, E. Dewey, 56

registration, mandatory, 63

Republican Party: control of Congress 1952–1953, 149, 168, 169; Grand Old Party, ix; image and the Army-McCarthy hearings, 226, 230, 234; Lincoln Day speeches, 79–85, *80*, 185–86; poll results for McCarthy, 183; pres. campaign platform 1952, 135; recruitment after WWII, 42; Republican National Comm., 199, 201, 259; rise in opposition to McCarthy, 192, 195, 199–202, 213; Senate defeat 1948, 68–69; Senate majority 1946, 59, *59*; Stalwarts, 43, 45, 47, 48; two

factions, 43, 45, 133, 195, 201, 256; Young Republicans, 42, 46–47, 51, 53

Reston, James, 201, 248

Rhee, Pres. Syngman, 112

Ridgway, Gen. Matthew B., 123, 124, 190

rights. *See* U.S. Constitution

Rombin, Hillevi, 269

Roosevelt, Eleanor, 94, 99, 170

Roosevelt, Pres. Franklin D.: death, 40; McCarthy vote for, 12; New Deal, 44, 45, 56, 62; nomination of Marshall, 126; second pres. campaign, 16, 17; Yalta Conference, 39, 160

Rosenberg, Ethel, 153–55, *154*, 173

Rosenberg, Julius, 153–55, *154*, 173, 177

Russia, 12. *See also* Soviet Union

Ryan, Gen. Cornelius, 182, 234–35

St. Clair, James D., 219, 239

Sayre, Very Rev. Francis B., Jr., 216

Schine, Berndt, 269

Schine, G. David, *166*; after McCarthy's death, 269; and the Army-McCarthy hearings, 214–17, 220–31, *231*, 234–35, 236–37, 242; background, 156; Govt. Operations Comm., *156*, 156–57, 165–67, 177; military service, 181–82, 185, 186, 208–9, 211–13; Voice of America investigation, 165–67, *166*, 172

Schmitt, Len, 139

Senate elections: 1946, 59, *59*; 1948, 68–69; 1950, 116–19, 129, 201, 224; 1952, 132, 133–34, 146–48, 149; 1954, 201, 226, 246, 249–50, 251; 1958, 260

Service, John Stewart, 75, 77, 84, 106–7, *107*, 108, 114

Shapley, Harlow, 84

Shawano, Wisc., 15, 16, 19, 20, 22

Smith, Sen. Clyde H., 109

Smith, Sen. Margaret Chase, 109–11, *110*, 132

Smith, Walter Bedell, 160

Snow, Edgar, 18
socialism, 12, 266
Solomon Islands, 28, *30*
South Korea (Republic of Korea), 112, 113, *122,* 150, 181. *See also* Korean War
Soviet Union: cold war, 211, 250, 251, 260; and espionage, 77–79, 81, 154; formation, 12; with Germany during WWII, 23, 27, 60; invasion by Germany, 27; under Khrushchev, 250; and the Korean War, 112, 123; nuclear weapons, 73, 77, 88, 154, 173, 260; and the Spanish Civil War, 17–18; under Stalin, 12, 23, 27; U.S. ambassador to, 159–60; as U.S. ally during WWII, 27, 39, 40, 41, 60
Spanish Civil War, *17,* 17–18, 23, 64, 92, 153
Sparkman, Sen. John J., 162
Spellman, Francis Cardinal, 261, *262*
spies. *See* espionage
Stalin, Joseph, Gen. Sec., *159;* collectives under, 12; death, 160, 250; labor camps, 23, 250; post-WWII, 56; Potsdam Declaration, 40, *159;* Soviet Union under, 12, 23, 27; war against Japan, 39–40, 41; Yalta Conference, 39, 160
Stassen, Harold, 134, 135
Stevens, Robert T., *182;* and the Army investigation, 174, 177, 179; and the Army-McCarthy hearings, 222, 223–24, 226, 227, 234; Eisenhower's support for, 196, 200; and the Peress investigation, 184, 185, 187, 190–92, 195–96, 200; power struggle with McCarthy, 177, 179, 195–96, 197–99, 222; and Schine's military service, 181–82, 186, 201, 212, 213
Stevenson, Sen. Adlai E., 129, 137–39, *138,* 142, 145, 149, 201
Stimson, Henry L., 96

stock market crash. *See* Great Depression
strategies. *See* political strategies of McCarthy
Stripling, Robert E., *65*
Surine, Donald, 91, 111, 115, 192, 204–5, 211, 215
Suzuki, P. M. Kantaro, 41
Swedish, Steve, 262
Symington, Sen. Stuart, 210, *210,* 211, 217, 235, 265

Taft, Sen. Robert, *67;* and the Bohlen nomination, 162, 163; and the housing comm., 67–68, 69; during McCarthy Senate hearings, 98; power in the Republican Party, 57; pres. campaign 1952, 132, 134, 135; Senate election 1950, 119; support for McCarthy, 101, 132; on Truman and the Korean War, 113
television: *Angels in America, 269;* industry, 66; McCarthy's rebuttal to Murrow, *218,* 218–19; *Meet the Press,* 158, 181; Murrow's report on McCarthy, *202,* 202–7, 213; *See It Now, 202,* 202–7, 211, *218,* 218–19
Ten Million Americans Mobilized for Justice, 251, 256
Tennessee Valley Authority, 62
terrorism, 266
Thomas, Rep. J. Parnell, 64, *65, 66*
Tobey, Sen. Charles, 161
Todd, Maj. Glenn A., 34
Tolson, Clyde, *90,* 91
torture, investigation, 70–73, 89
Truman, Pres. Harry S., *61;* and atomic bombs, 41, 78; attempted China truce, 74; and Gen. MacArthur, 124, 127–28; housing shortage and housing bills, 67, 69, 70; and hydrogen bomb, 173; during the Korean War, 113, 123–24,

132; opposition to McCarthy, 83, 84, 85, 89, 98, 100, 135; order for investigation of govt. workers, 60–61; Potsdam Declaration, 40, *159*; pres. election 1948, 68; presidency after Roosevelt's death, 40; support for "Declaration of Conscience," 111; views on HUAC, 83

Trump, Donald, 268

Tydings, Sen. Millard E., *118*; chrmn. Senate Armed Services Comm., 72; chrmn. Senate hearings 1950, 89, 91, 94, 95, 98, 101–2, 105, 114–15; and review of the loyalty files, 105–6, 114; Senate campaign 1950, 116–19, 129–30, 201, 224; on Smith, 111

Underhill Elementary School, 1, 2, *3*

unemployment: blacklists, 66, 163; due to culture of fear, 163; due to HUAC, 66; due to "taking the Fifth," 179, 180, 185; due to the Depression, 7, 11; govt. employees, 180–81

unions, labor, 147

United Nations: Commission on the Status of Women, 94; forces in Korea, *112*, 113, 120, 122–23, 131; investigation of personnel, 163; and Korean armistice, 150; Security Council, 113

United States: atomic bombings of Japan, 41–42; attack by the Japanese, 26, 28, 29; and the Chinese Civil War, 74–75; cold war, 211, 250, 251, 260; culture of fear, 60, 71, 73, 77, 88, 104, 111, 163–65, 173, 206, 251; isolationist view prior to WWII, 22–23, 44; Korean War, 111–13, 119–25, *121*, 131–32, 148–49, 150, 181; nuclear weapons, 41–42, 173, 260; occupation of S. Korea, 112, 113; possibility of "McCarthyism" today, 266–67; post-war foreign policy, 46; pres. elections (*see* presidential elections); and the Spanish Civil War, *17*, 18, 92, 153; Vietnam War, 270; during WWII, 27, 28, 31, 39–42, 70–73, 126

U.S. Air Force, 203–6

U.S. Army: Army-McCarthy hearings, 214, 215, 217, 220–42, 274; document on Siberia, 174–75; Fort Monmouth lab investigation, 176, 177–80, *178*, 207, 227–29; McCarthy-Cohn hearing, 208–9, 214–17; McCarthy's threat to Stevens' authority, 195–96, 197–99, 201, 208–9; Moss investigation, 192–95, *194*, 209–11; Peress investigation, 183–86, 187–92, 195–96, 200; report on Cohn and Schine, 208–9, 211–13

U.S. Congress: bills during Johnson admin., 269–70; Democratic control 1955, 258; Gen. MacArthur's address to, 124–25; housing bills, 67–68, 69–70; Republican control 1952, 149

U.S. Constitution: Bill of Rights, 138, 267; due process of law, 61, 144, 206; Fifth Amendment, 65, 179, 180, 183, 185, 195, 200; and mandatory registration, 63; pres. as commander-in-chief, 124; separation of powers, 233; Sixth Amendment, 179; and Truman's order for background investigations, 61

U.S. Information Agency, 168

U.S. Marines, 27, 28, 29, *264*

U.S. Office of War Information, 101

U.S. Senate: Armed Services Comm., 57, 59, 72; Army-McCarthy hearings subcomm., 214, 215, 217, 219, 220–42; Banking and Currency Comm., 59–60, 68–69; "Declaration of Conscience," 109–11; elections (*see* Senate elections); Expenditures in the Executive Departments Comm., 59, 69, 72;

U.S. Senate *(cont.)*
Foreign Relations Comm., 160–63; Govt. Operations Comm., 151, 153, 155–57, 258; Internal Security Subcomm., 158, 163; investigation of McCarthy to expel, 130–31, 134, 140–41, 148, 150, 244; McCarthy censure comm., 246–47; McCarthy's claims against 1951, 131; McCarthy's hearings 1950, 76–85, 86–95, 96–104, 105, 114–15; Permanent Subcomm. on Investigations, 151, 159–68, 169–75, 177–86, 187–96, 213, 217; rise in opposition to McCarthy, 172, 191, 201–2, 210, 234

U.S. State Department: loyalty board *(see* loyalty review); McCarthy claims against, 76–85, *80,* 86–95, *87,* 96–104, 212; Voice of America radio, 100, 163, 165–68

Van Susteren, Margery, *52*
Van Susteren, Urban: friendship with McCarthy, 25, 26–27, 215, 241, 261; on McCarthy's image, 20; and McCarthy's Senate campaign 1946, 48, 50
Vietnam War, 270
Voice of America (VOA), 100, 163, 165–68
Voy, May, 15

Wallace, V. Pres. Henry, 101
Walters, Barbara, 268
Wander, Jerome, 31
Watkins, Sen. Arthur V., *248;* Eisenhower's support for, 258; McCarthy censure hearings, 247, 248, 249, 251, 254, 255, 258
Waupaca, Wisc., 12–13, 14
Wayne, John, 139
Wedemeyer, Gen. Albert, 128
Welch, Joseph N., *221;* after McCarthy's death, 269; counsel during Army-McCarthy hearings, 219, 220, 223–27, *225,* 234, 236–40, 241
Welker, Sen. Herman, 141, 252
Werner, Judge Edgar V., 19, 20, 21–22, 24
Wershba, Joseph, 204–6
Wherry, Sen. Kenneth S., 90, 100, 105
Wiley, Sen. Alexander, 26, 34, 37, 57, 101
Williams, Edward Bennett, 249
Willkie, Wendell, 170
Wilson, Charles E., 207, 208–9, 233
women's issues, 43, 109
World War II: Battle of the Bulge, 71; events during, 27–28, 31, 39–40; events leading up to, 22–23; Marshall Plan, 128; Potsdam Declaration, 40, *159;* torture investigation, 70–73, 89; two fronts, 39–42; U.S. involvement, 26; Yalta Conference, 39, 160

Zhou Enlai (Chou En-Lai), 106
Zwicker, Brig. Gen. Ralph W., *188;* aftermath of McCarthy's bullying, 191–92, 199–200, 244, 247, 249, 255, 256; during Army-McCarthy hearings, 189–90, 195; background, 188–89